Critical Perspectives on Work and Organisations

Series editors:
David Knights, Department of Management, University of Keele, UK
Chris Smith, School of Management, Royal Holloway, University of London, UK
Paul Thompson, Department of Human Resource Management, University of Strathclyde, UK
Hugh Willmott, Cardiff Business School, University of Cardiff, UK

This series offers a range of titles examining the broad areas of work and organisation within a national and global arena. Each book in the series is written by leading experts and covers a topic chosen to appeal to students and academics. Originating out of the International Labour Process Conference, the series will be informative, topical and leading edge.

Published:
Alan Felstead and Nick Jewson
GLOBAL TRENDS IN FLEXIBLE LABOUR

Bill Harley, Jeff Hyman and Paul Thompson
PARTICIPATION AND DEMOCRACY AT WORK

Craig Prichard, Richard Hull, Mike Chumer and Hugh Willmott
MANAGING KNOWLEDGE

Andrew Sturdy, Irena Grugulis and Hugh Willmott
CUSTOMER SERVICE

Paul Thompson and Chris Warhurst
WORKPLACES OF THE FUTURE

Chris Warhurst, Ewart Keep and Irena Grugulis
THE SKILLS THAT MATTER

Chris Warhurst, Doris Eikhof and Axel Haunschild
WORK LESS, LIVE MORE?

Critical Perspectives on Work and Organisations Series

Series Standing Order ISBN 0-333-73535-8

You can receive future titles in this series as they are published by placing a standing order. Please contact your bookseller or, in case of difficulty, write to us at the address below with your name and address, the title of the series and the ISBN quoted above.

Customer Services Department, Macmillan Distribution Ltd, Houndmills, Basingstoke, Hampshire RG21 6XS, England

---

Also by Chris Warhurst
THE SKILLS THAT MATTER
WORKPLACES OF THE FUTURE

Work Less, Live More?

Critical Analysis of the Work-Life Boundary

Edited by

**Chris Warhurst,
Doris Ruth Eikhof and
Axel Haunschild**

Editorial matter, selection and Introduction © Chris Warhurst, Doris Ruth Eikhof and Axel Haunschild 2008.
Individual chapters © contributors 2008.

First published 2008 by
PALGRAVE MACMILLAN
Houndmills, Basingstoke, Hampshire RG21 6XS and
175 Fifth Avenue, New York, N.Y. 10010
Companies and representatives throughout the world

PALGRAVE MACMILLAN is the global academic imprint of the Palgrave Macmillan division of St. Martin's Press, LLC and of Palgrave Macmillan Ltd. Macmillan® is a registered trademark in the United States, United Kingdom and other countries. Palgrave is a registered trademark in the European Union and other countries.

ISBN-13: 978-0-230-53560-2   paperback
ISBN-10: 0-230-53560-7   paperback

This book is printed on paper suitable for recycling and made from fully managed and sustained forest sources. Logging, pulping and manufacturing processes are expected to conform to the environmental regulations of the country of origin.

A catalogue record for this book is available from the British Library.

A catalog record for this book is available from the Library of Congress.

10   9   8   7   6   5   4   3   2   1
17   16   15   14   13   12   11   10   09   08

Printed and bound in China

Contents

List of Figures

List of Tables

Acknowledgements

At the 2005 *Annual International Labour Process Conference* hosted by the University of Strathclyde, Madeleine Bunting was an eloquent plenary speaker. In talking about how long working hours were ruining lives, she was preaching to the converted. Many in the audience were researching that very subject; some had even provided the basic data from which Bunting drew her arguments. In short, she came, she spoke, she found a willing audience. How right she is, they chorused afterwards; it's a scandal, some proclaimed; it's the capitalist system, others argued; before they all traipsed off home that weekend to sit at their PCs and catch up on their work as they also did most weekday evenings. Whether by design or default, academics are not good at maintaining work-life balance. We are no exception, and there are many among our family and friends to whom we pay insufficient attention. We promise to do better in the future and apologise to them now: Martin Whitehead, Esther Neill, Olivia Vincent, George Warhurst; Helga, Johann and Christian Eikhof; and Irene, Janne and Nele Kenzler. We would also like to thank Ursula Gavin at Palgrave for keeping the faith with the book series; it too needs, and will receive, more attention – because it's worth it.

Notes on the Contributors

Stinne Aaløkke Ballegaard is currently a doctoral student at the Center for Pervasive Healthcare, Information and Media Studies at the University of Aarhus, Denmark. She holds an MA in ethnography. Her research focuses on IT and organisational change, particularly within the health sector and knowledge-intensive companies. Her doctoral research focuses on the role of pervasive healthcare within independent living. She has has published several papers on this topic in international conference proceedings, primarily within the area of human-computer interaction.

Jeanne de Bruijn is Rector Magnificus at the University of the Netherlands Antilles. Her research focuses on gender changes in the labour process, and international comparative research on women's labour force participation and work-care arrangements. She has published on women's work issues such as sexual harassment, work and care, women's participation policies, equal pay and job evaluation.

Rachel Lara Cohen is a British Academy Postdoctoral Research Fellow based in the Department of Sociology at the University of Warwick. Her research focuses on work relations and the labour process. Her doctoral thesis, *Styling Labour,* analysed the effect of hairstylists' varied work relations on their relations with clients, workplace social relations, temporality, mobility and work-life boundaries. Her current project, a comparative analysis of car mechanics and accountants, develops these themes.

Doris Ruth Eikhof is Lecturer in Organization Studies at the Department of Management, University of Stirling, and Research Associate at the Wirtschaftsuniversität Wien, Austria. Her research interests include creative industries, changing forms of work and organisation, organisational boundaries, organisations and lifestyles and social theories in organisation studies. She has

published in international and German academic books and journals, including *Journal of Organizational Behavior, Creativity and Innovation Management* and
in edited volumes to be published by Palgrave Macmillan and Routledge.

Anne Bøgh Fangel is a Researcher and Advisor at the Center for New Ways of
Working at The Alexandra Institute in Aarhus, Denmark. Her work focuses on
innovation, collaboration and the development of new working styles. Apart
from her research activities, she also works as an advisor and facilitator for
companies and is an expert speaker in the fields of new ways of working and
processes of change. She has authored several academic and non-academic
articles published in Danish.

Sandra Groeneveld is Assistant Professor in the Department of Public Administration at the Erasmus University, Rotterdam. She has published on the
labour market position of ethnic minorities in general and ethnic minority
women in particular. Public personnel management and diversity issues are
the subjects of her most recent work.

Axel Haunschild is Professor of Work, Employment and Organization at the
University of Trier. His research interests include changing forms of work and
organisation, creative industries, the institutional embeddedness of work and
employment, organisations and lifestyles, and organisational boundaries. He
has published in a variety of journals, including *Human Relations, British Journal
of Industrial Relations, International Journal of Human Resource Management* and
Journal of Organizational Behavior.

Annette Henninger is Senior Research Fellow at the Social Science Research
Center Berlin (Wissenschaftszentrum Berlin für sozialforschung). Her research
interests include labour market and social policy, female employment and
changing gender arrangements. She has authored a number of publications
on work and gender arrangements in the German new and old media industry, including an article on freelancers in the German new media industry
(*Critical Sociology*, with Karin Gottschall).

Arlie Russell Hochschild is Professor of Sociology at the University of
California, Berkeley. She is the author of numerous articles and several books,
including *The Time Bind* (Henry Holt & Co, 1997), *The Second Shift* (Viking,
1989) and *The Managed Heart* (University of California Press, 1983). Her current
research centres on the relationship between market culture and life, analysing, for instance, the commercialisation of intimate life and market culture as a
potential carrier of personal identity.

Jeff Hyman is Professor of Human Resource Management in the Department of Management Studies at the University of Aberdeen Business School.
His main research interests include the future of work, work-life issues and

industrial democracy. He is also a Research Associate of the Scottish Centre for Employment Research at the University of Strathclyde.

Jan Ch. Karlsson is Professor of Sociology at the Department of Working Life Science, Karlstad University, Sweden. His research during recent years has focused on the development of work organisation and consequences thereof for employees. He has published widely on these issues, for example in the books *Gender Segregation: Divisions of Work in Post-Industrial Welfare States* (Ashgate, 2006) and *Flexibility and Stability in Working Life* (Palgrave Macmillan, 2007). He is also interested in the methodology of the social sciences, publishing *Explaining Society: Critical Realism in the Social Sciences* (Routledge, 2002).

Tilda Khoshaba has a BA in Industrial Relations from the University of New South Wales, a Masters (Hons) in Industrial Relations from the University of Sydney and recently completed her doctorate at the same institution. She is a lecturer in the Employment Relations Programme at the University of Western Sydney and a Director and current Secretary of the Rugby League Professionals Association (RLPA). Her research interests include employment relations in sport, in particular trade unionism, individual and collective bargaining and player education and welfare.

Camilla Kylin is a doctoral student in the Work and Organizational Psychology Division of the Department of Psychology at Stockholm University, and was recently appointed as researcher in the Department of Management and Leadership, Swedish National Defence College, Karlstad. Her research interests focus on the interaction between work and other life domains and consequences for individuals' health and well-being in the context of changing spatial and temporal boundaries. She is co-author of a number of articles, including (with T. Hartig, C. Kylin and G. Johansson). 'The Telework Tradeoff: Stress Mitigation vs. Constrained Restoration', *Applied Psychology*, 56:2 (2007), 231–53.

John MacInnes is Professor of the Sociology of Europe at the University of Edinburgh and investigador associat at the Centre d'Estudis Demogràfics, Universitat Autònoma de Barcelona. He 'works' on the relationship between families and the labour market in 'Western' societies; on the demographic origins of social change, especially gender relations, in modern societies; and on 'identity' in its various dimensions (ethnic, national, gender and class) and its (mis)use in contemporary social science. His daughter Jana is his 'life'. He published *The End of Masculinity* (Open University Press, 1998).

Rozemarijn de Man was awarded her doctorate from the Fee University in Amsterdam. Her research focuses on contemporary work and the combination of work and care. She is currently working as a policy advisor for the Dutch Ministry of the Interior and Kingdom Relations.

Abigail Marks is a senior lecturer in employment at Heriot-Watt University, Edinburgh. She has undertaken research and published within the areas of identity, teamwork, work centrality and the construction of professions.

Ulrike Papouschek is Senior Researcher at the Working Life Research Centre in Vienna. Her research interests include female employment and changing gender arrangements, work organisation and changes of work. Since 2004 she has been a member of the 'High Level Group of Experts on Gender, Social Inclusion and Employment' (EGGSIE). She co-edited *Herausforderungen der Arbeitswelt. Beiträge zu neuen Arbeitsformen, Geschlecht, Informationstechnik* (2001).

Barbara Pocock is Professor and Director of the Centre for Work + Life at the University of South Australia. She has been researching work for over 25 years and is widely published. Her recent books include *The Work-Life Collision* and *The Labour Market Ate My Babies: Work, Children and a Sustainable Future* both published by Federation Press.

Paul Ransome is Lecturer in Sociology at the University of Wales, Swansea. In addition to his ongoing research into the sexual/gender division-of-labour paradigm, and concepts of work-life balance, he is interested in the development of social theory and epistemological issues in the social sciences. His main publications include *The Work Paradigm* (Avebury, 1996), *Sociology and the Future of Work* (Avebury, 1999) and *Work, Consumption and Culture: Affluence and Social Change in the Twenty-first Century* (Sage, 2005). He is currently writing *Reviewing Social Theory*, also for Sage.

Natalie Skinner is a Research Fellow at the Centre for Work + Life at the University of South Australia. Her primary research interests are around health and well-being in the workplace. She has conducted research on a range of issues, including stress and burnout, job satisfaction, work overload and more recently the interaction between work and life.

Chris Warhurst is Professor of Labour Studies and Co-Director of the Scottish Centre for Employment Research at the University of Strathclyde in Glasgow. His research and publications focus on work and employment issues and developments. He has published over 30 articles, including in *Administrative Science Quarterly* and *Sociology,* and he is currently co-editor of

Work, Employment and Society. He has authored, co-authored and co-edited 12 books, including *The Skills That Matter* (Palgrave Macmillan, 2004), Emerging *Human Resource Practices* (Akademiai Kiado, 2003) and *Looking Good, Sounding Right* (Industrial Society, 2001).

Philippa Williams is a Research Fellow at the Centre for Work + Life at the University of South Australia. She has studied a range of social, psychological and health phenomena over the past 16 years and is now working on a large multi-method study exploring how people fit work, home and community together in urban Australia. Her background is in psychology and public health.

Out of Balance or Just Out of Bounds? Analysing the Relationship between Work and Life

Chris Warhurst, Doris Ruth Eikhof and Axel Haunschild

Introduction

The relationship between work and life, articulated as work-life balance, has become a key feature of much current government, practitioner and academic debate. The need for good work-life balance is the main message of this debate. The issue then becomes ensuring this balance so that workers can satisfactorily combine paid work with private life and, moreover, gain satisfaction in both. With the point of departure for labour process analysis in the 1970s being the degradation of work (Braverman 1974), that current debate is about enabling workers to gain satisfaction in and through their jobs has to be welcomed. However, the current work-life balance debate is dissatisfying for three reasons.

Firstly, research shows a gap between employers' work-life balance intentions and employees' work-life balance experience. This gap is most prominently illustrated in Hochschild's (1997) study of a Fortune 500 company in the US: offering work-life balance provisions does not automatically result in a positive work-life balance experience for employees. In Hochschild's study, a poor uptake of work-life balance provisions was due to (female) workers' flight *to* work, which offered opportunities for success and satisfaction. By contrast their private lives were a constant struggle with unmanageable demands and offered less personal achievement and reward. Several other studies have indicated how work-life balance provisions or family-friendly policies fail to provide balanced, positive and – most important for the employer – productive workers (for example Fangel and Aaløkke in this volume). Such research suggests that work-life 'balance' fails to adequately capture empirically key aspects of work and life. Secondly and relatedly, the current work-life balance articulation of the relationship between work and life is conceptually limited because work and life are assumed to constitute distinct spheres. This assumption is relatively new, it was not until the industrial revolution and the shift from handicraft and domestic production to production in large-scale organisations that work and life emerged as distinct spheres separated by time and space (Türk et al. 2002; Thompson 1984). With the rise of paid employment outwith the household, the emergence of large-scale organisations and the imposition of middle class norms and values, work and non-work/life evolved as distinct spheres in Western countries during the late nineteenth century and throughout the twentieth. It is not surprising therefore that work-life balance presumes that work and life constitute two distinguishable and separable spheres that can or should be 'balanced'. However, that work and life might not be distinct and neatly bounded is overlooked. Analyses within what was then termed 'industrial sociology' would suggest that such distinctions are, at best, questionable. This research showed how jazz musicians, policemen and even factory workers were part of communities within occupations in which work relations and practices extended into life outwith the workplace, and how for occupations within communities such as mining and fishing, community life impacted workplace relations and practices (for example Cain 1964; Cavendish 1982; Mayo 1946; Roy 1973; Salaman 1974). Such analyses disappeared with the decline of manu-facturing and the demise of primary industries. Although too readily forgotten, the importance of this earlier body of research is that it challenges the con-ceptualisation of work and life as two distinct and detached spheres, and also reveals that interpenetration of the two can be beneficial to workers. Thirdly, the work-life balance debate also rests on particular readings of work and life in themselves (see also Eikhof et al. 2007). Work is regarded as a sphere of physical and mental demands that steals time and energy from employees' 'real' lives and thus has to be contained. Life, on the other hand, is mostly equated with caring responsibilities (see also MacInnes' and Ransome's contributions to this volume) and features as a haven of personal fulfilment, love and joy. Such myopic readings of life and work importantly overlook work as a source of satis-faction and life as encompassing more than just (child) care. In other words, not all work is perceived as bad and not all life revolves around children.

In short, the current work-life balance debate is limited both empirically and conceptually. As a consequence, it fails to provide an adequate understand-ing of work, life and the relationship between the two. The contributions to this volume aim to address this inadequacy. Drawing on a range of secondary literature, some from the authors, this opening chapter examines the relation-ship between work and life. The first three sections critique the work-life balance debate, analysing its central claims and drivers. Following from this critique, the fourth section evaluates an influential alternative articulation – that of the work-life boundary. The subsequent section develops this articulation by outlining and illustrating analysis of work-life patterns. The concluding remarks signal how this new approach might inform future research on the relationship between work and life.

'In Business, Life Sucks': unpacking the claim for work-life balance

In *The Apprentice*, a popular BBC reality television show, a wannabe but distraught candidate is fired by her potential employer, the successful businessman and entrepreneur Sir Alan Sugar, and told to go back home to the child that she misses. The message to her is that she cannot expect to work for and be like Sugar *and* have a meaningful home life: 'In business, you get homesick. In business, you miss your children. In business, life sucks. It [home] should never, ever affect what you're doing [at work]', he says, 'Go home and see your daughter' (quoted in Banks-Smith 2007: 31). Such statements illustrate the concern at the core of the current work-life balance debate: too busy working lives are detrimental to private life, particularly family life.

A central assumption behind this concern is that there exists a pervasive and debilitating long working hours culture (IDS 2000). In Italy this concern with working time features in Basso's (2003) *Modern Times, Ancient Hours*, in the US in Schor's (1991) *The Overworked American* and in the UK in Bunting's (2004) *Willing Slaves*, in which it is claimed, playing on the latter book's subtitle, work is not just ruling but ruining our lives. In France campaigns for reducing working time have rallied around the phrase 'work less, live better' (cited in Fagnani and Letablier 2004). Some self-selecting survey data seems to indicate that there does exist a long working hours culture – in the UK at least – resulting in 'the intrusion of work into many workers' home lives' (French and Daniels 2005: 27). Moreover, just over half of French and Daniels' respondents claimed that they sometimes felt unable to cope with work demands and almost a third claimed to suffer from consequential health problems – an outcome that features heavily in the accounts of Bunting's respondents. As such, in work-life balance debate and practice it is the – more or less explicit – premise that work is bad and to be contained, with working time the point of intervention, creating a 'burgeoning demand for more flexible working lives' Bolchover (2005: 134) claims.

There are two flies, however, in the ointment of this argument about long working hours and employee demands to spend more time with their children. Firstly, it appears that the long working hours culture is a myth. It is true that UK working hours are *relatively* high in the EU and that significant numbers of men (29 per cent) and women (9 per cent) work longer than 45 hours per week. However, working hours for both men and women in the UK have steadily fallen in the post-war years to below 40 hours per week (Mason et al. 2008; for other, similar European data see Roberts 2007). In a nuanced review of a range of statistical data, Roberts consequently asserts that 'it is doubtless the case in all countries that some individuals, and probably particular occupational groups, have lengthened their hours of work. However, there is no country, not even the USA, in which there is uncontested evidence of an overall lengthening of work schedules in the late-twentieth century' (p. 336). What have increased in many countries are female part-time paid working hours. Secondly, while there are some employees, 26 per cent for example in the UK, who want to work fewer hours, almost 70 per cent – that is, the vast majority – are content with their working hours, and women appear more content than men in this respect (Hooker et al. 2007). Moreover, for those employees who do wish to work fewer hours, theoretically that option is available to them, usually through part-time work; and employees' 'right to request' (albeit on employers' terms) is now a feature of UK employment law. Furthermore, and contrary to the rhetoric of the work-life balance debate, taking into account the range of options available (part-time, flexitime, school term-term etc. working), Hooker et al. found a high level of additional, informal flexible working such that most employees (56 per cent) across occupations were or had been working flexibly within the last 12 months. Similarly across Europe, it should be noted that even among *working women with dependent children*, 82 per cent report satisfaction with their working hours (European Foundation for the Improvement of Living and Working Conditions 2007: 72–3; see also Pocock et al. in this volume for similar findings in Australia). To sum up, most employees do not want to work fewer hours and those who do want or have to work fewer hours, already have options to do so.

The labour market hates my babies, but I love my job … well, sometimes

If long working hours are not the problem, what drives work-life balance debate and practice? The stock critique centres on employer and government concern with families. This concern limits the conceptualisation of 'life', narrowly equating it with childcare or caring in general, with subsequent practice nearly exclusively targeting working mothers (Eikhof et al. 2007; also MacInnes in this volume). The reason for this focus is not difficult to discern. Despite the rhetoric of job satisfaction, for both government and employers childcare *is the issue*. Government is concerned not with workers having better lives but with breeding new lives; more specifically the reproduction of the future labour force at a time when birth rates are in decline and most population increase occurs through migration rather than reproduction (EC 1999, 2004). In the UK

alarmist headlines scream of a 'baby crisis' and the 'potentially disastrous consequences as work pressures force young women to shelve plans for a family'
(Hinsliff 2006: 1). If government is concerned with employees not having
children, conversely the problem for employers is that employees (read female
employees) do have children and, again, with a shrinking labour force, measures need to be taken to keep these mothers at work. Thus the 'foundations'
of the work-life balance debate lay with employers and their perceived recruit-
ment and retention problems caused by 'parents ... who have to fit their working
lives around their childcare responsibilities' claims IDS (2000: 1). The solution
is seen in the introduction of 'family-friendly' flexible employment, which, it
should be noted, has to be compatible with superordinate business needs (IDS
2000), is introduced as employer financial circumstances allow (Schneider et al.
2006) and typically only meets statutory minimal provision set by government
(Hyman and Summers 2007).

A second driver of the work-life balance debate relates to changes to the
labour process, not just labour markets. In this respect, Roberts (2007) suggests
that it is not the extension of work but the intensification of work that is caus-
ing problems. As organisations become lean and mean, employees are being
required to do more with less, and lunch and other breaks are disappearing
as employees play catch-up at their desks. As Roberts states: 'even if they are
not working longer, people are likely to feel that their work is making greater
demands on them and having a greater impact (for good or ill) on their overall
quality of life' (p. 340). Of course, that work can be debilitating of life is not new.
Debate about the hidden injuries of work occurred in the early 1970s. Studs Terkel's (1972) influential book *Working* starts thus: 'This book, being about work,
is, by its very nature, about violence – to the spirit as well as to the body. ... The
scars, psychic as well as physical, brought home to the supper table and the TV
set, may have touched, malignantly, the soul of our society' (p. xiii). By way of
example, one of his respondents, a hotel clerk, notes how after busy work days,
'it takes me about an hour and a half to unwind. I just want to sit there and pick
up a book or a paper or something. Just to get away from it all' (p. 333).

However, while it can be debilitating, work is not all bad, either now or in
the recent past. Aside from its instrumental benefits, such as pay and consequently enabled consumption, paid work can be a source of satisfaction and
self-fulfilment. Indeed, most workers seem to like their jobs. Although there
will be variations amongst individuals, occupations, industries and countries,
the *European Working Conditions Surveys* over 1995–2005 consistently reveal
that over 80 per cent of respondents are satisfied or very satisfied with their
work (European Foundation for the Improvement of Living and Working Conditions 2007:77). Even Terkel's bottom-of-the-occupational-hierarchy hotel
workers can experience their jobs positively, as Sherman (2007) reveals. She
found workers 'engaged in their work and want[ing] to do it well' (p. 15) and

deriving – 'borrowing' (p. 159) in her words – prestige from the employing luxury hotels. Likewise, workers in intermediate occupations, such as those of the skilled trades, enjoyed and still enjoy a positive relationship with their jobs; they also derive social prestige as well as self-respect and personal and social identity from their work (see for example Pomlet 1969; Sennett 2004). The same can also be true for professional workers at the top of the occupational hierarchy such as lawyers and medical doctors for whom work is said, by Parsons (1951) to be a 'calling' with a defined 'moral desirability' (Becker 1970: 90) bridging work and life.[1] The point is that, as Isles (2004: 23) notes, 'work can make a major contribution – for some *the* major contribution – to overall life satisfaction'.[2] Significantly, such satisfaction from work is independent of hours of work as Booth and van Ours (2005) find from analysis of the Household Income and Labor Dynamics in Australia Survey. Such data emphasize that work can offer rewards, both intrinsic and extrinsic, and that the flight *from* work, assumed in the work-life balance articulation of work and life is too simplistic.

Where have all the good times gone? The chattering classes' lament

If it is being driven by government and employers for reasons other than job satisfaction, and many workers are already satisfied with their working hours (and jobs), the obvious question to ask is why work-life balance discourse still resonates. The answer might lie in another important point raised but not subsequently explored by Roberts (2007) when he suggests that the current debate on work-life balance is being driven by the so-called 'chattering classes' and their current experience of paid work. This claim finds support in British social attitudes survey data, which reveals that senior management and professionals are the most likely to report that work interferes with their family life (Park et al., 2007). While Roberts notes that these better-educated male and female professionals and managers work the longest hours, the nature of their work also makes boundary management more difficult. Moreover, as the numbers of professionals and managers grow (Wilson et al. 2006),[3] so too therefore does the number of workers for whom this boundary management is a problem. In addition, the nature of professional labour is also changing, with consequences for the anticipated relationship between work and life.

As predominantly white-collar workers high in the occupational hierarchy, the chattering classes are spatially and temporally more 'available' to work, as Bergman and Gardiner (2007) reveal in a comparative study of a paper and pulp mill, a bank and a university college in Sweden. In this study, the work of professionals in the college was found to be most 'disconnected' from the workplace, often undertaken at home and involving business journeys away from home; for blue-collar manufacturing workers in the mill the boundaries between work and life were most 'intact'; the bank, where many workers were associate professionals and managers, was closer to that of the college than to the mill. Consequently, these authors conclude that 'availability patterns are strongly influenced by position in the occupational structure. The higher the position, the greater the associated availability for work, irrespective of gender and organisation' (p. 412). While Roberts (2007) argues that this availability is self-inflicted, Bergman and Gardiner's findings indicate that it also reflects the intangibility of some of the work of the chattering classes. Manufacturing workers cannot roll pulp into paper at home but professionals (and managers) can take their 'mental' labour home with them and many other tasks, such as administration and networking, can also be undertaken anywhere, any time. This spatial and temporal blurring of the work and life boundary is often, but not solely, ITC-enabled and neatly illustrated by the so-called 'CrackBerry' addiction. A survey by AOL and Opinion Research in the US found that 60 per cent of respondents use their BlackBerry to send emails while in bed and 83 per cent used their BlackBerry to check for emails while on holiday (Pilkington 2007).

In addition, we would argue that three particular occupational changes impact the chattering classes' work-life relationship. First, while the 'higher' or traditional professions such as lawyers, medical doctors and architects have expanded, these occupations have also fragmented intra-occupationally and, not unconnected, experienced greater (quasi-)market pressures – whether private sector or public sector based. For example, with there now being a mass education of lawyers through universities, Muzio (2004) notes there is an emergence of a new division of labour among solicitors, with polarisation of career opportunities, pay and tasks between two groups: partners and salaried solicitors, with the former economically exploiting the latter. Elsewhere medical doctors complain of 'feel[ing] under siege from a culture of controls', of being buried by bureaucracy and having reconfigured (and less comprehensive) training opportunities so that deprofessionalisation appears to loom large (Puttick 2007: 1). Architects too feel that the era of the 'gentlemanly architect' is coming to an end with increased competition and industry re-organisation (Fowler and Wilson 2004). Generally, UK skill surveys report consistent and continual declining job control and task discretion among professional occupations (Felstead et al. 2007). As a result, some traditional professionals are experiencing dissonance between their anticipated and actual work and associated lifestyles. Second, while the alleged source of economic and jobs growth, the 'new' creative industries professionals experience 'bulimic' or 'volatile' employment. This 'precariate' lurch between famine and feast: between having no work and having to work long hours. New York new media workers, for example, move from project to project with different employers, with typical job tenure only six months (Batt et al. 2001). This project-based employment can create personal and familial financial insecurity and stress. In the UK, the de-regulation of the television industry has led to market uncertainty, production companies cutting costs, skeleton staff operating independent production companies and precarious employment among freelance creative production workers (Dex et al. 2000). Workers feel 'demoralised'. Almost half of one of Dex et al.'s samples required alternative sources of income outwith the industry and one worker reported that 'it is difficult to imagine a long-term involvement in the industry compatible with a healthy personal life' (p. 302). Third, while 'lower' or associate professions, such as nursing and other allied medical occupations, are also expanding, much of these occupations' 'professionalisation' is often little more than a labour market strategy involving a rebranding of training from further to higher education and categorisational relocation up the occupational hierarchy with the attainment of that 'degree' level education (see Anderson 2007; Warhurst and Thompson 2006). Not surprisingly, these workers do not have, to borrow Ferris' (2007) phrasing, traditional professionals' 'way-of-life work' but, instead, 'means-to-ends work'. In other words, such workers may have discarded the label of *vocational training* but have not acquired the *vocational calling* of the traditional professionals while they yet ape the latter's labour market strategy. As such it might be that this labour is more 'proletarianised' than professionalised; having an instrumental rather than moral engagement with work, and regarding work and life practices as not interpenetrating but demarcated.

Such developments indicate that the work-life balance debate is also fuelled by the chattering classes' dissatisfaction with their work and life, and that the cause of this dissatisfaction is not long working hours or unmet demands for flexible working hours but instead rooted in changes to the nature of professional labour. That a key public debate about jobs should be influenced by the chattering classes' experience is not unprecedented. Despite the more voluminous and vicious downsizing redundancies of the 1980s that decimated steel and auto towns, docklands and mining villages, it was not until the 1990s as bank managers, civil servants and media professionals became redundant through delayering that the 'death of the job' became a public issue (rather than industrial relations) – despite job tenure remaining remarkably stable (Auer and Cazes 2003).

Beyond indicating that the middle classes can mobilise their private crises as public concerns, the analysis of the intensification of work and the reconfiguration of professional labour reveals that what distorts workers' work-life experience is not a mere lack of balance that could be restored by family-friendly or flexible working. Negative work-life experiences are due to deeper changes in the relationship between work and life that relate to the nature of work and employment and the fit between labour and lifestyle. This complex configuration thus suggests that work and life can be interpenetrating rather than distinct and balanceable.

Analysing the work-life boundary

The above discussion suggests that the relationship of work and life is not best articulated as one of balance (see also Pocock et al. in this volume) because interpenetration occurs between work and life. The forms, processes and outcomes of this interpenetration are salient again, as they once were in industrial sociology, because of a number of recent developments. The most obvious and most commonly cited are ITC-enabled temporal and spatial workplace changes (see for example Felstead et al. 2005). Precision is difficult but around 7–10 per cent of the UK's working population are regular home-located workers. The penetration of workplace technology into the home is 'fraught', claim Felstead et al., with a majority probably wanting spatial and temporal separation between home and work. However other developments are also having or have the potential to affect the boundary between work and life. There is, for example, speculation that employer attempts to prescribe clothing and appearance standards may well undermine or infringe employees' rights to freedom of expression. Currently it is unclear how the European Human Rights Act 1998 (HRA), which confers rights to respect for private life and freedom of expression, will impact on organisational dress codes and appearance standards. The same is true for new European directives on employment equality that include sexual and religious proclivities and which also have the potential to create clashes between workers' own identities and lifestyles and those prescribed by employing organisations. The wearing of tattoos, piercings and certain items of jewellery and clothing, and even corporate uniforms, are now potential or actual legal flashpoints as workers' human rights and self-expression are pitted against corporate strategies that require particular forms of employee public presentation (Hay and Middleman 2003; see also the British Airways case in Dinwoodie 2007). Relatedly, there is also growing appreciation that employers are now not only concerned with appropriating and transmuting workers' knowledge as a feature of the scientific management identified by Braverman (1974) but also workers' feelings, corporeality and even lifestyles, as the expanding academic literature on emotional, aesthetic and creative labour illustrates (see for example Hochschild 1983, Nickson et al. 2005 and Florida 2004 respectively). Indeed, as Hyman and Marks point out in this volume, the attraction of 'new economy' workplaces was precisely the offer to employees of better work-life balance, which for employers would offer the mutual gain of enhanced employee commitment. Similarly, Hebson et al. (2003) and Cunningham (2005) respectively argue that there exist distinct public sector and voluntary sector ethos as features of individuals' *Weltanschauung* and which influence the job orientation of particular workers, so that a matching occurs between job types and individuals' values and beliefs. This list is not exhaustive but does emphasize that the relationship between work and life is more expansive than that offered in the work-life balance articulation. It also indicates a complex interplay of choices and constraints, as well as different, sometimes competing, interests, in how the relationship between work and life is shaped and experienced.

What is required therefore is another analytical framework for understanding the relationship between work and life. This task has been championed most prominently by Nippert-Eng (1996a, 1996b), who focuses on what she describes as 'boundary work'. Nippert-Eng's premise is that workers can be classified as 'segmentors' or 'integrators'. Boundary work is the active mental management and organisation of practices and artefacts so as to create the segmentation or integration of home and work. Integration occurs when '"home" and "work" are one and the same, one giant category of social existence, for no conceptual boundary separates its contents of meaning' (1996a: 567). Segmentation occurs when the boundary between work and home is 'clear and impregnable ... everything belongs to "home" or "work"' (p. 568). In between the two classifications lies a continuum, though the trend over the past hundred years is towards segmentation. However, no matter where individuals are along this continuum, all are actively engaged in boundary work. Segmentors have two key rings for example, one for work keys, the other for house keys; integrators affix all keys to one key ring. For segmentors, changing into different clothes for work and home is crucial; integrators have an all-purpose home and work wardrobe. Segmentors keep two wall calendars, one at home, the other at work, with no overlapping contents; by contrast, integrators maintain just one pocket calendar.

Re-focusing the analysis, Nippert-Eng's articulation of the relationship between work and life in terms of 'boundary' represents a useful step forward. Nevertheless, four problems are immediately apparent with her particular conceptualisation of boundary work. First, although purporting to present an account of how boundaries are negotiated in everyday *life*, the analysis is again focused firmly on only one aspect of that life – the home. Life, however, involves more than just the home; it encompasses a myriad of activities including leisure, socialisation, and community and voluntary activities. Second, for Nippert-Eng, boundary work is infused with rational 'choices' in which 'detailed decisions' are made solely in the heads of individuals at points at which home and life meet (p. 579). That there might be external constraints or impositions upon boundary work is ignored. So, with regard to Nippert-Eng's example of money, US tax regulation may require a separation of work and home accounts and expenses for self-employed workers; not doing so would probably incur punishment so is not really a choice. Given that such rational decision-making requires information, the third and related problem – the lack of context to boundary work - is puzzling. Beyond generalities, very little detail is offered by Nippert-Eng about her hypothetical cases' terms and conditions of employment or nature of work. Yet, as Felstead et al. (2005) point out, home-located workers are required to be more accountable to their employers than office based employees, and their invisibility to management can be detrimental to their career and pay prospects. As it is so often, the devil is in the detail. How boundaries are 'worked' requires appreciation of external constraints and impositions. Indeed much boundary work, in its broadest sense, involves a third party other than employees and employers – sometimes trade unions – as Mason et al. (2008) point out for the regulation of working time; most typically the state – as work-life balance initiatives demonstrate. These three conceptual problems, however, are made explicable by the fourth – that boundary work is regarded by Nippert-Eng as a personal, individualised endeavour. Drawing on the approach of Georg Simmel, who anticipated phenomenology (Frisby 1981), boundary work is essentially concerned with identity work and the project of the self; in Nippert-Eng's words, to 'evoke the sense of self' (p. 569). It is about 'creating and maintaining ... "territories of the self" amid "our physical, tangible surroundings"' (p. 569) – presumably those keys, wardrobes and calendars but not the managerial imposition, work intensification or acts of resistance that arise through the employment relationship and wage-effort bargain. This latter point is important. There are material conditions, most obviously associated with class, that shape not only individuals' experience of and opportunities at work but also life experience and opportunities, as well as the experience of and opportunities within the relationship between work and life. Within this interplay of interests, expectations and opportunities both choices and constraints exist. Opting for part-time paid work to enable more time for family and friends, leisure or voluntary work has opportunity costs, principally less pay and prospects. Sometimes these costs are worth paying; sometimes they outweigh the benefits. For this reason, downshifting is more topical than typical. As Roberts (2007: 344–5) notes:

> The German time pioneers ... who had voluntarily chosen to downshift substantially and who had accepted commensurate drops in their earnings, remain very rare exceptions, and were regarded as peculiar by most of their German colleagues. The real constraint ... is that they would be unable to downshift while retaining their current jobs, status, salaries and career prospects. In other words, their situation is not one of 'no choice' but of preferring the balances of advantages and problems that accompany their current ... packages.

Boundaries are important therefore in the analysis of the relationship between work and life, and feature not just in Nippert-Eng but also in some contributions to this volume (for example Cohen, de Man et al., and Fangel and Aaløkke).

In this respect, the distinguishing between segregation and integration should not be abandoned because of Nippert-Eng's conceptual weaknesses. However understanding how boundaries are worked requires a more comprehensive account of the complex interplay of interests, expectations and opportunities through which personal choices and material constraints shape the relationship between work and life.

Work-life patterns: moving beyond balance and boundary

Simply locating workers on a continuum of separation and integration overlooks the fact that workers can occupy the same position on that continuum but experience that position differently – positively or negatively most obviously. A more nuanced approach is therefore needed. This approach is provided by Bourdieu's (1990) theory of individuals as producers of social practices, which, we suggest, constitute *work-life patterns*. These patterns comprise any practices that an individual produces: those related to job descriptions and contractual obligations, commuting, education and training, family activities and maintaining friendships, pursuing sports and leisure activities or political and religious interests. While work-life patterns can be externally observed, how they are experienced can vary for the individuals concerned.

Significantly, for Bourdieu, individual practice and experience have to be contextualised. For the analysis of work-life patterns, this approach has four implications. Firstly, the focus on practices prompts an analysis of work practices themselves and the effect they have on work-life patterns. Secondly, to understand work-life patterns, the structural constraints that shape them have to be examined. Such constraints are set by an individual's monetary, cultural and social resources (economic, cultural and symbolic capital) as well as by the structures within which individuals work and live (employment relationship, markets, industries, nations). Both resources and structures can enable and restrain individual practice and thus work-life patterns. Thirdly, individuals' practices are influenced by their lifestyles. Lifestyles include values, beliefs and perceptions related to work and employment and thus influence work-life patterns. Fourthly, Bourdieu points out that practices are produced following context-specific logics. While work centres on the paradigms of paid labour and working to earn one's living, life encompasses a multitude of logics, such as the reciprocity of friendships, unconditional love for family members or the hedonism of consumption. Analysing the different logics and potential tensions between them usefully advances understanding of work-life patterns and experiences. In the following section, we draw on our own and others' research to outline and illustrate these four influences on work-life patterns.

Work practices and the adaptation of work and life

Following Bourdieu's focus on practices, work itself influences work-life patterns. As noted before with Bergman and Gardiner (2007), if work practices are tangible and immobile, then the work-life pattern is likely to exhibit a distinction between work and life. Supporting these findings, Cohen's study of hair stylists (in this volume) demonstrates how hairdressing, as mobile work, leads to work-life patterns in which work and life mix heavily. As stylists work on friends' and family's hair after working hours and outwith the salon, the stylists' work-life boundaries blur with respect to space, time and social interaction. Such work practices tend to require an *adaptation* of work and life, as individuals actively (re-)configure work and life to meet the demands of the respective other. Household chores are slotted into work breaks, furniture and room layouts are adapted to work needs, home-located work is organised around family routines and while wearing a dressing-gown instead of shirt and tie (see for example Fangel and Aaløkke, and Kylin and Karlsson in this volume).

Research by de Man et al. (in this volume) shows how working outwith the standard workplace generally leads to work-life patterns in which work and life mix heavily. Consequently, adaptation to work-life patterns requires considerable personal micro-management of work and life, as done by Musson et al.'s (2006) worker who covered up her PC with a blanket on Friday to erase traces of work from her living room over the weekend. Some workers welcome mobile and intangible work as it enables flexible working and opportunities to coordinate the demands of work and life (Fangel and Aaløkke in this volume). However, workers' preferences are subordinate to the nature of the work to be undertaken. For example tele-workers who might prefer to segment work and life are unable to do so, according to de Man et al., and find themselves having to adapt either their life to their work or vice versa. As a consequence, adaptors do not experience work and life as separable, and work-life balance provisions premised on work-life separation are inappropriate for them.

Structural factors and the accommodation of work and life

The structural embedding of individual practices (Bourdieu 1990) also influences work-life patterns by providing the framework within which individuals accommodate work and life. While MacInnes (in this volume) argues that there are limits to the outsourcing of life practices, it is clear, firstly, that work-life patterns depend on the economic, social and cultural resources of an individual (see the difference between Gail and Rosa in Pocock et al.'s contribution to this volume). Economic capital, for instance, can buy additional time for work (for example by hiring a nanny) or for life (for example by enabling part-time employment). Likewise, individuals' cultural resources, such as educational qualifications influence work-life patterns as they affect employment opportunities (Bourdieu et al. 1981). Lastly, social resources such as extended families or social networks shape work-life patterns and influence work-life experiences by, for example, meeting childcare needs (Williams 2007).

Secondly, the structural context of paid labour influences work-life patterns. Terms and conditions of employment such as flexible working or shift-working can create precarious work-life patterns and negative work-life experiences (see for example Henninger and Papouschek, and Hyman and Marks in this volume). In addition, as Henninger and Papouschek point out, it is those flexible workers commanding the least financial resources who feel most pressured. Work-life patterns are also crucially influenced by the availability or absence of work-life balance provisions, be it the more usual flexible working hours and part-time work or the less usual employer-provided laundry services or 'mother and kid' workplaces (Nuri 2006). However, work-life balance provisions depend not only on employers' goodwill (Schneider et al. 2006) but also on the wider societal context of government policies (Burgess et al. 2007), union representation (Hyman and Summers 2007) and occupational specificity (Moore 2007).

No matter whether workers are segmentors or integrators, how they accommodate work and life depends on a number of structural factors. However, as outlined above, structural factors are largely absent from current work-life boundary debate. Analysing the influencing factors of work-life patterns rather than focusing on individual boundary work can systematically re-integrate these important variables. Importantly, as Ransome (in this volume) suggests, such analyses can illuminate how individuals' choices and constraints occur within work-life patterns.

Lifestyles and the amalgamation of work and life

Lifestyles encompass an individual's 'ensemble of the partners, goods and practices an actor has chosen for himself' (Bourdieu 1998: 21) as well as beliefs, norms and values – about, among other aspects, work. Research on the link between lifestyle and work-life patterns dates back to Weber (1930), who claimed that religious beliefs and values resulted in particular work-life patterns. More recent research has identified the Bohemian lifestyle of artists to promote what can be called *amalgamation* work-life patterns: work and life are blended to such an extent that singling out the respective practices would be a purely academic and analytical undertaking (Murger 1988). Driven by the aim to integrate work and life into one work of art, theatre artists, for example, regard work as life and life as work, providing self-fulfilment in the production of art for art's sake. Friendships and (love) relationships remain within the occupational community; activities outside theatre are reduced to a minimum and geared towards work (Eikhof and Haunschild 2006). An adverse case of work-life amalgamation occurs with Australian rugby league athletes. Initially 'living the dream', these athletes' work-life experience is dramatically changed for the worst as new doping regulations prescribe athletes' activities and behaviours, and enable physical invasion of their home life by the regulatory authorities, according to Khoshaba (in this volume).

As with adaptation work-life patterns, examples of work-life amalgamation indicate that work-life experiences cannot be understood with a simplistic model of work and life as separated spheres. For amalgamators whose lifestyles revolve around their work, work-life balance policies are neither appropriate nor desired; they would not know what to balance. However, while adaptors and amalgamators would both be classified as integrators by Nippert-Eng, their work-life experiences are different. Adaptors perceive work and life as different and often conflicting, whereas amalgamators tend to view the blurring of work and life as positive and beneficial – even rugby athletes initially. Such distinctions are crucial but invisible within the work-life boundary articulation of the relationship between life and work.

Logics of practice and work-life patterns between alternation and absorption

Social practices are driven by what Bourdieu terms field- or context-specific logics. Work practices are produced following the logics of paid labour and of earning one's living, embedded in the general logics of market exchange and return on investment prevalent in the economic field. Life, on the other hand, comprises a variety of logics such as altruism, love or hedonism. Depending on the work itself and its context, these logics of work and life can coexist without interference, allowing workers a fairly frictionless *alternation* between the two distinct spheres. The obvious example is Goldthorpe et al.'s (1968) Luton car workers, who had an instrumental orientation to their jobs; they disliked many aspects of their work but were 'satisfied' with that job because of the level of salary. This salary then provided opportunities in terms of consumption and lifestyle – the famous cars, washing machines and holidays – that had been denied to their parents. Work enabled the life that they wanted to lead.

In work-life patterns with mixed work and life practices, work and life logics can exist as alternatives for the same practices. If both logics advocate the same practices, as for instance in the case of amalgamation work-life patterns, these workers too will not experience conflict (Eikhof and Haunschild 2006). However, as Hochschild (in this volume) demonstrates, the logic of work can crowd out life logics and reconfigure life practices. In Hochschild's example, a management performance evaluation tool is now being incorporated into some US workers' home lives. The practices of being a father and a spouse then become governed by the logic of 'efficiency'. While other of her worker types simply endured – putting relationships on hold for example – these 'busy bees' had a work-life pattern of *absorption* of life by work rather than the alternation between work and life of the Luton car workers. In the work-life boundary articulation, absorber work-life patterns would be classified as integration and the differences between absorption and other integrated patterns, such as adaptation and amalgamation, become indiscernible.

Incorporating the characteristics of work practices, structural constraints, lifestyles and logics into the analysis makes more comprehendible why individuals have certain work-life patterns and different work-life experiences. Employing a practice-theory approach to discern work-life patterns not only extends analysis of the boundaries between work and life but also reveals that there is more to the work-life relationship than either boundary or balance.

Concluding remarks

Whether a concern of workers, employers or government, work-life balance is intuitively a worthy cause. We would not deny that some workers are looking to devote more time to non-work activities and interests, including their families. However our critique reveals the work-life balance debate as empirically and conceptually flawed. Claims of a long hours culture and pent-up demands for more family time appear to be countered by evidence of decreasing working hours and an already common existing flexibility for workers in those hours. Moreover, many workers enjoy their work. Instead the work-life balance debate appears to have two drivers. On the one hand, there appears to be a convergence of government and employer interests centred on labour markets. On the other hand, for some workers there is work intensification rather than work 'extendification' but for others, professional labour, occupational changes are creating dissatisfaction with their work-life experience. The chattering classes' lament also indicates that work and life are not necessarily distinct, balance-able spheres. Other conceptualisations of the relationship between work and life have attempted to focus on the boundary between work and life (Nippert-Eng 1996a, 1996b). This approach is useful though analytically limited. It fails to adequately appreciate that workers with the same degree of integration or segmentation between work and life often have very different work-life experiences. Drawing on Bourdieu (1990), we have suggested that these conceptual deficiencies can be overcome by articulating the relationship between work and life as work-life patterns. These patterns are shaped by the characteristics of work practices, structural constraints, lifestyles and logics.

This articulation stimulates new research agendas about the relationship between work and life. As a starting point, as some of the contributions to this volume make clear, work-life patterns can differ by occupation and industry.

More comparative research is therefore required, which, we would add, might also include comparisons between countries. The means of assessing similarities and differences are important here, as indeed they are for examining the work-life patterns offered in this chapter – adaptation, accommodation, amalgamation, alternation and absorption. It should also be recognised that much current analysis of the relationship between work and life, whether articulated as balance or boundary, has a 'snap-shot' approach, capturing only particular moments or at best short spans of workers work and life (usually that time when they have young children), ignoring the fact that work-life patterns can change as individuals' work and life cycles progress. In order to understand work-life patterning more thoroughly, it would be beneficial to know why, how and when such changes occur. We consider Schmid's (1995) modelling of transitional labour markets to be a useful starting point on which to build this research.

Such research agendas arise once the analytical limitations of the work-life balance articulation of the relationship between work and life are recognised and addressed. Starting with chapters that critique the work-life balance debate, the contributions to the remainder of the book seek to advance analysis and understanding of the relationship between work and life. They reveal that the relationship is not a zero-sum game, that to work less is not necessarily to live more.

Notes

1. Parking at this point debates about 'professionalism' being a labour market strategy (see for example Johnson (1972) but returning to it later in the chapter.
2. Emphasis in the original.
3. In the 20 years to 2004, most percentage occupational growth in the UK has involved professionals (3.4 per cent) and associate professional and technical workers (4.2 per cent; at the bottom, personal service occupations also grew by 3.4 per cent) (Wilson et al. 2006).

REFERENCES

Anderson, P. (2007) 'Stuck in the middle of a metaphor: Intermediate occupations and some limitations of the hourglass economy thesis', paper to the *Work, Employment and Society Conference*, University of Aberdeen.

Auer, P. and Cazes, S. (eds) (2003) *Employment Stability in an Age of Flexibility*, Geneva: ILO.

Banks-Smith, N. (2007) 'In *The Apprentice*, events took an unexpected turn – Sir Alan showed his nice side', *Guardian*, 24 May, 31.

▶

▶

Basso, P. (2003) *Modern Times, Ancient Hours*, London: Verso.

Batt, R., Christopherson, S., Rughtor, N. and van Jaarveld, D. (2001) *Net Working*, Washington: Economic Policy Institute.

Becker, H. (1970) *Sociological Work*, Chicago: Aldine.

Bergman, A. and Gardiner, J. (2007) 'Employee Availability for Work and Family: Three Swedish Case Studies', *Employee Relations*, 29:4, 400–14.

Bolchover, D. (2005) *The Living Dead*, Chichester: Capstone.

Booth, A.L. and van Ours, J.C. (2005) 'Hours of Work and Gender Identity: Does Part-time Work Make the Family Happier?', Centre for Economic Policy Research, Australian National University.

Bourdieu, P. (1990) *The Logic of Practice*, Cambridge: Polity.

Bourdieu, P. (1998) *Praktische Vernunft. Zur Theorie des Handelns*, Frankfurt: Suhrkamp.

Bourdieu, P., Boltanski, L., de Saint Martin, M. and Maldidier, P. (1981) *Titel und Stelle: Über die Reproduktion sozialer Macht*, Frankfurt a.M.: Suhrkamp.

Braverman, H. (1974) *Labor and Monopoly Capital*, New York: Monthly Review Press.

Bunting, M. (2004) *Willing Slaves*, London: Harper Collins.

Burgess, J., Henderson, L. and Strachan, G. (2007) 'Work and Family Balance through Equal Employment Opportunity Programmes and Agreement Making', *Employee Relations*, 29:4, 415–30.

Cain, M. (1964) 'The Life of a Policeman and His Family' in B. Whittaker (ed.) *The Police*, London: Penguin.

Cavendish, R. (1982) *Women on the Line*, London: Routledge and Kegan Paul.

Cunningham, I. (2005) 'Struggling to care: Employee attitudes to work at the sharp end of service provision in the voluntary sector', paper to the *23rd Annual International Labour Process Conference*, University of Strathclyde.

Dex, S., Willis, J., Paterson, R. and Sheppard, E. (2000) 'Freeelance Workers and Contractual Uncertainty: The Effects of Contractual Changes in the Television Industry', *Work, Employment and Society*, 14:2, 283–305.

Dinwoodie, R. (2007) 'U-turn by BA in row over cross', *Herald*, 20 January, 1 & 3.

Eikhof, D.R. and Haunschild, A. (2006) 'Lifestyle Meets Market. Bohemian Entrepreneurs in Creative Industries', *Creativity and Innovation Management*, 13:3, 234–41.

Eikhof, D.R., Warhurst, C. and Haunschild, A. (2007) 'What Work? What Life? What Balance? Critical Reflections on the Work-Life Balance Debate', *Employee Relations*, 29:4, 325–33.

European Commission (1999) *The Future European Labour Supply*, Luxembourg: Office for Official Publications of the European Communities.

▶

▶

European Commission (2004) *Employment in Europe 2004*, Luxembourg: Office for Official Publications of the European Communities.

European Foundation for the Improvement of Living and Working Conditions (2007) *Fourth European Working Conditions Survey*, Dublin: European Foundation.

Fagnani, J. and Letablier, M-T. (2004) 'Work and Family Life Balance: The Impact of the 35-hour Laws in France', *Work, Employment and Society*, 18:3, 551–72.

Felstead, A., Gallie, D., Green, F. and Zhou, Y. (2007) *Skills at Work 1986–2006*, ESRC Centre for Skills, Knowledge and Organisational Performance, Universities of Oxford and Cardiff.

Felstead, A., Jewson, N. and Walters, S. (2005) *Changing Places of Work*, Basingstoke: Palgrave Macmillan.

Ferris, J. (2007) 'Nine to five', *Guardian*, Review, 21 April, 4–5.

Florida, R. (2004) *The Rise of the Creative Class*, New York: Basic Books.

Fowler, B. and Wilson, F. (2004) 'Women Architects and Their Discontents', *Sociology*, 38:1, 101–19.

French, S. and Daniels, G. (2005) 'Work-Life Balance: Evidence from across the UK', *European Industrial Relations Review*, No. 380, 27–9.

Frisby, D. (1981) *Sociological Impressionism*, London: Routledge and Kegan Paul.

Goldthorpe, J.H., Lockwood, D., Bechhofer, F. and Platt, J. (1968) *The Affluent Worker*, Cambridge: Cambridge University Press.

Hay, O. and Middleman, S. (2003). 'Fashion Victims, Dress to Conform to the Norm, or Else? Comparative Analysis of Legal Protection against Employers' Appearance Codes in the United Kingdom and the United States', *International Journal of Discrimination and Law*, 6, 69–102.

Hebson, G., Grimshaw, D. and Marchington, M. (2003) 'PPPs and the Changing Public Sector Ethos: Case Study Evidence from the Health and Local Authority Sectors', *Work, Employment and Society*, 17:3, 481–501.

Hinsliff, G. (2006) 'Overwork triggers £11 billion baby crisis', *Observer*, 19 February, 1 & 3.

Hochschild, A. (1983) *The Managed Heart*, Berkeley: University of California Press.

Hochschild, A. (1997) *The Time Bind*, New York: Henry Holt & Co.

Hooker, H., Neathey, F., Casebourne, J. and Munro, M. (2007) 'The Third Work-Life Balance Employee Survey: Main Findings', *Employment Relations Research Series No.58* London: Department of Trade and Industry.

Hyman, J. and Summers, J. (2007) 'Work and Life: Can Employee Representation Influence Balance?', *Employee Relations*, 29:4, 367–84.

▶

▶

IDS Studies (2000) *Work-Life Balance*, No. 698, November.

Isles, N. (2004) *The Joy of Work*, London: Work Foundation.

Johnson, T. (1972) *Professions and Power*, London: Macmillan.

Mason, G., Mayhew, K., Osborne, M. and Stevens, P. (2008) 'Low Pay, Labour Market Institutions and Job Quality in the UK' in C. Lloyd, G. Mason and K. Mayhew (eds) *Low Wage Work in the UK*, New York: Russell Sage Foundation.

Mayo, E. (1946) *Human Problems of an Industrial Civilisation*, New York: Macmillan.

Moore, F. (2007) 'Work-Life Balance: Contrasting Managers and Workers in an MNC', *Employee Relations*, 29:4, 385–400.

Murger, H. (1988 [1851]) *Scènes de la vie de bohème*, Paris: Gallimard.

Musson, G., Tietze, S. and Scurry, T. (2006) 'Feeling guilty, being left behind and letting bureaucracy in by the backdoor: the hidden aspects of home-based telework and managing the work-life boundary', paper to the *24th Annual International Labour Process Conference*, University of London.

Muzio, D. (2004) 'The Professional Project and the Contemporary Re-organization of the Legal Profession in England and Wales', *International Journal of the Legal Profession*, 11:1–2, 33–50.

Nickson, D., Warhurst, C. and Dutton, E. (2005) 'The Importance of Attitude and Appearance in the Service Encounter in Retail and Hospitality', *Managing Service Quality*, 15:2, 195–208.

Nippert-Eng, C. (1996a) 'Calendars and Keys: The Classification of "Home" and "Work"', *Sociological Forum*, 11:3, 563–82.

Nippert-Eng, C. (1996b) *Home and Work*, Chicago: University of Chicago Press.

Nuri, M. (2006) 'Work-Life-Balance in Kassel', *Personalwirtschaft*, 1, 12–14.

Park, A., Curtice, J., Thomson, K., Phillips, M. and Johnson, M. (2007) *British Social Attitudes: the 23rd Report*, London: Sage.

Pilkington, E. (2007) 'Six in 10 US BlackBerry users check emails in bed, survey finds', *Guardian*, 28 July, 4.

Pomlet, J. (1969) 'The Toolmaker' in R. Fraser (ed.) *Work 2*, Harmondsworth: Penguin.

Puttick, H. (2007) 'Doctors "feel under siege from culture of controls"', *The Herald*, 2 August, 1.

Roberts, K. (2007) 'Work-Life Balance – the Sources of the Contemporary Problem and the Probable Outcomes: A Review and Interpretation of the Evidence', *Employee Relations*, 29:4, 334–51.

▶

▶

Roy, D. (1973) 'Banana Time, Job Satisfaction and Informal Interaction' in G. Salaman and K. Thompson (eds) *People and Organisations*, Harlow: Longman.

Salaman, G. (1974) *Occupation and Community*, Cambridge: Cambridge University Press.

Schmid, G. (1995) 'Is Full Employment Still Possible? Transitional Labour Markets as a New Strategy of Labour Market Policy', *Economic and Industrial Democracy*, 16:3, 429–56.

Schneider, N., Ruppenthal, S., and Haeuser, J. (2006) 'Lippenbekenntnis zur Work-Life-Balance?', *Personalwirtschaft*, 1, 26–9.

Schor, J. (1991) *The Overworked American*, New York: Basic Books.

Sennett, R. (2004) *Respect*, London: Penguin.

Sherman, R. (2007) *Class Acts*, Berkeley: University of California Press.

Terkel, S. (1972) *Working*, New York: Avon.

Thompson, E.P. (1984) 'Time, Work-Discipline and Industrial Capitalism' in A. Giddens and D. Held (eds) *Classes, Power and Conflict*, Houndmills: Macmillan.

Türk, K., Lemke, T. and Bruch, M. (2002) *Organisation in der modernen Gesellschaft*, Wiesbaden: Westdeutscher Verlag.

Warhurst, C. and Thompson, P. (2006) 'Mapping Knowledge in Work: Proxies or Practices?', *Work, Employment and Society*, 20:4, 787–800.

Weber, M. (1930) *The Protestant Ethic and the Spirit of Capitalism*, London: Allen & Unwin.

Williams, P. (2007) 'Understanding how physical and social infrastructure at work and at home can facilitate or impede the development of healthy communities: Findings from the work, home and community study', paper to the *Work, Employment and Society Conference*, University of Aberdeen.

Wilson, R., Homenidou, K. and Dickerson, A. (2006) *Working Futures 2004–2014: National Report*, Wath-on-Dearne: Sector Skills Development Agency.

2 Work-Life Outcomes in Australia: Concepts, Outcomes and Policy

Barbara Pocock, Natalie Skinner and Philippa Williams

Introduction

As with most OECD countries, Australia is a place of change in relation to paid work and households (Charlesworth et al. 2002; HREOC 2007; Pocock 2003). Australian experiences are governed by a range of factors. Three features seem especially important: firstly individual preferences, expectations and aspirations; secondly the institutions that govern life at work and around work (including labour law and its institutions of care, workplaces); and thirdly the cultures which shape the lived experiences of households and communities, including care arrangements, the family, and gendered workplace, household cultures and practices (see Pocock 2003).

This chapter considers some conceptual issues around 'work-life' analysis before reviewing some empirical outcomes of existing arrangements for Australian workers, along with their households. The chapter explores factors that underpin work-life outcomes and, building on empirical findings, offers a model depicting some of the key contributors to work-life outcomes. We argue that an ethic of care needs to accompany Australia's well developed ethic of work, and that new arrangements are necessary to govern their simultaneous realisation in Australia if negative interaction between the spheres of work and the rest of life are to be minimised.

The chapter is in three parts: firstly we discuss the conceptualisation of work and life issues; secondly the state of work and life in Australia; and thirdly some reflections on ways in which better policy settings at work can result in better outcomes. Material for the review of current work and life outcomes for Australians draws on a recent survey, the Australian Work and Life Index (AWALI) (Pocock et al. 2007a).

Conceiving work and life

Understandings about the interaction between work and life have become more sophisticated over the course of the past 20 years. Analysts increasingly apply a life-course approach and better data are being collected in a range of countries. However, the discussion is marked by some conceptual grey areas.

Firstly, it is helpful to define what we mean by 'work' and by 'life' and consider their relationship with work and family. We define work as paid work and life beyond work as the activities outside paid work including household activities and those activities with family, friends and community, including care activities and voluntary activity. We do not assume that 'work' is distinct from 'life': given the growing reach of work into the lives of Australians, this distinction would be absurd, but in order to better understand how work affects the rest of life, it is important to analytically distinguish the activities of paid work from the rest of life beyond the workplace.

This definition subsumes 'family' activities within the definition of 'life' activities beyond work, so that in our definition work-life policy discussion subsumes the very significant field of 'work and family' policy. We do this because for many people without their own children or living in any familiar form of nuclear family, work-life issues are having important effects, not least upon their steps towards family formation and their social fabric. A life-cycle approach demands a broader consideration of the interaction of work with life outside work and outside family, beyond the years of direct family formation and child-rearing, if it is to be broadly useful to social policy analysts.

Secondly, it is important to consider the scope of work-life issues which some suggest are narrowly about time and thus particularly about the 'fit' of working time to time for life and activities outside work (see for example Ungerson and Yeandle 2005). This is certainly an important aspect of work and life, but it does not capture the full interaction. Work-life issues are broader and deeper than work consuming more of our time (although growth in the average length of the working week for full-time Australians over the past 30 years certainly makes this important). Some aspects of work have effects beyond working hours: for example, demanding jobs can affect health and mental and emotional well-being. Indeed it is this kind of spillover from the nature of parents' jobs that many children notice (Galinsky 1999; Pocock 2006). Children in Galinsky's (2005: 229) US study were often very alert to 'the level of stress and exhaustion that parents bring home from work' – effects that are created not only by the hours of work but also by its conditions. In this light, work-life discussion should not focus only upon temporal aspects of work-life interaction but upon both time and other general forms of interference.

Finally, how should we think about work-life interaction? Are they distinct spheres that can be held in balance? This is an important question. It lies at the heart of the common question: how can I get the balance right – as a mother, a worker, a manager? This question implies a frame – to use George Lakoff's (2007) language – which places the individual 'coper' at the fulcrum of 'getting it right'. As Lakoff says, dominant frames are very powerful: 'People think in frames ... To be accepted, the truth must fit people's frame. If the facts do not fit a frame, the frame stays and the facts bounce off' (p. 17). The frame of 'balance', for example, obscures the role of job quality. Even as individual women struggle in daily life to 'get a balance', even as they hear from other women and so many self-help books that getting a balance is pretty hard for many people, they still frame the problem as one they must get right individually, through their personal efforts. This frame has powerful force, partly because it is partly true. What individuals do – during their hours of work, their material aspirations and their patterns of thinking – affect their experiences of work and life. What is more, many individuals cannot do very much about larger public policy settings so they concentrate, very sensibly, on what they can control.

The concept of balance is not helpful given its implication that at the centre of such balance exists a clever or lucky individual who manages to keep things 'in balance'. This framing denies the complex range of actors and forces at work in constructing work-life outcomes. The dominant metaphor of 'balance' overstates the place of the individual in the work-life picture. The metaphor of 'the juggle' is not much better. While balance and juggle are the dominant discursive metaphors, discussions with people about their life and the complex interactions of work and life beyond work do not support the notion of balance and independent spheres. We agree with Halpern and Murphy (2005: 3) when they reject the balance, juggling and separate spheres metaphors and point to the positive (as well as negative) *interactive* nature of work and life:

> Work and family are not a zero-sum game. Although there are reasonable limits to all activities, there are many benefits that accrue to people who both work and have families and other out-of-work life activities. It is time to change the metaphor.

We suggest that the metaphor of 'collision' is more accurate (Pocock 2003). Work and life are not dichotomies but interactive fields, with spillover between them. The boundaries between work and life are not closed but porous. This porosity is at once spatial (with work increasingly undertaken away from the workplace – in the car, on the train, in the home and walking down the street or over food), temporal (with work and care undertaken at the same time) and interactive (with the effects of one sphere affecting the other). For these reasons the term 'interaction' seems superior to 'fit' (given the latter's implications that the two spheres of life sit alongside each other).

Work-life interaction and inequality

Popular public discussion often implies that finding the 'balance' is a matter of canny self-organisation. This perspective denies the gendered, class and ethic differences that shape work-life outcomes for individuals. The individual road to work-life balance is often asserted about senior, successful public figures. In Australia, for example, Gail Kelly, CEO of St George Building Society (until August 2007 when she became CEO of Westpac, one of Australia's largest banks), is often held up as a model of someone who manages it all. Under her leadership, St George's implemented some significant work and family initiatives, including 13 weeks paid maternity leave, the chance to purchase extra leave and career breaks, opportunities for part-time work on return from parental leave flexible working hours for older workers and, most recently, 12 months unpaid leave for grandparents. With respect to work-life balance provisions this made the company a leader in the finance sector in Australia.

Gail Kelly is often held up as an icon of work-life success for women (most recently in *Charter*, an industry magazine for accountants). According to Parker and Lipman (2007: 52) while at the helm of St George, the company 'experienced enormous growth ... At the same time, Kelly has managed to raise four children [including triplets], keep herself in tremendous shape and ensure she is personally accessible to staff. Not surprisingly, she is reported to sleep just four hours per night.' In 2007 Gail Kelly's income from St George was reported at A$4.4 million. This income gives her very considerable resources, alongside those provided by her employer, to secure reasonable work-life outcomes.

However, compare her situation with that of Rosa, a sole parent living in Sydney, recently interviewed as part of a research project investigating the nature of low pay in Australia.[1] Rosa is a sole parent who provides for herself and her five dependent children by working two days a week as a room attendant at a luxury hotel. She was at that time being paid A$14.33 an hour. Rosa also works an additional 16 hours a week at a shop, where she is paid the below award rate of A$10.70 an hour, generating a yearly income of about A$30,000 including around A$10,000 of government allowances, rent subsidy and tax benefits. Rosa's work-life situation, with her long commute and high household demands, is poor. She is time as well as income poor. Gail Kelly earns four times Rosa's annual salary every week.

For both Rosa and Gail, their personal strategies matter, but they are unlikely to determine outcomes. Inequality defines their difference. Professional workers rely on workers such as Rosa to undertake long commutes, daily juggles around multiple jobs and to live on their low pay to sustain the work-life 'balance' of professional and better paid workers like Gail Kelly. The latter often require a much more complex juggle of those they rely on than they undertake themselves, given their material differences in resources.

Such gaps in 'work-life' circumstances raise issues about what Tronto (1993) and Williams (2001) have highlighted as an 'ethic of care' which is necessary to complement our over-developed 'work ethic'. This ethic of care has its international and racial dimensions as many social scientists have discussed (see Salazar Parrenas 2001). Gail Kelly raised her triplets as babies while living in South Africa where the circuits of racialised paid work and care are underpinned by the wide use of low paid servants.

Clearly, the discussion around work-life outcomes is also highly gendered. It is no coincidence that most circuits of 'work-life' and its discussion are primarily built around and conducted by women. Men are often shadowy figures in this world. Every picture of the competently balancing woman should properly include a crowd of ghosts: men – employers, fathers, partners, sons, government ministers – who shape outcomes (for better or worse) for workers such as Gail and Rosa but are all too rarely either visibly or conceptually central. They should be much more central, along with the army of helpers – cleaners, carers – who maintain and support Australia's increasing rate of labour market participation. All these ghosts shape outcomes much more than the volumes of work-life tips that the self-help industry profitably sells women in bookshops and airports.

There are those who think that work-life issues are at the warm and fuzzy end of the human resources industry and policy spectrum – a long way from the hard edges of industrial law making. They are wrong: the rewriting of industrial law in Australia through WorkChoices since 2005 is having important effects on work-life outcomes for many Australians, especially those on lower incomes and on the lower rungs of the labour market. We now turn to some of these outcomes.

Work-life interaction in Australia

What is the state of work-life outcomes in Australia? We recently conducted a survey about work-life interaction in Australia. The AWALI 2007 sample is a national stratified random sample of 1435 Australian workers conducted through computer-assisted telephone interviews over two weekends in early 2007.[2] The survey provides a good representation of the Australian labour force and the analysis is weighted by age, schooling, sex and geographic area to reflect population distributions.

We consider four main findings which have significant policy implications in the Australian context: overall patterns of work-life interaction, outcomes in rclation to hours, and hours preferences and the effect of poor quality jobs on work-life outcomes.

Spillover from work to life, and from life to work: work takes more than life

We asked people about the frequency with which work interferes with activities outside work, with time for family and friends, with community connections. We also asked respondents how frequently the reverse occurs: how often personal life interferes with work activities and restricts time spent at work Confirming international findings, we find that work interferes with life much more than the other way around. For example, 70.0 per cent of both women and men felt that personal life never or rarely interferes with work activities, compared to the 45.1 per cent of men and 50.2 per cent of women who felt that work never or rarely interferes with activities outside work.

It is interesting to note that workers often try to protect their workmates from the effects of stress on the home front: they talk of keeping it to themselves. However, they are not always so able to protect those with whom they live with from stress arising from work. As a woman interviewed by *The Australian* newspaper put it when our results were published: 'I'm an angel at work and a devil at home' (quoted in Lunn 2007: 3). It seems that we work hard to perform ourselves as even-tempered at work, while spilling tensions on those we live with in the hope that our private reserves of love and affection will absorb what we cannot spill at work. This emotional and social 'bank' has its limits as many discover and as research among children shows (Galinsky 1999; Pocock 2006).

Work-to-community interaction is widespread

Public policy and academic debate about the relationship between work and life outside work tend to focus on the reconciliation of work and family, occasionally focusing on workers' capacity to pursue personal and social interests. However, the impact of work on workers' capacity to develop and maintain connections in their community is generally overlooked. These effects include the impact of work on social networks, social cohesion and social capital. Putnam (2000) has drawn attention to these complex and multi-faceted concepts and the links between them. We asked respondents how often work interferes with their capacity to develop or maintain connections and friendships in their community as a broad indicator of the spillover of work onto the broader community fabric. Our findings on this issue indicate that work's interference with community connections is surprisingly widespread (see Table 2.1). Just under half the respondents (47.3 per cent) felt that work interferes with their capacity

Table 2.1   Work interferes with community connections by gender and work status, employees, AWALI 2007 (%)

	Never/ Rarely	Sometimes	Often/Almost always	Total
Men				
Full-time	47.3	30.0	22.7	100
Part-time	74.7	17.1*	8.2*	100
Total	51.2	28.1	20.7	100
Women				
Full-time	48.9	26.2	24.9	100
Part-time	61.5	30.9	7.5	100
Total	54.6	28.4	17.0	100
All				
Full-time	47.8	28.7	23.5	100
Part-time	65.2	27.0	7.7	100
Total	52.7	28.3	19.0	100

Note: Data weighted by Australian Bureau of Statistics data on age, highest level of schooling completed, sex and area. *Estimate not reliable. Hours usually worked per week used to categorise full-time (35 or more hours) and part-time (34 or less) work status. Table excludes self-employed persons.

to build and maintain community connections and friendships to some extent (sometimes, often or almost always).

Feeling rushed or pressed for time: women feel it most

Over half the respondents report frequently (often or almost always) feeling rushed or pressed for time (52.5 per cent, see Table 2.2). Women report more frequent feelings of time pressure (55.6 per cent) than men (49.9 per cent). Given that women are more likely to work part-time and that part-timers overall are less often rushed or pressed for time, this effect for women is pronounced. Working part-time offers men more relief from time pressure than it does women. Overall, women working full-time are most likely to experience high levels of time pressure in their daily lives.

Work-life satisfaction: most employees are satisfied with their overall work-life balance

Most respondents (75.4 per cent) are satisfied with their work-life balance (see Table 2.3). There are small statistically significant associations with gender and part-time/full-time work status. Women (77.2 per cent) were more likely to report feeling satisfied than men (74 per cent) and part-time employees (84.6 per cent)

Table 2.2 Rushed or pressed for time by gender and work status, employees, AWALI 2007 (%)

	Never/Rarely	Sometimes	Often/Almost always	Total
Men				
Full-time	17.0	29.8	53.2	100
Part-time	34.0	35.4	30.6	100
Total	19.4	30.6	49.9	100
Women				
Full-time	8.2	32.4	59.4	100
Part-time	15.8	33.1	51.0	100
Total	11.6	32.7	55.6	100
All				
Full-time	14.0	30.7	55.3	100
Part-time	21.0	33.8	45.3	100
Total	15.9	31.6	52.5	100

Note: Data weighted by Australian Bureau of Statistics data on age, highest level of schooling completed, sex and area. Hours usually worked per week used to categorise full-time (35 or more hours) and part-time (34 or less) work status. Table excludes self-employed persons.

more frequently report satisfaction than full-timers (71.8 per cent). Overall, women working part-time are most likely to be satisfied with their work-life balance.

Work-life interaction and working hours

In the past 30 years the patterns of working hours in Australia have changed significantly, with growth in both part-time and extended full-time working hours. In November 2006, 36.8 per cent of Australian employees worked over-time (40.8 per cent of men and 32.5 per cent of women) and almost half of these employees (48 per cent) were not paid for these hours (ABS 2006b). In our survey, 33.4 per cent worked more than 45 hours a week (20.3 per cent of all those surveyed worked 50+ hours a week and 7.7 per cent worked 60+ hours). Different working hours are associated with sizeable and significant differences in work-life outcomes.

Long hours

The most striking finding is the consistent association between long (45–59 hours) and very long hours (60+) and poorer work-life outcomes. This associa-tion is very pronounced for men and women. More than twice as many men working very long hours often or almost always perceive that work interferes with non-work activities, compared with men working around a full-time week

Table 2.3   Satisfaction with work-life balance by gender and work status, AWALI 2007 (%)

	Not satisfied	Satisfied	Total
Men			
Full-time employees	27.4	72.6	100
Part-time employees	17.7*	82.3	100
Total	26.0	74.0	100
Women			
Full-time employees	29.7	70.3	100
Part-time employees	14.4	85.6	100
Total	22.8	77.2	100
All			
Full-time employees	28.2	71.8	100
Part-time employees	15.4	84.6	100
Total	24.6	75.4	100

Note: Data weighted by Australian Bureau of Statistics data on age, highest level of schooling completed, sex and area. *Estimate not reliable. Hours usually worked per week used to categorise full-time (35 or more hours) and part-time (34 or less) work status. Table excludes self-employed persons. Response range on satisfied with work-life balance: 1 'not at all satisfied' 2 'not very satisfied', 3 'somewhat satisfied', 4 'very satisfied'. Responses 1 and 2 categorised as 'not satisfied', responses 3 and 4 categorised as 'satisfied'.

(35–44 hours). The effect is three times greater among women, although the number of women working long hours is small and the result should be treated with caution.

This effect is most clearly seen in relation to the index of work-life interaction. We construct this index by averaging responses across five measures of work-life interaction: the frequency that work interferes with activities outside work, with time for family and friends, with community connections; the frequency of feeling rushed or pressed for time and the overall work-life satisfaction.[3] The average score is set at 100 with a standard deviation of 15 (very similar to the treatment of standard IQ scores). A score higher than 100 indicates a worse than average work-life outcome and a score lower than 100 indicates a better than average work-life outcome.

When we look at this index in relation to working hours there is a consistent statistically significant association between longer work hours and poorer work-life outcomes ($P < 0.001$) for both men and women. As Figure 2.1 shows, there is a clear relationship between worse work-life outcomes and longer hours. Long hours are consistently associated with worse outcomes relative to the average score of 100 and this effect persists as hours increase from standard full-time to moderate long hours to extended long hours. Work hours account for 10 per cent of the variation in work-life outcomes as measured by the work-life index.

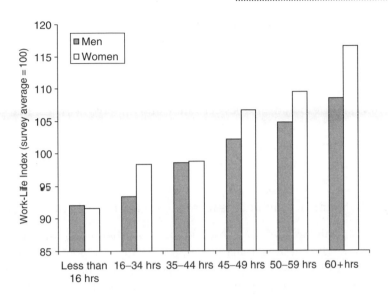

Figure 2.1 Work-life index by hours of work, AWALI 2007

Note: Data weighted by Australian Bureau of Statistics data on age, highest level of schooling completed, sex and area. Estimate for women working 60 or more hours is not reliable. Figure excludes self-employed persons.

With the exception of employees working short part-time hours (< 16 hours) or standard full-time hours (35–44 hours), women consistently have worse work-life outcomes than men as they work longer hours. Overall, women working very long hours (60+) have the worst work-life outcomes. However, the findings for this group should be interpreted with caution as the cell size is small.

Part-time work

The picture is interesting when we turn to part-time work. Much more than in most OECD countries, many Australian women attempt to reconcile work and family through part-time work. Most of them work long part-time hours (two-thirds of all female part-timers in our sample). Overall, part-time hours (< 35 hours per week) are associated with better work-life outcomes. But part-time work hours have different effects for men and women ($P < 0.001$), suggesting that part-time work is not a very effective protector against negative work-life spillover for women. Long part-time hours are associated with significantly worse work-life outcomes for women compared to short part-time hours. Further, there is no difference in work-life outcomes for women working long part-time or standard full-time (35–44) hours. In contrast, work-life outcomes for men do not differ between short and long part-time hours, and men working long part-time hours have better work-life outcomes than men working standard full-time hours (35–44 hours).

These results suggest that, relative to full-time work, extended part-time hours – the work-life mechanism of choice for many Australian women, much more widely used in Australia than in most OECD countries – may not be an effective shield from time pressures or frequent negative work-life spillover. This finding might be explained by a range of factors including the possibility that part-time jobs are low quality jobs (a relationship explored below) or that part-timers have less external support (from partners, the market or the extended family) than full-timers enjoy – which might in turn reflect their internalised belief that as part-timers they should *need* less support.

The fit between actual and preferred hours and work-life outcomes

Many Australian workers work more hours than they want to, while others work less. The latest Australian data on working time preference refers to Queensland (ABS 2006c). In that state in 2006 just over half of all wage and salary earners worked their preferred hours, while one-third wanted to work less and 14.1 per cent wanted to work more. In our study, 40 per cent of those surveyed had a good fit between their actual and preferred hours, which we defined as one hour or less difference between their actual and preferred hours per week (changing this definition to two hours or less made little difference to our analysis). Sixty per cent did not have a good fit, and – as for the ABS data – most of these wanted to work less. Overall, 43.5 per cent of employees wanted to work less. Another group of about 16 per cent wanted to work more.

This result is perhaps surprising given that the survey was conducted at a time of low official unemployment when conditions might be expected to favour a good fit between workers' preferences and outcomes through worker mobility or negotiating strength. International studies suggest that workers who have a good fit between their working time regime and their preferences are likely to have better work-life outcomes (Fagan and Burchell 2002; Messenger 2004). From the perspective of the International Labour Organisation, Messenger has included the notion of 'employee say over working time' as a key element of 'decent work'. Indeed some countries have taken steps to attempt to make this better fit possible for workers through facilitative labour laws that confer on employees a right to request a change in hours of work. The Australian Industrial Relations Commission took a step in this direction in its 2005 family leave test case decision. This ruling has since been removed as a general right through WorkChoices changes to federal labour law under the conservative Howard Government. Our data provide good evidence in support of the proposition that a good fit between hours of work and preferences improves work-life outcomes, reinforcing studies in other countries.

Significantly better work-life outcomes occur for those workers who can get a better fit between the hours they work and their preferences (see Table 2.4). Most employees who prefer more hours are working part-time (65.7 per cent compared

Table 2.4   Working hours preferences and work-life outcomes, AWALI 2007 (%)

	Never/ Rarely	Sometimes	Often/ Almost always	Total
Work interferes with activities outside work				
Actual and preferred hours match	55.7	31.5	12.8	100
Prefer more hours	54.5	30.0	15.5	100
Prefer fewer hours	36.9	35.7	27.5	100
All	47.3	33.1	19.6	100
Work interferes with enough time with family or friends				
Actual and preferred hours match	49.1	36.0	14.9	100
Prefer more hours	44.2	34.6	21.1	100
Prefer fewer hours	27.8	38.3	33.9	100
All	39.1	36.8	24.1	100
Work interferes with community connections				
Actual and preferred hours match	64.1	24.2	11.7	100
Prefer more hours	56.2	32.3	11.5	100
Prefer fewer hours	40.8	30.6	28.6	100
All	52.7	28.3	19.0	100
Feel rushed or pressed for time				
Actual and preferred hours match	20.8	33.9	45.4	100
Prefer more hours	17.6	38.4	43.9	100
Prefer fewer hours	10.9	26.4	62.8	100
All	16.0	31.3	52.7	100

Satisfaction with work-life balance	Not satisfied	Satisfied	
Actual and preferred hours match	15.1	84.9	100
Prefer more hours	25.1	74.9	100
Prefer fewer hours	33.1	66.9	100
All	24.5	75.5	100

Note: Data weighted by Australian Bureau of Statistics data on age, highest level of schooling completed, sex and area. Hours match defined as 1 hour or less difference between actual and preferred hours per week. Table excludes self-employed persons.

to 34.3 per cent working full-time), and most employees who prefer fewer hours are working full-time (89.4 per cent, compared to 10.6 per cent working part-time).

Satisfaction with overall work-life balance is very high among those who have a good fit: around 85 per cent are satisfied, compared with around 75 per cent of those who would like to work more hours and only two-thirds of those who would like to work less. Gender differences within these groupings are small. For those respondents with a good fit between their hours and preferences, only 12.8 per cent often or almost always feel that work interferes with their activities outside work, compared to 27.5 per cent of those working more hours than they prefer. Those respondents who would like to work more hours are not much different from those with a good fit to preferences.

Similarly, work interferes with time for family or friends often or almost always for a third of those who would like to work less, compared to 14.9 per cent of those with a good hours fit. Only a fifth of those who would like to work more say that work often or almost always interferes with their time for family or friends.

Not surprisingly, those with a good fit of hours to preferences (as well as those who would like to work more) have much less work-to-community spillover than those who would like to work less. The latter group are more likely to be working longer hours. Over a quarter of those who would like to work less find that work frequently interferes with community connections.

In sum, the proportion of those with a good hours fit who experience frequent work to life interference is small, especially among women. For example, only 9.6 per cent of women whose working hours match their preferences often or almost always experience interference from work to activities outside of work or to their community connections, compared to 15.4 per cent and 13.5 per cent of men, respectively. On all measures of work-life interference, men are more likely to perceive frequent interference than women, whether their hours match their preferences or exceed or fall short of them.

However, the reverse occurs around feeling rushed: women are more likely than men, to experience frequent feelings of being rushed regardless of the fit of their actual and preferred hours. For example, 67.3 per cent of women who preferred fewer hours felt often or almost always rushed compared to 59.3 per cent of such men; 47.6 per cent of women who sought more hours felt often or almost always rushed for time (40.8 per cent men), not much different from the proportion of 'rushed' women (46.9 per cent) whose hours matched their preferences.

In terms of the overall work-life index, there are significant differences between those respondents with a good fit and those who seek more or seek less hours ($P < 0.001$; see Figure 2.2). Those with a good match of actual and preferred hours have the best work-life outcomes. Those who are working less than they want also have better than average outcomes. Those who are working more than they want, however, have the worst outcomes. This effect is partly explained by the fact that many who want to work less are working long hours.

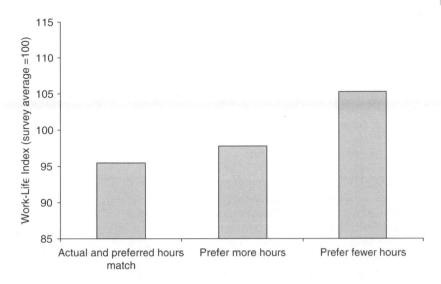

Figure 2.2 Work-life index by fit between actual and preferred hours, AWALI 2007

Note: Data weighted by Australian Bureau of Statistics data on age, highest level of schooling completed, sex and area. Hours match defined as one hour or less difference between actual and preferred hours per week. Original data shown (not adjusted for work hours). Figure excludes self-employed persons.

However, when we control for differences in hours this pattern, while moderated, is sustained. Controlling for hours, the adjusted work-life index scores are 95.9 for those with a good fit, 100.8 for those who would prefer to work more hours and 103.6 for those who would like to work less. This pattern is observed for men and women. Figure 2.2 shows the original (unadjusted for hours) index scores.

Job quality and work-life outcomes

What difference does the quality of the job make to work-life spillover? Many aspects of a job can affect work-life outcomes, including the demands that a job makes (for example workload) and the resources it supplies (for example flexibility and satisfaction). AWALI assesses six job characteristics: work overload, job insecurity, time and task autonomy, work schedule flexibility and overall job satisfaction. Our findings confirm what a large body of literature has already established: job security, load and employee control affect work-life outcomes and the general well-being of workers.

On each of the job quality measures, substantial proportions of employees report low quality working conditions and experiences (see Table 2.5). Specifically, 54.5 per cent of employees agreed somewhat or strongly that they are overloaded

Table 2.5   Job quality outcomes by gender, AWALI 2007 (%)

	Strongly or somewhat disagree	Strongly or somewhat agree
Men		
Work load (often seem to have too much work to do)	43.9	56.1
Job security (worry about the future of the job)	65.9	34.1
Flexible working time (working times can be flexible to meet own needs)	34.6	65.4
Freedom when to do work (a lot of freedom to decide when to do work)	48.8	51.2
Freedom how to do work (a lot of freedom to decide how to do work)	27.0	73.0
Job satisfaction (satisfied with present job)	15.7	84.3
Women		
Work load (often seem to have too much work to do)	47.6	52.4
Job security (worry about the future of the job)	72.4	27.6
Flexible working time (working times can be flexible to meet own needs)	27.7	72.3
Freedom when to do work (a lot of freedom to decide when to do work)	50.8	49.2
Freedom how to do work (a lot of freedom to decide how to do work)	28.0	72.0
Job satisfaction (satisfied with present job)	11.9	88.1
All		
Work load (often seem to have too much work to do)	45.5	54.5
Job security (worry about the future of the job)	68.8	31.2
Flexible working time (working times can be flexible to meet own needs)	31.6	68.4
Freedom when to do work (a lot of freedom to decide when to do work)	49.7	50.3
Freedom how to do work (a lot of freedom to decide how to do work)	27.5	72.5
Job satisfaction (satisfied with present job)	14.0	86.0

Note: Data weighted by Australian Bureau of Statistics data on age, highest level of schooling completed, sex and area. Table excludes self-employed persons.

at work, 31.2 per cent are worried about the future of their jobs (job insecurity), 31.6 per cent have low flexibility around their schedules (job schedule flexibility), 27.5 per cent have little freedom to decide how to do their jobs (work task autonomy), 49.7 per cent have little freedom about when to do their jobs (work time autonomy) and 14.0 per cent are strongly or somewhat unsatisfied with their jobs (job satisfaction). Each of these indicators of poorer quality jobs is associated with worse assessments of work-life interference.

Spillover from work into activities outside work is greater for those in poorer quality jobs, and this finding holds consistently for all six job quality measures and across the five work-life measures. For example, 27.7 per cent of those who experience work overload often or almost always feel that work interferes with activities outside work, compared to only 10.5 per cent of those with no overload. Workers who are worried about the future of their jobs are more likely to experience frequent spillover (26.7 per cent) from work to activities outside work, compared to 16.6 per cent who have secure jobs. Similarly, those with less flexible work schedules are more likely to experience spillover from work to activities outside work (27.4 per cent) than those who have flexibility (16.5 per cent). Freedom about when work is done and how it is done has a similar set of associations. Similar findings of negative work-life spillover are evident for low levels of job security and autonomy. With the exception of job satisfaction, over 60 per cent of employees with poor job quality are also dissatisfied with their overall work-life balance. The relationship between job satisfaction and work-life balance satisfaction appears to be slightly weaker, with 58.7 per cent of dissatisfied workers also reporting dissatisfaction with their work-life balance.

Good quality jobs across a range of job characteristics are thus associated with better work-life outcomes. Lower work overload, more secure employment, more schedule flexibility, more autonomy at work and higher job satisfaction are all associated with less negative work-life spillover, having enough time with family and friends, less interference with community connections, less chance of feeling rushed or pressed for time and better self-assessments of work-life balance.

The overall work-life index scores confirm this picture. There is a consistent and significant difference between employees with good quality jobs compared to poor quality jobs ($P < 0.001$). Those with poor job quality on each of the five measures had the worst work-life outcomes. This effect is particularly strong for work overload, which accounted for 16 per cent of the variation in work-life outcomes. These effects are consistent for men and women. It is interesting to note that on each of the job characteristics, those in poor quality jobs reported longer working hours. However, statistically controlling for work hours does not result in any meaningful changes to the figures reported or the interpretation of the data.

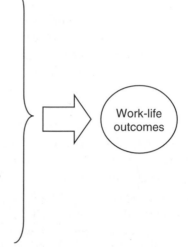

Factors influencing work-life outcomes

Resources: including financial, personal & domestic resources

Demands: including personal aspirations, care and unpaid responsibilities

Job quality: (Some settings act as demands, others as resources)
- *Workload*
- *Job security*
- *Job schedule flexibility*
- *Task autonomy*
- *Work-time autonomy*
- *Job satisfaction*

Worker voice: (Enabling/disabling, for example, fit between actual and preferred hours)

Gender:

Hours worked: (Some settings act as demands, others as resources)

Work-life outcomes

Figure 2.3 A conceptual map of some significant influences on work-life outcomes

These findings have implications for the conceptualisation of work-life issues and the ways in which they are researched. While we have investigated only some factors that might be expected to shape work-life outcomes (leaving aside other likely contenders, for example, personal care responsibilities and the overall state of the labour market), we have found that gender, issues around job quality, hours and the fit between actual and preferred hours are important in constructing work-life outcomes for individuals. We contend that our conceptualisation of the factors affecting work-life outcomes should recognise these factors and their possible moderators. We set out these factors in Figure 2.3, giving some prominence to job characteristics, alongside other likely causal factors.

In this figure we suggest that personal resources and aspirations are relevant to work-life outcomes, but that many other factors well beyond the control of the individual are also influential, including various dimensions of job quality and especially workers' capacity to exercise voice to affect their jobs and their hours. Some of these factors are not independent of each other. For example, job security shapes worker voice: workers without secure employment hesitate to ask for changes in working time. In another example, long working long hours are often associated with dimensions of job quality such as work overload. We also suggest in this model that the resources and demands that individuals deploy or face (whether financial, personal or domestic) shape work-life outcomes, as does gender. A well paid, male worker on a permanent contract and with a high level of domestic support, minimal care responsibilities, a good boss who responds to worker requests, exercising control over working time, task and hours will have much better work-life outcomes that a casually employed, low paid mother with a boss who does not listen – especially if she unwillingly works overtime. This model suggests that greater attention should be paid to aspects of job quality, working hours and worker voice in researching work-life issues.

Public policy options in Australia

What do our empirical findings mean for policy in Australia centred on the reconciliation of work and activities outside it? Work and family issues have been particular sites of lively political debate in recent electoral cycles. However, while the 2001 and 2004 Australian federal elections involved considerable public debate about busy households and stresses on working mothers, very little changed in their aftermath beyond some increases in financial benefits for families and a financial bonus for those families having babies. While these changes are not insignificant, they have been offset by a range of other changes – especially in relation to labour law – that have worked in the opposite direction, making it more difficult for many workers to reconcile work and family especially and resulting in a deterioration in the quality of jobs especially among the low paid.

Changes in industrial law and work arrangements since the 2004 election have reduced minimum standards underpinning workplace agreements, reduced workers' voice at work, lowered payments for working unsocial working time and increased employment insecurity through changes in unfair dismissal law (Elton et al. 2007; Elton and Pocock 2007; Peetz and Preston 2007; Pocock 2006). These especially affect those in service sector employment and low paid jobs. If left in place, these laws are likely to significantly change working conditions, affecting a broad range of workers across the labour market.

As the data that we have presented show, issues of control over working time, influence over working life and job quality have very important effects on the nature and dimensions of work-life interaction. Changes in unfair dismissal regulation in particular cast a long shadow over security and voice at work (Elton and Pocock 2007; Elton et al. 2007). The unconstrained prerogative of employers to dismiss on a whim in companies with less than 100 employees has a powerful effect on workplace climates, especially where employees are unsure of their rights and increasingly un-unionised.[4]

The prospects for more worker influence, especially in smaller and medium-sized companies, are poor in this new climate for those with weak labour market power, including many workers with sizeable caring responsibilities. Where tight labour market conditions exist, this voice might be bolstered but there are few signs of such tightening in many areas of lesser skilled employment.

WorkChoices swims in the wrong direction for better work and life outcomes especially in relation to job quality and say over working time. It has resulted in very significant losses in income for workers on individual agreements in non-managerial employment. Australia's working carers deserve concerted action from all levels of government if they are to work and care under arrangements that recognise and better reward their dual contributions. An economy that openly relies on greater contributions out of households to labour supply – indeed mandates it for certain family forms such as single parent households – must provide decent minimum labour standards and supports. Without them, women and children in particular are the unsung shock absorbers of the current economic boom. Labour and social policy has to be better framed for social justice objectives including a better social settlement for children, low income earners and women. These new policies require new framings, better research and more use of the virtuous circle of good research: piloting, review, full implementation and further rounds of new research.

In 2007 the Work and Family Policy Roundtable, a grouping of academics from diverse disciplinary backgrounds released a set of benchmarks on work and family policy in an attempt to encourage evidence-based policy change on work-life questions (see www.familypolicyroundtable.co.au). These include policy ideas to improve the quality of part-time work, limit long hours and increase government-supported paid maternity, paternity and parental leave. Following European examples, the Roundtable also recommended the creation of a right to request changes in working time arrangements (conferring upon employers a duty to reasonably consider such requests). This recommendation is for a general 'right to request' for all employees with care responsibilities. However, such a right can only be effective if arbitrary dismissal by employers is not possible. The best right to request laws will mean nothing in an environment without dismissal remedies (as now exists in companies with less than 100 employees) and where casual work prevails.[5] A right to shift from casual work to permanent work past a qualifying period is also recommended.

It is clear from our survey results, that current arrangements create pressure points for some workers. Current work-life arrangements in Australia are distinguished by luck – especially around finding a good boss, by an individual's social and financial resources and by their union coverage. Statutory standards (such as minimum wages and penalty rates) and facilitative rights (such as the right to request changes in hours or to convert from casual to permanent work) are examples of policy options that can assist workers to meet their work-life challenges in ways which remove unfairness.

Australia is a rich, happy nation enjoying an exceptional boom. However, work to life spillover is affecting many households while the Australian industrial and policy regime lags behind other OECD countries. This spillover and its consequences are likely to remain pressing social policy issues well into the future.

Notes

1. Interview by Jude Elton in 2006 as part of a collaborative research project involving the Brotherhood of St Laurence, the Liquor Hospitality and Miscellaneous Workers Union and the Centre for Work + Life at the University of South Australia.
2. The survey was conducted by a professional polling company and will be repeated annually. Respondents were selected by means of a stratified random sample process. The concepts, methods, literature, measures and pretests underpinning AWALI are outlined in Pocock et al. (2007b).
3. The scale has a satisfactory internal consistency (Cronbach's alpha = 0.81).
4. Union density in Australia is just over 20 per cent (ABS 2006a).
5. A quarter of Australian workers now work on casual contracts of employment without any formal job security (ABS 2006d).

REFERENCES

Australian Bureau of Statistics (2006a) Employee Earnings, Benefits and Trade Union Membership, catalogue number 6310.0, Australian Bureau of Statistics, Canberra.

Australian Bureau of Statistics (2006b) Working Time Arrangements, Australia, catalogue number 6342.0, Australian Bureau of Statistics, Canberra.

Australian Bureau of Statistics (2006c) Preferred Working Hours of Wage and Salary Earners, Queensland October 2006, catalogue number 6365.0, Australian Bureau of Statistics, Canberra.

Australian Bureau of Statistics (2006d) Forms of Employment, Australia, catalogue number 6359.0, Australian Bureau of Statistics, Canberra.

Charlesworth, S., Campbell, I., Probert, B., Allan, J. and Morgan, L. (2002) 'Balancing Work and Family Responsibilities: Policy Implementation Options', A Report for the Victorian Department of Premier and Cabinet and Department of Innovation, Industry and Regional Development, Centre for Applied Social Research, Royal Melbourne Institute of Technology University.

▶

▶

Elton, J., Bailey, J., Baird, M., Charlesworth, S., Cooper, R., Ellem, B., Jefferson, T., Macdonald, F., Oliver, D., Pocock, B., Preston, A. and Whitehouse, G. (2007) *Women and WorkChoices: Impacts on the Low Pay Sector*, Centre for Work + Life, University of South Australia.

Elton, J. and Pocock, B. (2007) 'Not fair, No Choice: The Impact of WorkChoices on 20 South Australian Workers', Centre for Work + Life, Hawke Research Institute, University of South Australia.

Galinsky, E. (1999) *Ask the Children*, New York: William Morrow.

Galinsky, E. (2005) 'Children's Perspectives of Employed Mothers and Fathers: Closing the Gap between Public Debates and Research Findings' in D.F. Halpern and S.E. Murphy (eds) *From Work-Family Balance to Work-Family Interaction: Changing the Metaphor*, London: Lawrence Erlbaum.

Halpern, D.F. and Murphy, S.E. (eds) (2005) *From Work-Family Balance to Work-Family Interaction: Changing the Metaphor*, London: Lawrence Erlbaum.

Human Rights and Equal Opportunity Commission (HREOC) (2007) *It's about Time: Women, Men, Work and Family*, Sydney: HREOC.

Lakoff, G. (2007) *Don't Think of an Elephant: Know Your Values and Frame the Debate*, Carlton South: Scribe.

Lunn, S. (2007) 'Part-time Work Not All Its cCacked up to Be', *The Australian*, 27 June, 3.

Messenger, J. (2004) *Working time and workers' preference in industrialized countries: Finding the balance*, Geneva, ILO.

Parker, S. and Lipman, N. (2007) 'Gail Force', *Mortgage Professionals Australia*, Issue 7:3, 52.

Peetz, P. and Preston, A. (2007) *AWAs, Collective Agreements and Earnings: Beneath Aggregate Data*, Industrial Relations Victoria, Melbourne.

Pocock, B. (2003) *The Work/Life Collision*, Sydney: Federation Press.

Pocock, B. (2006) 'The Impact of "WorkChoices" on Australian Working Families', Centre for Work + Life, University of South Australia.

Pocock, B. (2006) *The Labour Market Ate My Babies*, Sydney: Federation Press.

Pocock, B., Williams, P. and Skinner, N. (2007a) 'Work, Life and Time: The Australian Work and Life Index 2007', http://www.unisa.edu.au/hawkeinstitute/cwl/default.asp.

Pocock, B., Williams, P. and Skinner, N. (2007b) 'The Australian Work and Life Index (AWALI): Concepts, Methodology and Rationale', http://www.unisa.edu.au/hawkeinstitute/cwl/publications.asp.

Pocock, B., Skinner, N. and Williams, P. (2007) 'Work, Time and Life, the Australian Work and Life Index', Centre for Work + Life, Hawke Research Institute, University of South Australia.

▶

▶

Putnam, R. (2000) *Bowling Alone: The Collapse and Revival of American Community*, New York: Simon and Schuster.

Salazar Parrenas, R. (2001) *Servants of Globalization: Women, Migration and Domestic Work*, Stanford: Stanford University Press.

The Work and Family Policy Roundtable (2007) Benchmarks for the 2007 Election, Work and Family Policy Roundtable, www.workfamilyroundtable. co.au.

Tronto, J. (1993) *Moral Boundaries: A Political Argument for an Ethic of Care*, London: Routledge.

Ungerson, C. and Yeandle, S. (2005) 'Care Workers and Work-Life Balance: The Example of Domiciliary Careworkers' in D.M. Houston (ed.) *Work-Life Balance in the 21st Century*, Basingstoke: Palgrave Macmillan.

Williams, F. (2001) 'In and Beyond New Labour: Towards a New Political Ethics of Care', *Critical Social Policy*, 21:4, 467–93.

3 Work-Life Balance: Three Terms in Search of a Definition

John MacInnes

Introduction

There has been a remarkable surge of interest in what has been termed work-life balance, reconciliation of work and family life or 'family-friendly' policies (hereafter this chapter uses the first term to cover all three). This interest exists across states with all types of welfare regimes (Esping-Andersen 1990) and within supra-state organisations (Council of the European Union 2000; OECD 2002). However, perhaps because the debate has been so policy driven and its concepts appear intuitively obvious, little attention has been paid to three underlying features of the debate: its analytical imprecision, its lack of reflexivity over its origins and the growing contrast between its burgeoning rhetoric and meagre results. After reviewing these three weaknesses this chapter proposes an alternative sociological theory of work-life balance and then uses this theory to conclude that while the debate's origins might lie in state's anxieties about the consequences of low fertility, the work-life balance debate has struck a popular chord because it appears to address a quite different issue: the fact that steadily rising standards of living in capitalist societies come to appear to the members of these societies as an increasing shortage of time.

Analytical imprecision

Beyond occupational psychology, there has been little sustained analysis of the three key terms used in the work-life balance debate and their analogues. Despite the clear distinction made by sociology between work and employment (for example Pahl 1988) the work-life balance literature routinely equates the two. As the male breadwinner system gives way to the dual earner family, rates of cohabitation and divorce rise and lone parent families become more

common; this conflation becomes unhelpful if we wish to analyse the redistri
bution of paid and unpaid work obligations between men and women in diver-
sifying family forms. The meaning of 'life' in the debate slides between unpaid
work obligations, specifically family commitments, leisure in general and ultimately anything that is not employment. Thus, while the OECD (2002: 9) clearly
defines work-life balance as the combination of employment and parenting,
'to earn an income while participating in the most important social activity
of modern life', Wise (2003: 3) asserts that '[e]ssentially, work-life balance is
about helping employees better manage their work and non-work time'. As we
shall see, this imprecision helps legitimate work-life balance policies, since it
obscures whether they affect everyone or specifically target parents.

Scheibl and Dex (1998: 587) avoid discussing the 'weaknesses' in the conceptualisation of 'family-friendly' arrangements because 'a full discussion ... would
be time consuming'. The introduction to Lewis and Lewis (1996: 4) at least
notes that 'families come in many different forms' and that the 'male model'
[*sic*] of work 'may have been family-friendly ... in the sense that it produced a
family wage'. However their remaining discussion proceeds on the assumption
that regardless of their form, or the divergent interests of their members, what
families need is time. Lewis and Lewis assert that the rather diverse objectives
of work-life balance – such as equal opportunities, organisational profitabil-
ity or quality of life – are 'interdependent rather than mutually exclusive' and
avoid analysing terminology in greater depth because '[r]eliance on one term ...
risks losing much of the richness and diversity of the various approaches'
(1996: 6), all of which rather begs such basic questions as what work-life balance
comprises, what its aims are and who is to be affected and whether all family
members do indeed share a common interest in more family 'time'.

By conflating 'work' and employment, work-life balance formulations
assume that the work sphere is essentially about constraints and alienation,
while 'life' is about self-realisation, liberty or the pursuit of happiness. This
assumption follows an often distinguished tradition (for example Thompson
1967: 93); however it is one rooted in a resolutely male breadwinner perspective,
tending to view the family as a 'haven in a heartless world' (Lasch 1977). This
can hardly be adequate for analysing work as the male breadwinner system
collapses. That people may wish to escape rather than facilitate unpaid family
work, that family may embrace abuse as well as loving support or that paid work
may bring financial independence or other rewards beyond income, tends to be
glossed over. As we shall see, it may prove profoundly mistaken to assume that
employment is simply a drain on increasingly precious 'free' time. Finally, as
Sayers (1988) and others have often pointed out, most empirical activities can
easily be defined as 'work', 'life' or both.

Approaches rooted in occupational psychology have at least attempted
to define and use terms in the debate consistently but their value has been

diminished by role theory perspectives that privilege the study of individual orientations at the expense of a more adequate consideration of power, resources and the wider system of social relations. Thus, Frone (2003: 145) defines work-family balance as comprising: 'low levels of inter-role conflict and high levels of inter-role facilitation', while Greenhaus et al. (2003: 123) discuss 'the extent to which individuals are equally involved in and equally satisfied with their work role and their family role'. However, even if we could accept the theoretical implications of role theory, the problems remain of defining the boundaries of such roles and understanding how their occupants choose to fashion them. Is earning the money that funds family life part of the 'family' role? Without the family, where would future generations of those who are to occupy work roles come from? When working parents anticipate role conflict and proceed to curtail or abandon, temporarily or permanently, one or both of these roles, does this not represent an 'inter-role facilitation' qualitatively distinct from that which might occur were employment and parenting more compatible? Conversely, on what grounds can balance be defined to require equal involvement in both work and family roles? And could we accept the absence of overt conflict as evidence of genuine, as opposed to constrained 'balance' (see for example Coser 1956; Lukes 2004)?

It is hardly surprising that role theory research produces micro-level conclusions. Greenhaus and Singh (2003: 6) argue that 'regardless of corporate and government initiatives ... people can attempt to work for employers with progressive work-family cultures ... In addition, self insight, the ability to prioritise life roles and the willingness to periodically re-examine goals and strategies are critical in managing the relationship between work and family'. Is this what the UK Department of Trade and Industry (2000: 4) has in mind when it describes work-life balance as 'something for everyone'? This spectacularly individualist perspective reduces social and structural issues to mere questions of personal preference.

The work-life balance debate also seems to pursue not only diverse ends, but contradictory ones. Once we move beyond the role theory literature, what comprises 'balance' and how it might be measured are rarely specified. Is the aim to make employment and careers more flexible in order to enable employees to spend more time as parents? Or vice versa: to make it easier for parents to be in employment? Is it to *increase* the labour supply by facilitating mothers' employment (fathers' employment rates are already high)? Or is it to safeguard the future supply of labour by facilitating employees' parenthood and thus addressing chronic low and declining fertility in Europe, but presumably, in the short term, *decreasing* the labour supply? If work-life balance policies are about gender equity, where does this leave fathers or women without dependents? Like peace, love and justice, who can decry 'balance' or family 'friendliness' ... until the devil arrives with the detail? Finally, who the parties are to the work-life balance debate is unclear. Does it concern personal life management skills (relevant to everyone) or employee-employer bargaining (relevant to those in paid work), or is it also about state regulation of employment or state provision of childcare and other 'family-friendly' services (relevant to parents)?

Origin and timing

Although the work-life balance debate often seems to deal in rather timeless platitudes, it has only recently surfaced. The 1981 ILO Convention 156 on 'Workers with Family Responsibilities', for example, uses no work-life balance language but by 2000 the *Guardian* (24 August 2000) could note that what had been 'a little known concept at the start of the 90s ... was tripping off the tongue of every politician, policy maker and commentator'. Taylor (2003: 6) notes that 'the flow of research monographs, seminars and conferences over this issue seems to have grown endless in a remarkably brief period of time'.

Three popular explanations for the rise of the debate are simply mistaken. The most common one is that economic change is devouring more of workers' time, energy or both, leaving them too 'time-poor', stressed or exhausted to enjoy 'life', including, of course, the reproductive activities of caring for children or other dependent family members (Schor 2001; Taylor 2003). In this scenario work-life balance simply responds to a new 'long-hours culture' (Kodz et al. 1998), especially in the UK. However, average hours of paid work have been declining in all European countries: by about one sixth across the EU 15 since 1970 (OECD 2004). The proportion of jobs with long hours has been falling in the UK since 1997 (TUC 2003). Averages conceal divergent experiences and changing schedules of work. It may have become more extensive or intensive for specific occupations, industries, labour market segments or groups of workers. Both Gershuny and Fisher (2000) for the UK and other countries and Robinson and Godbey (1999) for the US have used time budget studies to show that, on average, what people think of as their 'leisure' time has increased steadily over the second half of the twentieth century.

A second explanation for the rise of the work-life balance debate is that a rising burden of childcare conflicts with employment. Because it is not the basis of a formal contract, it is harder to measure time and effort devoted to this aspect of 'life'. However, we can estimate the changing volume of family activity in the simple sense of the number of children being raised. The total fertility rate (TFR) gives a synthetic, if imperfect, measure of the children born to an 'average' woman at any point in time. In the 15 countries of the EU it halved from around 2.8 at the height of the post-war baby boom in the early 1960s to around 1.4 by 2005. The demographics of parenthood have also changed. More women remain childless, and those who have children have fewer of them, do so later, in increasingly diverse family forms, with male partners who gradually do more housework and childcare, and with a greater input of both state funded and private services (Esping-Andersen 1999; Irwin 2000; Palomba 2003). Moreover, parents are more likely now to have one or both of their own parents not only alive but in a condition to actively help with childcare (Peréz Diaz 2003). Grandparents are the most important source of childcare for most families after the parents themselves. Income transfers to parents have increased, in theory allowing parents to devote more resources to time-saving bought-in products rather than domestic labour (disposable nappies, ready cooked meals) (OECD 2001). Thus any increasing inability to balance work and family cannot be due to any aggregate increase in the burden of childcare, except insofar as parents choose or are constrained to make it more burdensome.

Third, it is often assumed that the increased demographic weight of parents in the workforce, caused by the decline of the male breadwinner system, has fostered the work-life balance debate by creating an army of worker-parents. Were we to stick to a role theory perspective we might imagine that work-life balance could only ever become an issue in the first place once work and family roles cease to be ascribed by sexual status in the manner theorised by Parsons (1956). However, the UK General Household Survey shows that the proportion of male workers below retirement age with dependent children at home fell from just over one half to just over one third between 1977 and 2002, while for women the fall was from 44 to 37 per cent (MacInnes 2006). Data from the European Social Survey 2002 show the proportion of those in paid work who were either a mother with a child under seven in their household or a father with such a child under seven and a partner at work varied from around one in ten in the Scandinavian countries and the Netherlands to one in twenty in Germany, Austria and Greece. Conversely, over one quarter of the workforce comprised workers who had never had a child living in their household (MacInnes 2006). More mothers may work, but owing to increases in childlessness and rapid increases in age at first birth fewer women of working age are mothers in the first place, while the proportion of workers who have not yet taken on family obligations is increasing.

The work-life balance debate must therefore have another origin. I shall argue below that it lies in states' fears about future demographic trends in the wake of the decline of the male breadwinner system. This becomes clearer if we analyse the latter not only as an employment system but also as a reproductive regime.

Rhetoric and practice

Beyond the wobbly concepts and problematic empirical evidence there has also been little critical reflection over why the volume of earnest official and academic prose about work-life balance has reaped the meagre results visible to any critical reviewer of developments. Research in Britain has observed little real change (Taylor 2003) beyond new forms of hours flexibility, which, according to Hyman et al. (2003: 237), require 'an element of detachment from the realities of contemporary work' to portray as any improvement in balance. Most 'change' in the UK has been driven by state intervention: new regulation of working hours, rights to consultation about hours reductions and extension of childcare provision.

However, any lack of progress is hardly because workers experience little work-life 'imbalance'. To argue that there is little evidence of its deterioration is not to suggest that no problem exists. Table 3.1 suggests that in Europe in 2002 half of those with some kind of family life (a partner, child or both) reported time pressure both at work and at home or reported frequently returning home too tired either to do chores or enjoy their leisure time properly. A 1997 survey on attitudes to work (ISSP 2001) and 1996 Eurobarometer survey (Reif and Marlier 2002) gave similar results. However, before we draw the conclusion that such evidence confirms the analyses offered by the work-life balance debate we should note the remarkable absence of any relationship between such perceived imbalance and family form, life course stage or type of employment (MacInnes 2006). It does not appear, for example, that many parents of young children in the UK want jobs with fewer hours but cannot find them (MacInnes 2005).

Table 3.1 Europe 2002: reports of work-life balance, workers with a partner, child or both (%)

	Agree or strongly agree
There are so many things to do AT HOME, I often run out of time before I get them all done.	54.5
There are so many things to do AT WORK, I often run out of time before I get them all done.	51.8
MY JOB is rarely stressful.	25.6
In the past three months it has happened that …	*Several times each week/month*
I have come home from work too tired to do the chores which need to be done.	51.3
It has been difficult for me to fulfil my family responsibilities because of the amount of time I spent on my job.	32.3

Source: Author's calculations from ISSP (2004). Countries: UK, Germany, Austria, Hungary, Ireland, Italy, Netherlands, Norway, Sweden, Czech Republic, Slovenia, Poland, Bulgaria, Spain, Latvia, Slovakia, France, Cyprus, Portugal, Denmark, Switzerland, Flanders (Belgium), Finland.

If we analyse what increases or decreases people's perceptions of time stress, hours, scheduling and intensity of paid work play some part but not in any simple way. By contrast, job satisfaction has a very strong and positive impact. It appears that people who enjoy their work can cope with long hours and substantial family commitments yet still consider themselves to have sufficient leisure time (Nazio and MacInnes 2007). As Roberts (2007) argues, affluence may bring both growing demands on time and also the resources to purchase time-saving services.

A theoretical framework for analysing work-life balance: activity, time, embodiment and technological progress

It is possible to see the work-life balance debate from a very different perspective if we first consider the definition of terms more rigorously and outline a more coherent sociological theory of what work-life balance might comprise. However, to do so requires a brief theoretical review of the relationship between time, activity, technology and embodiment.

In order to avoid problematic assumptions about where any boundary might lie between work and life, or production and consumption, and avoid frustratingly circular discussions of reproduction, we can think in terms of activities. Activities take time. No matter how universal the development of the market, time itself cannot be commodified. Buying immortality still resembles a camel passing through the eye of a needle. However, buying the use of others' activity for a definite period of time is not only possible but constitutes the essence of employment. The price of such time is wages. Technological progress raises the value of labour and thus also raises the value of time. The inexorable obverse of rising affluence is thus increasing shortage of time, leaving abundance of time as the dubious privilege of those trapped in absolute poverty (Linder 1970). This point is recognised by theorists as diverse as Marx (1976) and Becker (1965).

As well as taking time, activities produce results. Even idleness may 'produce' a rested, potentially more productive, worker. The results of an activity can be distinguished according to whether or not they can be physically alienated and thus transferred to another person and by the rules governing such transfer (such as custom, kinship obligations, market exchange, state regulation). The duration of an activity can be distinct from its formal market exchange if its results are not physically alienable, that is when either the producer or consumer must be physically present to undertake it or reap its benefit. Part 4 of *Capital* Volume 1 is Marx's analysis, in terms of time, of the transformation of the market exchange of labour-power (sold by workers) into labour undertaken by them (managed by its new owner but never physically separable from workers' bodies). If I grow potatoes I can pass on one result of this activity – the potatoes themselves – to others. However, only the actual grower can 'consume' the inalienable results produced by the activity itself: physical fitness, tiredness, a bad back, bucolic enjoyment of the potato patch, pleasure at watching the potatoes flourish. Similarly, paying someone to change my child's nappies may save me time, but deprive me of the loving (or disgusting) experience of the activity itself. While working for others is central to the labour market, most consumption is physically non-alienable. Rarely can one consume something on behalf of another. It makes little sense to employ others to watch films, read books, eat fine meals, play or watch sport, relax, travel, visit friends or relations or, as Linder (1970) suggested, clean one's teeth. Finally, personal services consumed in the moment of their production (for example a meal in a restaurant, education, hospital treatment, a haircut) require the presence not only of the consumer but the producer too.

Marx (1976) first pointed out, and Baumol (1967) rediscovered, that technological progress must, paradoxically, raise the proportion of time in a society devoured by 'technologically non-progressive' activities (where innovation has been slower or is by its nature impossible). Although technological progress benefits almost every activity directly or indirectly, thus reducing the time devoted to it, technologically non-progressive activities come to appear ever more expensive compared to those cheapened more rapidly by innovation: their opportunity cost increases. Since embodied human beings find it as hard to be in two places at once as to live for ever, activities with physically unalienable results are usually intensely technologically non-progressive, because the actor must be present. As Baumol (1967) makes clear, most personal services (including childcare), many of which are managed by the state, are thus technologically non-progressive and prone to trend increases in their relative but not absolute cost, no matter how 'efficiently' they are undertaken.

Needs are the mother not only of invention but also of constraints. Technological progress, rationalisation and science vastly increase the volume of needs satisfied by any given duration of activity. The global proportion of time devoted to activity that satisfies needs directly or indirectly will thus depend on the ratio of such productivity increase to the rate of discovery or invention of new needs. Only if technological progress outstrips the evolution of needs will a population's average proportion of 'free' time increase. However, any such increase in the proportion of free time will not lead to a decrease in its opportunity cost. Precisely that technological progress which keeps in check the proportion of time devoted to satisfying needs must also *increase* the value and thus opportunity cost of any individual unit of time.

Activities exist on a continuum from the freely chosen to absolutely constrained. Following Weber's definition of power, as elaborated by Lukes (2004), activities are more 'constrained' the less any person is able to avoid doing them when their immediate subjective preference is to do something else. The term 'immediate' is unfortunately necessary. It is possible to prefer not to do something as an end in itself but nevertheless have a great interest in it as a means to another end. Sleep might be regarded as a waste of time, but accepted as an unavoidable means to other ends. Many activities flow more or less inexorably from others. 'Freely' choosing to become a parent implies foreseeing (or discovering) that various constraints follow (disrupted sleep for example). To the extent that such calculation of the relationship between means and ends is conscious and consequences can be anticipated or calculated we could define some activity that appears to be constrained as having a greater element of choice and vice versa. To the extent that such links are unconscious or invisible or consequences unanticipated we might continue to focus on the means as an end in itself.

Such consciousness and visibility are largely socially and normatively defined. Childcare obligations may be seen as stemming from the 'free choice' of individuals to become parents and therefore as a means to an end freely chosen by them. Conversely, if childcare is understood as a matter of social reproduction, parents' apparent 'choice' may be seen as a socially regulated and constrained means to this greater end. Free activity has elements of constraint insofar as it reproduces capacities necessary for constrained ones (such as employment that provides the basis of one's livelihood for example). Conversely little constrained activity is totally bereft of fulfilment nor fails to reproduce some capacity for choice by facilitating free activities. I might buy groceries, work dawn to dusk, iron my partner's shirts or change my infant's nappy as, among other things, an act of love that gives me pleasure. I might suffer rapacious exploitation in a poorly paid, physically demanding, mentally alienating and dangerous job but nevertheless find niches of self-expression or comradeship within its confines or 'freely' choose it as a preferable alternative to absolute poverty or an abusive family life. We could take individual and social attitudes to various activities and their social contexts as an approximate guide to placing them on a continuum from freedom to constraint, recognising that there need be no correspondence between the judgment of any given individual or social group or between the views of the same social group over time.

If the value of labour increases over time, so too does its cost of production. However a less noticed correlation of technological progress (as much cause as result) has been a countervailing, largely one-off, leap in the efficiency of the production of human beings (Peréz Diaz 2003). Because they now last around twice as long as they did before the 'demographic transition' (and especially because very few now die before reaching their own fertile years), the proportion of social activity dedicated to reproducing the population has fallen. This reveals another paradox. While the real 'cost' of children in technologically advanced societies has steadily been reduced, the appearance has been the opposite: that of their unprecedented cumbersomeness and expense, above all in terms of their opportunity cost.

A little noticed precondition of societies dominated by 'possessive individualism' is that reproductive sex escapes the general rule that ownership of an activity (and of objects consumed in its performance) confers ownership upon any physically alienable results. Rather than being owned as commodities by their parents, infants can look forward to becoming independent owners of their own capacities as commodities in their own right. However, their journey towards this destiny from their initial total dependence is marked by a number of key features.

Pregnancy, childbirth and infant care are technologically very non-progressive. Pregnancy cannot be shortened, nor would the use of reproductive technology to encourage multiple births be medically responsible. Some of the relevant routine tasks involved in childcare may be quickened or cheapened by technological progress and by the commodification of household subsistence activity (automatic washing machines, disposable nappies, commercially prepared milk and baby-foods, microwave ovens and so on). Some may be made more compatible with other simultaneous activity within and beyond the household or nursery (baby alarms, videos, gameboys, internet supervision). However, there is a finite, rather low, limit to the number of children one adult can responsibly and safely supervise. More importantly, a close, time-consuming relationship with one or two adults (whether or not the biological or social parents of the infant and regardless of their sex) that develops over a lengthy period and is rooted in their physical presence – 'attachment' – is widely believed to be crucial to the psychological health of both parties to the relationship (Winnicott 1965). The *ascribed* status of parents is paramount. Children, especially infants, need someone they know and trust: much more so even than employers. They need consistency over time and cannot be tossed into the nearest available crèche. This parental engagement severely limits the potential commodification of parenting, explains the ubiquity of the family across all known societies (although social arrangements may deliberately attempt to attenuate its influence – as in the kibbutz) and renders its 'industrialisation' impossible. In a dynamic, mobile, market society, this makes children cumbersome (Myrdal 1939). While it is possible to imagine the daily reproduction of individual employees being organised on an entirely market or bureaucratic basis it is no accident that those imagining generational reproduction in this way have done so in the context of futuristic dystopias which feature reproductive technological change, such as Huxley's (1932) hatcheries, Orwell's (1989 [1949]) wonderful 'abolition of the orgasm' in *1984* or Kingsley Davis's (1937) 'professionalisation of childrearing'.

How might 'balance' between different activities be defined? Any definition in terms of some equalisation of time devoted to qualitatively different activities by an individual is logically impossible. Balance must refer to *comparisons* between individuals or groups. One possibility is for each member of a society, across their life course, to undertake a roughly similar ratio of free to constrained activity. Given that economic and demographic change will alter this ratio over time, there still exist complex issues of intergenerational equity to resolve. Moreover, argument over the definition and measurement of 'freedom' and 'constraint' will increase alongside the extension of the social division of labour, as scientific progress makes the relationship between effort and result more opaque and a public with limited time to invest in information-gathering relies increasingly on expert knowledge. Another possibility is for 'balance' to comprise the 'fair' application of norms (for example patriarchy, meritocracy, 'natural' rights), rules of public order (for example rights to private property, inheritance rules) or kinship obligations that determine the basis on which the results of activity are alienated, insofar as such norms and rules command popular legitimacy. In a liberal society, balance in this second sense might comprise such norms and rules as lead to 'balance' in its first sense.

Any activity can be placed on a continuum of constraint and freedom, making the working assumption that all preferences exist within some social or psychological context ('structure'), while most structural constraints are sustained over time by some form of subjective legitimacy which is at least in principle open to rational scrutiny and debate (even if individuals themselves need not be consciously aware of the range of implicit and explicit 'choices' they routinely exercise). No matter how 'liquid' we might wish to imagine 'late' modernity to be (Baumann 2000), analysis must take account of the weight of 'traditional' social action: behaviour and belief determined by routine and repetition. People do not continuously re-calculate their preferences from scratch.

Whatever practical answers we propose to these questions, they reveal that the analogy of 'balance' that appears to be about the contrast between 'work' and 'life' is in essence about the power relationship between different social groups and how their contribution to social activity ought to map on to the distribution of its results. It is about comparisons between those currently with or without caring obligations towards dependent family members; those satisfied or not by the distribution of those obligations between themselves, their partners (if they have one) and the state; those satisfied or not by the supply of effort and hours bargains currently available on the internal and external labour markets and those with or without skills that command an income to meet their needs.

Thus the analogy of 'weight' implied in the term 'balance' can be used only to describe some condition of equality between different groups such that their respective 'work-life balances' are 'fair' or equitable according to some normative order. Beneath its frequently unitarist and individualist language, work-life balance arguments actually turn on older and recognisable problems of the definitions of justice, equity, comparability, proper reference groups and 'balance' between the obligations and rewards of such social groups as the owners of different kinds of labour and capital, men and women, young and old and parents and non-parents about 'Who pays for the kids?' (Folbre 1994) and the whole gamut of questions addressed by collective bargaining and labour market regulation. Thus to represent work-life balance as an issue of personal time management is to fall prey to a spectacularly subjectivist vision of the world.

The origin of the work-life balance debate and demographic fears

The theory sketched above sheds light on the original three problems. Both the timing and 'top-down' nature of the debate is explained by European governments' twin anxieties about the short- and long-term labour supply: they wish to increase the share of employment in total activity. Declining male participation rates (especially for older men) have shifted the policy focus towards raising female labour force participation. This is reflected in the EU's 'Lisbon Strategy' objective of increasing the female employment rate to 60 per cent by 2010 (see http://europa.eu/scadplus/glossary/lisbon_strategy_en.htm). In practice this targets working mothers, because other women already have activity rates similar to men. In the UK, government has focused attention on the low employment rates for lone parents. Similarly, the OECD (2001: 129) argues that 'the main policy concern ... is that of encouraging a higher participation by mothers in paid employment'.

States' second fear concerns the long-term labour supply. Fertility rates across Europe have been low and falling for over a generation. Deaths now exceed births in many EU states (Fahey and Speder 2004). Low fertility raises the prospect of worsening dependency ratios (the proportion of the currently employed, social security and tax paying population to the retired, sick, elderly, young and those in education), population 'ageing' and the longer-term spectre of population collapse (Demeny 2003). Governments also therefore hope to raise fertility by increasing the share of total activity taken by parenting. However, they worry that measures designed to promote the employment of (potential) mothers might further depress fertility. Work-life balance is regarded as the magic wand simultaneously delivering *both* higher employment *and* more parenting. Hence most governments discuss work-life balance, with 'work' meaning formal employment that sustains tax and social security contributions, while 'life' means caring and parenting responsibilities relevant to labour force reproduction.

Governments' interest in work-life balance measures as a way of maximizing both employment and parenting faces three problems however. The first is that moves to reconcile employment and parenting appear better able to raise mother's employment rates than what might be regarded as women workers' mothering rates (Sleebos 2003). Across Europe, the decline in the latter has outpaced the rise in the former, so that the demographic weight of both mothers and fathers in the European workforce is declining. The second problem is that there are two critical constraints on further increasing the share of parenting costs. Governments need to persuade non-parents to accept the required increase in public spending and taxation; however, states in Europe have hitherto continually increased not only the provision of parental benefits and leaves, but also public education, childcare and health systems. In direct contradiction to the argument that the expanding state threatens liberty (Brittan 1975) it could be argued that social reproduction depends upon just such an expansion, given that the state controls so much technologically non-progressive activity. However, the greatest constraint is that, as the theory expounded in this chapter has suggested, some parenting activities are difficult or impossible to transfer, especially those connected to the development and maintenance of attachment, because they are physically inalienable. Moreover, changing norms about what constitutes responsible parenting (for example involved fatherhood, closer supervision) may *increase* the volume of these activities.

Alarmed by the implications of low fertility, states have become interested in identifying the determinants of the latter. This is not the place to comment on this fast expanding research area, except to note one implication of our theory. In contrast to the lay and academic consensus, it suggests that there is no trend increase in the 'cost' of children. Children occupy a declining proportion of parents' time away from employment over the life course. This reduced time may indeed carry an increasing value but so does *all* time. It is not at all clear that work-life balance measures could reduce this time enough to make parenting so much more attractive as to alter fertility rate trends, as such a reduction must soon hit against the physically non-alienable aspects of parenthood. Moreover, there is increasingly abundant evidence that few potential parents pay much attention to state's efforts to alter the time or money costs of children (MacInnes and Peréz Diaz 2007).

The third problem, given the fiscal pressures governments face, is a conflict with employers over who should shoulder the costs of reducing workers' parenting time. Employers wishing to compete in a global economy need not see why they should pay for an activity with overwhelmingly public ends. In a gender egalitarian labour market, why might an employer faced with a choice between workers with or without parental obligations ever choose the former? Employers might collectively wish to secure the reproduction of the labour force but it is in any individual employer's interests to avoid paying for workers' parenting time. Parents spending time away from employment may lag behind in the accumulation of social or human capital and lose familiarity with innovations in knowledge or technology. These factors help explain the meagre results of exhortation upon employers (see for example Evans 2001).

Conversely, it would be a truly Herculean task to take parental obligations 'out of competition' in the labour market, so that their cumbersomeness did not impact upon workers' labour market careers. Such a situation would demand much more than parental leave, dismissal protection or flexibility of working hours and schedules. It would require potential parents to expect any family formation decisions to have no impact on their education and training, employment and career prospects. Nevertheless, we know that fast rising ages at first birth are determined in large part by longer periods in education and potential parents' desire to first consolidate some labour market security (Frejka and Calot 2001).

The explanation of the popularity of the work-life balance debate must lie elsewhere. The theory here suggests that it is popular because it appears to address an almost universal perception of shortage of time. It does so because of the vagueness of the debate's terminology, which allows it to offer 'something for everyone' by using the term 'life' to mean anything from parenting obligations to leisure. However, the theory here also suggests that such time shortage has causes that lie beyond anything work-life balance policies might address, since its roots lie in economic progress as such. As Gershuny and Fisher (2000) point out, Keynes speculated on what the working classes might do with 'leisure' as he assumed that they had little or none. However, as we have seen, leisure time may accompany increase in time 'stress'. Time becomes short and will continue to get shorter because the range of time consuming leisure opportunities workers can afford grows at a faster rate than their leisure time. This helps to explain the paradox that in a world of both shorter working lives and weeks, perception of time shortage increases. This might be seen as an iron law of technological progress. Such work-life 'imbalance' is not caused by lengthening work hours and will not be eradicated by their reduction.

The impact of economic progress on time shortage explains the lack of any robust connection between perceived work-life balance, or its absence, and either employment situation, family form, life course or state policy. It is also why the UK Labour Force Survey shows not only the participation rate but also the workers' weekly hours falling steadily once these workers reach around age 50, that is 15 years before the 'official' retirement age. In an age of relative affluence, increasing numbers of workers can afford to swap income for leisure.

This point brings us to a contradiction at the heart of work-life balance policies and a fourth problem for governments. Work-life balance policies may have distinguished themselves from 'family-friendly' policies and enjoyed greater popular appeal because 'life' is so vaguely defined. Insofar as work-life balance is 'something for everyone', policies that facilitate reduced working hours may work against states' objectives of increasing the labour supply. Conversely, to the extent that they specifically target parents, they risk losing the support of other workers who might see privileges for parents hindering their own interest in more leisure time.

The rhetoric of work-life balance also has policy effects. Language that foregrounds social actors' choices rather than the changing social processes, institutions and constraints within which such choices are made tend to present public issues as private troubles with personal solutions. Encouraging social actors to bring some imagination to bear on what may be long established attitudes may not be problematic. However, conducting the debate in these terms has real consequences for its outcome. It obscures the technological, economic and social forces which have hitherto drawn the state ever further into the reproduction of the population and the way in which the male breadwinner system functioned not only to maintain gender inequality in employment but also systematically constrained women to 'choose' motherhood over employment.

Conclusions

This chapter started out by noting that it is difficult to account for the rapid rise to prominence of the work-life balance debate in the terms of the reasons participants in the debate usually adduce: an increase in time-stress caused by long hours, the demands of family life or an increase in the proportion of workers with parenting responsibilities. The work-life balance debate is indeed about the difficulty of combining employment and parenting in that it originated in states' fears (whether justified or not) that low and falling fertility rates will prevent continuing growth in the labour supply. Governments are unlikely to find an easy resolution of the work-life balance debate for four reasons however. First, work-life balance measures may facilitate hours reductions for affluent workers with the money but not the time for their leisure pursuits. Indeed it may well be this circumstance that has made work-life balance such a popular theme. Second, there is no obvious precedent for state action successfully raising fertility rates in the long term, nor robust evidence that it has been the cost of children in either time or money that has lowered fertility. Third, states will either have to convince employers to subsidise parenting time or convince taxpayers that the costs of parenting should be further socialised. Fourth, to the extent that the work-life balance debate's language continues to focus on micro solutions and individual choice, it will tend to deflect attention from the underlying macro issue: in a gender egalitarian labour market, what form of state regulation of employment and public support for parenting might best 'balance' the rights and obligations of parents and workers across the life course. The latter is indeed a debate that is needed once the superficialities that characterise most work-life balance debate have been cleared away.

REFERENCES

Baumann, Z. (2000) *Liquid Modernity*, Cambridge: Polity.

Baumol, W.J. (1967) 'Macroeconomics of Unbalanced Growth: The Anatomy of Urban Crisis', *American Economic Review*, 157, 415–26.

Becker, G.S. (1965) 'A Theory of the Allocation of Time', *Economic Journal*, 75, 493–587.

Brittan, S. (1975) 'The Economic Contradictions of Democracy', *British Journal of Political Science*, 5, 129–59.

Coser, L.A. (1956) *The Functions of Social Conflict*, London: Routledge.

Council of the European Union (2000) *Council Conclusions on the Review of the Implementation by the Member States of the European Union and the European Institutions of the Beijing Platform for Action: Relationship between Family Life and Working Life*, 13481/00, Brussels: Council of Europe.

Davis, K. (1937) 'Reproductive Institutions and the Pressure for Population', *Sociological Review*, 29, 284–306.

Demeny, P. (2003) 'Population Policy Dilemmas in Europe at the Dawn of the Twenty-first Century', *Population and Development Review*, 29:1, 1–28.

Department of Trade and Industry (2000) *Creating a Work-Life Balance. A Good Practice Guide for Employers*, London: HMSO.

Esping-Andersen, G. (1990) *The Three Worlds of Welfare Capitalism*, Cambridge: Polity Press.

Esping-Andersen, G. (1999) *The Social Foundations of Post-industrial Economies*, Oxford: Oxford University Press.

Evans, J.M. (2001) 'Firms' Contribution to the Reconciliation between Work and Family Life', *Labour Market and Social Policy Occasional Papers*, Paris: OECD.

Fahey, T. and Speder, Z. (2004) *Fertility and Family Issues in an Enlarged Europe*, Luxembourg: Office for the Official Publications of the European Communities.

Folbre, N. (1994) *Who Pays for the Kids?*, London: Routledge.

Frejka, T. and Calot, G. (2001) 'Birth Calendar Changes by Generation in the Low Fertility Countries at the End of the 20th Century', *Population*, 56:3, 397–420.

Frone, M.R. (2003) 'Work Family Balance' in J.C. Quick and L.E. Tetrick (eds) *Handbook of Occupational Health Psychology*, Washington DC: American Psychological Association.

Gershuny, J.I. and Fisher, K. (2000) 'Leisure in the UK across the 20th Century' in A.H. Halsey and J. Webb (eds) *British Social Trends*, London: Macmillan.

▶

▶

Greenhaus, J.H., Collins, K.M. and Shaw, J.D. (2003) 'The Relation between Work-Family Balance and Equality of Life', *Journal of Vocational Behaviour*, 63, 510–31.

Greenhaus, J.H. and Singh, R. (2003) 'Work Family Relationships' in C.D. Spielberger (ed.) *Encyclopedia of Applied Psychology*, San Diego: Elsevier.

Huxley, A. (1932) *Brave New World*, London: Chatto and Windus.

Hyman, J., Baldry, C., Scholarios, D. and Bunzel, D. (2003) 'Work Life Imbalance in Call Centres and Software Development', *British Journal of Industrial Relations*, 41:2, 215–39.

International Social Survey Programme (2001) *Work Orientations II, 1997* [computer file] 1st edition, ZA3090, Zentralarchiv für empirische Sozialforschung Köln.

International Social Survey Programme (2004) *Family and Changing Gender Roles III, 2002* [computer file] 1st edition, ZA3880, Zentralarchiv für empirische Sozialforschung, Köln.

Irwin, S. (2000) 'Reproductive Regimes: Changing Relations of Inter-dependence and Fertility Change', *Sociological Research Online*, 5:1, U151–U167.

Kodz, J., Kersley, B., Strebler, M.T. and O'Regan, S. (1998) *Breaking the Long Hours Culture*, Report 352, London: Institute for Employment Studies.

Lasch, C. (1977) *Haven in a Heartless World*, New York: W.W. Norton and Co.

Lewis, S. and Lewis, J. (eds) (1996) *The Work-Family Challenge*, London: Sage.

Linder, S.B. (1970) *The Harried Leisure Class,* New York: Columbia University Press.

Lukes, S. (2004) *Power: A Radical View*, Basingstoke: Palgrave Macmillan.

MacInnes, J. (2005) 'Work-Life Balance and the Demand for Reduction in Working Hours: Evidence from the British Social Attitudes Survey 2002', *British Journal of Industrial Relations*, 43, 273–95.

MacInnes, J. (2006) 'Work Life Balance: Baby Bust Response or Baby Boomers' Reward?', *European Societies*, 8:1, 223–49.

MacInnes, J. and Peréz Diaz, J. (2007) '"Low" Fertility and Population Replacement in Scotland', *Population, Space and Place*, 13:1, 2–21.

Marx, K. (1976) *Capital*, Vol. 1, Harmondsworth: Penguin.

Myrdal, A. (1968 [1939]) *Nation and Family*, Cambridge MA: MIT Press.

Nazio, T. and MacInnes, J. (2007) 'Time Stress, Well-being and the Double Burden' in G. Esping-Andersen (ed.) *Family Formation and Family Dilemmas in Contemporary Europe*, Bilbao: Fundación BBVA.

OECD (2001) 'Balancing Work and Family Life: Helping Parents into Paid Employment', OECD *Employment Outlook*, 129–66.

OECD (2002) *Babies and Bosses, Reconciling Work and Family Life*, Vol. 1, Paris: OECD.

▶

▶

OECD (2004) 'Clocking in (and out): Several Facets of Working Time', *OECD Employment Outlook*, 17–59.

Orwell, G. (1989) *1984*, Harmondsworth: Penguin.

Pahl, R. (1988) *On Work*, Oxford: Basil Blackwell.

Palomba, R. (2003) 'Reconciliation of Work and Family', *European Population Papers*, Strasbourg: Council of Europe.

Parsons, T. (1956) 'The American Family: Its Relations to Personality and to the Social Structure' in T. Parsons and R.F. Bales (eds) *Family Socialization and Interaction Processes*, London: Routledge and Kegan Paul.

Peréz Diaz, J. (2003) *La madurez de masas*, Madrid: Observatorio de las Personas Mayores & IMSERSO.

Reif, K. and Marlier E. (2002) *Eurobaromter 44.3OVR Employment Unemployment and Gender Equality*, February–April 1996 [computer file], ZA2830, GESIS, Köln.

Roberts, K. (2007) 'Work-Life Balance – The Sources of the Contemporary Problem and the Probable Outcomes: A Review and Interpretation of the Evidence', *Employee Relations*, 29:4, 334–51.

Robinson, J.P. and Godbey, G. (1999) *Time for Life*, Pennsylvania: Pennsylvania State University Press.

Sayers, S. (1988) 'The Need to Work: A Perspective from Philosophy' in R. Pahl (ed.) *On Work*, Oxford: Basil Blackwell.

Scheibl, F. and Dex, S. (1998) 'Should We Have More Family-friendly Policies?', *European Management Journal*, 16:5, 586–99.

Schor, J. (2001) 'The Triple Imperative: Global Ecology, Poverty and Worktime Reduction', *Berkeley Journal of Sociology*, 45, 2–16.

Sleebos, J. (2003) 'Low Fertility Rates in OECD Countries: Facts and Policy Responses', *OECD Social Employment and Migration Working Papers* No. 15, Paris: OECD.

Taylor, R. (2003) *The Future of Work Life Balance*, Swindon: Economic and Social Research Council.

Thompson, E.P. (1967) 'Time, Work Discipline and Industrial Capitalism', *Past and Present*, 38, 56–97.

Trades Union Congress (TUC) (2003) *Things Have Got Better – Labour Market Performance 1992–2002*, London: TUC.

Winnicott, D.W. (1965) *The Maturational Processes and the Facilitating Environment*, London: Hogarth Press.

Wise, S. (2003) *Work-Life Balance Literature and Research Review*, Employment Research Institute: Napier University.

4 The Boundary Problem in Work-Life Balance Studies: Theorising the Total Responsibility Burden

Paul Ransome

Introduction

This conceptual chapter asks whether, in concentrating largely on the experiences and concerns of women in family households with infant children, current academic discourse on work-life balance uses an unnecessarily narrow model of what is involved when people try to reconcile the various aspects of work and life. An alternative model is proposed, based on the idea of the *total responsibility burden*, which attempts to shift the focus away from how responsibilities are divided up *ex post* and towards how the burden is arrived at in the first place. 'Total responsibility burden' is defined as the sum of the responsibilities that members of households have set for themselves and which they need to discharge successfully in order to maintain the fabric of the household and the well-being of household members, and to the standards which they expect and/ or aspire to. These standards will vary from one type of household to another. In most cases, household members who discharge these responsibilities will be adults, the main exception being young-carer households. Although work-life balance research generally focuses on family households, the principles of total responsibility burden can also be applied to single-person households. It is not just couples and families who seek to 'balance' their necessary and recreational labour but also single persons. Approximately a third of households in the UK are made up of single-person households (Social Trends 2005: Table 2.5).

The chapter begins with a critical review of why the current, narrow division-of-labour model has become dominant in the work-life balance discourse before describing the principles and key constituents of an alternative model. Of particular importance is the inclusion of a third realm of *recreational labour* to emphasise that there is much more to work-life balance than paid work and unpaid caregiving. It is also suggested how, by enabling new kinds of comparison between one type of household and another, the alternative model can inform the future research agenda in this field.

The narrow division-of-labour model

The narrowness of the current model of work-life balance can be traced back to its origins in earlier discourses centred on the sexual/gender division of labour (for example Crompton 2002; Crompton et al. 2005; Irwin 2003; Walby 1997, 2004). The strength of this 'division-of-labour' model is that it has produced detailed empirical research into the contexts and responses of family women and especially of those carrying the double burden of paid work and infant care (Dex and Bond 2005; Duncan et al. 2003; Houston 2005; Marks and Houston 2002; Warren 2004). Its corresponding weakness, however, is that the division-of-labour model, which was developed to look specifically at the situation of women in family households with young dependent children, is not easily transferable to the *majority* of households which do not conform to this specific type. At any given moment in the UK in 2006, for example, approximately 22 per cent of households fall into the category presumed by the model, while a further 60 per cent are accounted for equally by family households *without* dependent children and households composed of *individuals* (single-parent family households account for 8 to 10 per cent of households). Even within this specific 22 per cent type of household, the scope of the division-of-labour model is further reduced when consideration is given to changes through the family life-course (Gardiner et al. 2007; McKie et al. 2002). The critical phases of work-life balance decision-making are relatively short and occur mostly in the early years of parenthood. Empirical evidence shows that levels of economic activity among female adult members of family households vary directly according to the number and age of dependent children (Social Trends 2005: Table 4.3).

A number of factors can be identified in explaining why the division-of-labour model dominates the current discourse on work-life balance. First, and looking at its ideological and political objectives, the sexual/gender division of labour paradigm is strongly influenced by a desire to shift the focus of academic research away from men and towards the concerns and experiences of women. If 1970s malestream sociology was all about male manual workers in industry, 1990s femalestream sociology was all about female carers in the home. The paradigm is thus motivated by a desire to advocate the social and political position of women. As I have argued elsewhere (Ransome 2007) however, these important steps forward in the analysis of social phenomena also impose a number of constraints on the analytical framework by naturalising the assumption that 'balance' (or 'equal division') can be used as a metaphor for 'equality'. Work-life balance thus becomes the latest way of theorising relations between women and men in society. As will be argued below, for those who set out from the presumption that gender relations are inherently unequal and exploitative, work-life balance is theorised as a manifestation of inequality, a mechanism through which inequality is perpetuated. Work-life balance can never be seen as a *solution* to the problem of inequality between gendered social roles, a way of looking afresh at the distribution of household responsibilities between adults/partners/carers because it is already characterised as an integral part of such inequalities.

A second issue, then, is that the current discourse tends to define work-life balance issues as mainly of concern to women. The objection against this design feature of the paradigm is not that men (or for that matter family women *without* dependents or single-person households) are never mentioned in the discourse because obviously they are. The point is that conceptually speaking, rather than being conceived as full and active participants in the work-life balance drama, men in particular often appear (or do not appear) as somewhat passive constituents of the background against which the real action is taking place. Part of the reason for this approach seems to be an assumption that, despite evidence to the contrary (Burchell et al. 2002), work-life balance is largely unproblematic for men and people without dependents, because they are willing participants in market work (see also MacInnes' and Pocock et al.'s contributions to this volume). They appear not to mind the long-hours culture and work intensification because the role of income getter is one with which they are universally happy. A similar query is raised by Hakim (2005: 55–6) who contends that much of the current discourse seems to presume that, if it were not for the constraints of sex discrimination and patriarchy, *women also* would automatically select full-time market working. The default setting of the discourse seems to be that paid employment is the surest way of achieving full citizenship and that, if it were not for the inconvenience of dependents of one kind or another, everybody would ordinarily prefer to be engaged full-time in paid employment.

A third issue is methodological and concerns uncertainty in the discourse over whether to theorise the situation people (and especially women with dependents) are in primarily as *individuals* or as members of family partnerships. This is particularly evident in accounts that pursue equality and social justice agendas (Lister 2002; McKie et al. 2002; Williams 2002), for whom welfare regimes constitute an essential part of the wider context of social rights in which work-life balance decisions are made (Crompton et al. 2005; Esping-Andersen 2002; Walby 2004; Windebank 2001). Equality and justice are, after all, properties of individuals not households. The rhetoric of the discourse is to support people's claims for individual rights but the pretext of work-life balancing is that partners have to forego some of their individual preferences in order to support the common household effort. Greater consideration could usefully be given to deciding, firstly, whether the correct 'unit of analysis' in studies of work-life balance is the individual or the household (see Wallace 2002), and, secondly, how to accommodate a notion of 'self-sacrifice', 'altruistic compromise' or even of 'rights-mediation' within models of the work-life balance decision-making process.

Fourth, the current discourse has also been affected by the policy context from which it has emerged. Academic commentators have been pulled in a particular direction in response to the current UK Labour government's desire to make everyone, women and men, responsible not only for market work but also for care work (Barlow et al. 2002; *Critical Social Policy* 2002; Gallie 2002; Scourfield and Drakeford 2002). While the intention of the earlier rhetoric of 'family-friendly policy' was to encourage employers to make it easier for women with dependent children to re-enter the labour market (www.dti.gov.uk/work-lifebalance, www.employersforwork-lifebalance.org), the rhetoric of 'work-life balance' implies attempts politically to get beyond 'natural assumptions' that men are the breadwinners and women are the carers, and to make women responsible for both (Bond and Sales 2001; McDowell et al. 2005; Williams 2001). Women are no longer chained to the kitchen sink; they are expected to take on responsibility for paid work *as well*.

The inevitable conclusion here is that although the principle of a non-gendered and more equitable division of responsibilities between adults in family households is agreed it will only become a reality if men are prepared to take on caring responsibilities to the same extent and with the same apparent enthusiasm with which women are taking on breadwinning responsibilities. As Esping-Andersen (2002: 70) puts it: '[It] is fairly clear that changes and adaptations in social behaviour have been pretty much limited to the female side of the coin. ... If we want more gender equality our policies may have to concentrate on men's behaviour.' McKie et al. (2002: 897) are similarly cautious about this possibility given that, even though there have been 'major shifts in family formation, women's participation in the labour market and debates about the changing role of men ... traditional assumptions about the relationship between femininity and caring remain relatively intact' (see also Doorewaard et al. 2004; Duncan et al. 2003).

While there is no question that work-life balance decision-making is interconnected with, and takes place in the context of, domestic and social divisions of labour, the conceptual design of the current model makes it very difficult to consider processes of domestic decision-making as *anything other* than a mechanism of the division of labour. This model will continue to provide empirical confirmation of the sexual/gender division of labour because this is what it is designed to do. From this perspective, the division-of-labour model is not 'narrow' but simply 'universal'.

Principles of the alternative model

Moving from critique to reconstruction, this section of the chapter recommends an alternative to the narrow division-of-labour model, based around the idea of the *total responsibility burden*. The overall aim of the alternative model is to develop a way of analysing and evaluating work-life balance decision-making that can be applied to all households and not just to those comprised of adult partnerships with infant dependent children.

The main difference between the alternative model proposed here and the narrow division-of-labour model is that rather than focussing on how the burden of responsibilities in households is divided up, greater consideration is given to understanding how that burden is arrived at in the first place. The model is theorised in such a way as to see the total responsibility burden as emerging from a complex, often circular process of decision-making rather than as a linear stimulus-response type model in which household members are simply expected to carry the burden that is somehow put in front of them by forces beyond their control. The active decision-making process might include such things as deliberate lifestyle and life-planning (family-planning) choices, and, especially important, preferences for the kind and level of activity household members are prepared to take on. Of particular note, and as will be discussed in more detail shortly, the alternative model tries to give proper consideration to the fact that people do not just aim to meet responsibilities for market and non-market necessary labour (the familiar constituents of the established paradigm), but also seek to express and satisfy needs for pleasure, leisure and enjoyment through the vital realm of *recreational labour*.

As these differences already suggest, the alternative model assumes that it is the household, rather than the individuals in it, which is the proper unit of analysis for investigating work-life balance decision-making. The basic design principle here is that it makes more sense to approach the question of how household members find ways of dividing the overall burden of household responsibility by looking at the overall size and shape of that burden first rather than by starting with its disbursements between individual household members. In the end, of course, it is individuals who have to meet the burden, but the allocation of the burden cannot be decided in advance of knowing what that burden *is*. As noted in the introduction, the total-responsibility-burden model also applies to single-person households because, clearly, work-life balance decision-making is not something which is only found in family households. Significant differences in the level and mix of responsibilities between one type of household and another should not affect the *applicability* of the model.

Support for this approach comes from the fact that age and number of dependent children is *the* crucial determinant of the total responsibility burden, a burden which, both in terms of sheer quantity and also in terms of the range of demands it makes, *sets the target* for the overall amounts of market and non-market labour that have to be supplied. It seems equally probable that, although the source and content of the burden will obviously vary from one household to another (it need have nothing to do with the care of infant children), people make assessments of the total responsibility burden in largely the same way, whether they are living in pensioner households, in young-couple households, in shared-accommodation households or in single-person households.

Methodologically, rather than regarding most households as somewhat inconvenient deviations from the ideal-typical 22 per cent type, the direction of comparison could be reversed. The decision-making strategies of households with dependent infants could be analysed in terms of how they compare with others of the same type and those households which have a quite different composition. The particular challenges faced by households with infant children, and more specifically still of the sub-type comprising single-parent households, could be explored in terms of ways in which they are *not able* to use the same kinds of decision-making strategies nor deploy their energies and resources in balancing different needs and responsibilities in the same way as other, possibly more prosperous, households. It might turn out that an *in*ability to apply 'best practice' work-life balance strategies might be a *cause* of anxiety and stress leading to further social disadvantage, rather than poor work-life balance choices being *caused by* anxiety, stress and lack of resources.

The total responsibility burden model

Looking a little more closely at the kinds of activities the total responsibility burden consists of, a basic typology of the model is provided in Figure 4.1.

A first part of the burden is made up of necessary labour that sub-divides into market and non-market work. As is common in all discussions of the nature of work in market societies, categorical distinctions relate less to inherent properties of the activity than to *where* it takes place and whether one gets *paid* for doing it (Ransome 1996). Also following conventional definition, non-market necessary labour is made up of the substantial realm of unpaid work which has to be carried out to maintain the structure and fabric of the household. Depending on household composition and on stage in the family life-course, the most demanding aspect of this category of activity is likely to be responsibility for unpaid care work. Although the most prevalent and visible form of unpaid care work (and, given the preoccupations of the current paradigm, the one which has attracted most attention in the research literature) is care for young dependent children, changes in the needs of household members over

Type	Sub-type	Utility	Contexts of choice
necessary labour	market work 'work' (paid) non-market work/'life' (unpaid)	extrinsic, practical outcomes	altruistic, other-directed, obligations structured by forces within and outside household
recreational labour	community activities, self-care, personal time, leisure, pleasure, enjoyment	intrinsic, personal satisfaction	self-oriented, self- directed, self-selecting, resource-dependent

Figure 4.1 Key elements in the total responsibility burden

the life-course produce a need for other kinds of care such as eldercare (Gardiner et al. 2007; Williams 2001).

In addition to direct care work the category 'necessary non-market work' encompasses a wide range of household tasks, including cleaning, washing, shopping and cooking as well as an array of further repair and maintenance duties for keeping the fabric of the household in good order (Cancican and Oliker 2000; Glucksman 2000; Williams 2002). Indicating the emergence in the research literature of a sense of dissatisfaction with the very loosely defined categories of the division-of-labour model (Lewis 2003; Pettinger et al. 2005; Taylor 2002, 2004), a number of contributors to the work-life balance debate have also identified some of the more ephemeral and subjective 'needs' or 'responsibilities' of household members. Drawing on Connell (1987), for example, Glover (2002: 255) lists responsibilities such as 'household management', 'direct' and 'indirect' care and 'emotional work'. Referring to Hochschild (1989), Bradley et al. (2005: 212) include the 'labour of emotional maintenance'.

Also responding to concerns with the limitations of the division-of-labour model, the alternative model includes a third distinct category of *recreational labour* to acknowledge the importance of activities whose primary aim is the satisfaction of individual and subjective needs rather than communal and objective ones. The basic principle of including this category is that life comprises more than necessary labour. Although the narrow model hints at the inclusion of these more subjective and distinctly pleasure-oriented activities in its category 'life', it can be argued that they are weakly theorised and treated as thoroughly subordinate to activities in the category of paid and unpaid 'work'. The category of recreational labour includes a range of beyond-the-household or community activities such trade union and political activity (Bradley et al. 2005; Taylor 2005). It also includes such things as sleep, leisure, meals, self-care and relationships which Ungerson and Yeandle (2005: 248) categorise as 'personal time' as distinct from 'work time' and 'care time'. Particularly impor-tant, and again as has been identified as a weakness of the division-of-labour model, is proper inclusion in the model of a range of activities aimed purely at leisure, pleasure and enjoyment (Ransome 2005).

The chief conceptual distinction between this new model and the old one is that activities that are lumped together in the poorly defined category of 'life' are specified much more clearly in the new model. The more personal, self-oriented and self-directed recreational activities are given a clear category of their own, while unpaid non-market 'life' activities, which includes most of the care work, are also recognised for what they are, that is *necessary* labour. As far as work-life balance decision-making is concerned, paid and unpaid necessary activities are given equal weight in the model (there is no presumption that paid market work is more important to the household than unpaid non-market work), while self-oriented and self-directed recreational activities are given the same status in the model as are activities in the category necessary labour. The model is not, therefore, prejudiced for or against any particular type of activity from the outset.

By opening up the model to include a broad and variegated range of activi-ties that, as the quality of life literature has shown, are obviously highly significant for people not only socially, but also personally and emotionally (Lewis 2003; Taylor 2004; Warren 2004; Williams 2001), it becomes possible to develop a much more integral understanding of how the total responsibility burden is arrived at. The key insight here is that by giving full consideration to all the activities that people engage in, rather than looking selectively at paid and unpaid work alone, this model offers criteria that can be usefully applied in analysing and comparing work-life balance decision-making in *all* types of households. The alternative model is also more democratic than the division-of-labour model that, paradoxically, tends to perpetuate a somewhat hierarchic perception of the relative significance in the mix between 'high status' paid work and 'low status' unpaid work. By giving equal analytical weight in the model to all activities, the work-life balance strategies that household mem-bers develop to meet the responsibility burden can be seen as supportive and enabling rather than as exploitative and disabling.

Sociologically, one would expect to find that the total responsibility burden in one type of household would be more similar in respect to others of the same general type than to those of a different type. Such categorical similarities are likely to be significantly influenced, in the first instance at least, by household composition. Looking at the ideal-typical 22 per cent type, for example, opportunities for recreational activity are likely to be much more restricted by the high demands of especially non-market care work than might be the case in young-couple households who have no dependents. Looking specifically at working-age female employees' perceptions of the leisure domain, Warren (2004: 115) concludes: 'Feeling financially comfortable, and then having no children, were the most important and consistent ingredients of a satisfactory leisure domain, which [is] a key indicator of quality of life.' A similarly high proportion of care work might be required in pensioner households as in single-carer household although the *kind* of care might be quite different. At the same time however, and acknowledging that households even in the same broad category are *not* identical in terms of their work-life balance decision-making and strategy, differences *between* *them* could also usefully be explained in terms of differences in how their total responsibility burden is arrived at. Differences in expectations about standard of living, lifestyle preferences and consumption activity and about levels of participation in the recreational realm are clearly significant elements in this mix (Ransome 2005).

Implications of the model

Motivation

It will be useful to make a few further comments about the model and the kinds of motivation and activities that might be associated with the various types and sub-types. First, the primary motivation for discharging energies in the form of necessary labour comes from the awareness that the practical sustainability of the household depends on it. Utility is extrinsic in the sense that it is weighted strongly towards practical outcomes. Clearly there are margins between, for example, having surplus earned income as opposed to having just enough to pay the bills, or between having a really clean house or one that is just habitable, but household members will be aware that any prolonged shortfall in the supply of necessary labour in its various forms threatens the sustainability of the household and the well-being of its members (or perhaps companion animals in single-person households).

The primary motivation for performing recreational labour comes from awareness of the need to find rewards and pleasures that go beyond an altruistic desire to help keep the household going. Borrowing Marxist topography, it could be said that the satisfactory discharge of necessary labour establishes the infrastructure of the household. As a result, members enjoy a platform for reaching the superstructural realm of leisure, pleasure and enjoyment. The personal dimension in what Williams (2001: 488) has usefully called 'personal time and space' is weighted towards intrinsic utility and personal satisfaction, in the sense that pleasure is essentially experiential and thus subjective. However, it can also be argued that the personal dimension may contribute to the infrastructural security of the household because happy household members are bound to be more productive than unhappy ones. Unlike the narrow model which tends to imply that non-work or leisure activities are not productive but trivial it can be noted that household members who become depressed as a result of having insufficient opportunity for recreational labour can add considerably to the total responsibility burden of the household. Therefore, first-order intrinsic benefits that accrue to the actor have a second-order, proto-extrinsic benefit to other members of the household. There might also be a similar balance between altruism and personal satisfaction in the performance of recreational labour through community activity.

Single-person households

One of the most serious limitations of the old model is the difficulty it has in accommodating different kinds of households and particularly single-person households. To the extent that the sexual/gender division of labour paradigm presumes that all divisions of labour are exploitative, the old model has little to say about the approximately one third of all UK households in which people make these 'divisions' alone. There are two points that can be made here: one conceptual and the other more practical. Taking the practical point first, the division-of-labour model does of course have important things to say about single-person households because, notwithstanding their single-person status, the choices that individuals make about the range and type of activities they want to engage in, and especially their employment preferences, are made in the context of the division of labour *in society*, not just the *domestic* division of labour. One of the clear advantages, then, of the narrow model, is that it highlights the linkages between the decision-making processes in households and the decision-making processes in society. Its weakness, as has already been suggested, is that in assuming that the latter more or less entirely dominates the former it has a rather narrow conception of the full range of choices and activities that people make in their households. These are deficiencies that the alternative model is designed to overcome by emphasising that the total responsibility burden is a joint undertaking, a shared entity arising from expressions of individual choice and preference. The conceptual point is that, unless it is assumed that members of single-person households only see their lives one-dimensionally in terms of necessary labour and especially of market work, then consideration should be given to how their balance of their activities is also determined by lifestyle preferences, expectations about standard of living, aspirations for recreation and consumption and so on. Just because the total responsibility burden of a household is not dominated by non-market care work does not mean that its members have no work-life balance decisions to make. Again, sociologically, it would be interesting to compare work-life balance decisions and decision-making processes in single-person households with those in other kinds of households in order to explore the extent to which personal preferences do or do not survive the decision-making process.

Choice

As noted at the start of this chapter, and as in more detail elsewhere (Ransome 2007), one of the reasons for developing an alternative model of work-life balance decision-making is to shift the emphasis away from seeing the burden as a *de facto* life situation which people are simply confronted with and towards seeing it as something that is intimately connected with previously made lifestyle preferences and choices. In much of the current debate however, and again drawing on the discourse of the sexual/gender division of labour paradigm, the tendency is to regard the work-life balance decisions as ringed-round by tight structural constraints (see for example the exchanges between Hakim 1998 and Crompton and Harris 1998; also Brannen et al. 2005). In the case of recreational labour, the choices household members make are 'free' but are nonetheless restricted by levels of disposable (surplus) income and disposable (surplus) or 'free' time (Gershuny 2000, 2002; McKie et al. 2002).

In one sense, having to provide market and non-market labour to secure the material well-being of the household does constitute a form of structural constraint, inasmuch as people agree to do things that they might otherwise not have done if they were not members of households with all the responsibilities and obligations this membership entails. Other constraints come in the form of prevailing conditions in the labour market or the global economy (Bond and Sales 2001; Burchell et al. 2002; Fleetwood 2007). For other academic commentators, constraint also comes in the form of gendered expectations about what a 'normal' division of responsibilities is supposed to be. As Barlow et al. (2002: 111) describe it, the decisions people make 'are not simply individual, therefore, but are negotiated in a collective way', and they are taken 'with reference to moral and socially negotiated views about what behaviour is expected as right and proper'. In this perspective, variation does not occur at the individual level at all but at the level of 'particular social groups, neighbourhoods and welfare states' (see also Brannen et al. 2005; Crompton et al. 2005; Duncan et al. 2003).

While accepting, as Glover (2002: 262) usefully puts it, that 'macro-institutional and structural factors' provide the general context of work-life balance decisions, the more immediate and specific context of households themselves must also be given due weight. A work-life balance decision 'is not solely an individual decision: it is a socially negotiated decision taken by an individual in the immediate context of the household, possibly together with other household members' (ibid.; see also Wallace 2002). Even within speci-fied segments of society where very much the same structural conditions are thought to apply, households are *not identical* but vary in respect of lifestyle choices and expectations: whether and when to have children; how much community activity they want to be involved with; aspirations for leisure, pleasure and enjoyment and so on. Warren has found, for example, a good deal of variation between different types of household and the kinds of decision-making which goes on there; variation that highlights 'some of the limitations of these gender-based approaches to the household division of labour' models that 'fail to emphasize distinct within-society variation' (2002: 108).

Unless one is proposing a highly dynamic concept of structural constraint that is flexible enough to account not only for variation between one house-hold and another but also for the emergence of new kinds of household and family partnership (Duncan et al. 2003), it seems sensible to accept that evi-dent variation arises in part from the capacity people have for making choices that really do affect their lives and society. In this respect at least, the alterna-tive model proposed here is much closer to ideas in Hakim's preference theory (2000) that proposes that women (and men) do make proactive lifestyle choices about whether to be home- or work-centred or whether to try to be adaptive and look for a balance between home and work. While acknowledging that Hakim's analysis remains controversial (although aspects of preference theory have been supported empirically, see Doorewaard et al. 2004; Houston and Marks 2005; McRae 2003), it has the potential to move the debate forward by drawing attention to the fact that work-life balance decision-making is not an isolated process which occurs *ex post* but is very much an integral consequence of decisions made at earlier stages. Adopting a more optimistic view of the role of choice in work-life balance decision-making, the model suggests that, even faced with unexpected changes in circumstances, household members do have the capacity to re-evaluate their decisions and to adjust their work-life balance strategy in light of what Giddens (1990: 38) calls 'incoming information'. At the risk of splitting conceptual hairs, it could be said that there is a significant dif-ference between 'self-restraint', which household members agree to impose on themselves, and external 'compulsion' which, to paraphrase Marx, signifies that one's labour is not 'free' but 'forced'.

Boundary issues

Finally, the argument returns to the issue of theorising where the 'boundary' lies between one category of activity and another, even of whether a satisfactory conception of 'boundary' can be achieved at all. In the division-of-labour model the battle lines are clearly drawn between paid work and unpaid care work. This separation preserves the analytical symmetry in the sexual/gender division of labour paradigm between men (paid workers) and women (unpaid care providers) (see for example Crompton 1999; Dex and Bond 2005; Walby 1997). As the significance of women's contribution to the household through involvement in market work has increased (Hakim 2000; Warren 2002), perceptions of where the boundary lies, and of 'the boundary problem' more generally, has tended to shift so that the boundary is now seen as partly between paid and unpaid activity but increasingly between women who do both paid and unpaid work and men who only do paid work (Houston et al. 2005). While this slippage certainly supports ideological and political initiatives to press for gender equality, it makes the model correspondingly *less* useful as a research tool for analysing how people combine the various aspects of their paid and unpaid, market and non-market, activity.

The alternative model offers a clear way out of this dilemma by treating the relations between one category of activity and another not in terms of borders and boundaries at all but in terms of bundles of activity. Bundles that might contain more of one type than of another type but which nonetheless amount to, and are seen in terms of, a share of the total responsibility burden. Following proposals made by Williams (2001: 'ethics of care'), Glucksmann (2000: 'total social organisation of labour'), Hakim (2000: 'adaptive households'), Irwin (2003: 'social configuration') and Taylor (2004: 'individuals' work domains'), the divisions of responsibilities by and between members of households are increasingly being conceptualised non-dichotomously and non-hierarchically as fluid assemblages of complementary activities. Although the division of activities will neither be easy to measure nor in any simple sense 'equal', notions of negotiation, cooperation and compromise, of reciprocity and complementarity might be better terms for what occurs here than 'balance'. The concepts of 'differentiation' and 'interdependency' which Le Feuvre (1999) and Irwin (2003) have deployed in reviewing ideas about the male breadwinner model provide useful points of departure here.

Conclusion

This chapter has argued for the replacement of the narrow division-of-labour model of work-life balance with a more flexible and universal model based on the idea of the total responsibility burden. Although useful when operating in rhetorical mode and when challenging broad policy agendas, the narrow model precludes a more energetic discussion of variation between individuals and households in respect of work-life balance decision-making and strategy. As a result, much current academic discourse on work-life balance generally refers only indirectly to the work-life balance decisions of most men, whether or not they are members of family households, family men and women who do not have dependents or women and men who live in non-family and single-person households. It has also had little to say so far about work-life balance issues for people who are below or beyond typical working age. In short, as long as work-life balance is only applied to family households with young dependent children and is subsequently generalised as a *de facto* confirmation of the normalised sexual/gender division of labour in society as a whole, the concept unfortunately loses any potential it might have for moving beyond such stereotypical perceptions of divisions of labour.

The alternative model proposed here allows important distinctions to be made between (i) the total responsibility burden that underpins work-life balance decision-making, (ii) the strategies households subsequently deploy for meeting those responsibilities and (iii) the actual work-life balance activity in which household members engage. Focusing in this chapter on the first of these three stages, the strength of the model is that it recognises that the final stage, the actual distribution of necessary and recreational labour, is not something that household members simply fall into, or is imposed on them by forces entirely beyond their control, but arises from a previous, and often quite complex process of making choices and decisions, of developing strategies and plans of action. Work-life balance is the *result* of the process, not the *beginning* if it.

Acknowledgements

The model proposed here follows earlier work exploring the limitations of the current work-life balance discourse (Ransome 2007) and, it is hoped, will provide the basis for a subsequent detailed analysis of the concept of recreational labour. I am grateful to the editors of this volume for their critical comments and support.

REFERENCES

Barlow, A., Duncan, S. and James, G. (2002) 'New Labour, the Rationality Mistake and Family Policy in Britain' in A. Carling, S. Duncan and R. Edwards (eds) (2002) *Analysing Families: Morality, and Rationality in Policy and Practice*, London: Routledge.

▶

▶

Bond, S. and Sales, J. (2001) 'Household Work in the UK: An Analysis of the British Household Panel Survey', *Work, Employment and Society*, 15:2, 233–50.

Bradley, H., Healy, G. and Mukherjee, N. (2005) 'Multiple Burdens: Problems of Work-Life Balance for Ethnic Trade Union Activist Women' in D.M. Houston (ed.) (2005) *Work-Life Balance in the 21st Century*, Basingstoke: Palgrave Macmillan.

Brannen, J.S., Lewis, A. and Nilsen, A. (2005) 'Individualisation, Choice and Structure: A Discussion of Current Trends in Sociological Analysis', *Sociological Review*, 53:3, 412–28.

Burchell, B., Lapido, D. and Wilkinson, E. (2002) *Job Insecurity and Work Intensification*, London: Routledge.

Cancican, F. and Oliker, S. (2000) *Caring and Gender*, London: Sage.

Connell, R.W. (1987) *Gender and Power: Society, the Person and Sexual Politics*, Cambridge: Polity Press.

Critical Social Policy (2002) Special Issue: 'New Divisions for Labour: Alternatives for Caring and Working', 22:1.

Crompton, R. (ed.) (1999) *Restructuring Gender Relations and Employment: The Decline of the Male Breadwinner*, Oxford: Oxford University Press.

Crompton, R. (2002) 'Employment, Flexible Working and the Family', *British Journal of Sociology*, 53:4, 537–58.

Crompton, R., Brockmann, M. and Lyonette, C. (2005) 'Attitudes, Women's Employment and the Domestic Division of Labour: A Cross-national Analysis in Two Waves', *Work, Employment and Society*, 19:2, 213–33.

Crompton, R. and Harris, F. (1998) 'Explaining Women's Employment Patterns: "Orientations" to Work Revisited', *British Journal of Sociology*, 49:1, 118–47.

Dex, S. and Bond, S. (2005) 'Measuring Work-Life Balance and Its Covariates', *Work, Employment and Society*, 19:3, 627–37.

Doorewaard, H., Hendrickx, J. and Verschuren, P. (2004) 'Work Orientations of Female Returners', *Work, Employment and Society*, 18:1, 7–27.

Duncan, S., Edwards, S., Reynolds, T. and Alldred, P. (2003) 'Motherhood, Paid Work and Partnering: Values and Theories', *Work, Employment and Society*, 17:2, 309–30.

Esping-Andersen, G. (2002) *Why We Need a New Welfare State*, with D. Gallie and M.J. Hemerijck, Oxford: Oxford University Press.

Fleetwood, S. (2007) 'Why Work-Life Balance Now?', *International Journal of Human Resource Management*, 18:3, 387–400.

Gallie, D. (2002) 'The Quality of Working Life in Welfare Strategy' in G. Esping-Andersen (ed.) *Why We Need a New Welfare State*, Oxford: Oxford University Press, 96–129.

▶

▶

Gardiner, J., Stuart, M., Forde, C., Greenwood, I., MacKenzie, R. and Perrett, R. (2007) 'Work-Life Balance and Older Workers: Employees' Perspectives on Retirement Transitions Following Redundancy', *International Journal of Human Resource Management*, 18:3, 476–89.

Gershuny, J. (2000) *Changing Times: Work and Leisure in Postindustrial Society*, Oxford: Oxford University Press.

Gershuny, J. (2002) 'Service Regimes and the Political Economy of Time', in G. Crow and S. Heath (eds) *Social Conceptions of Time: Structure and Process in Work and Everyday Life*, Basingstoke: Palgrave Macmillan.

Giddens, A. (1990) *The Consequences of Modernity*, Cambridge: Polity Press.

Glover, J. (2002) 'The "Balance Model": Theorising Women's Employment Behaviour' in A. Carling, S. Duncan and R. Edwards (eds) (2002) *Analysing Families: Morality, and Rationality in Policy and Practice*, London: Routledge.

Glucksman, M. (2000) *Cottons and Casuals: The Gendered Organisation of Labour in Time and Space*, Durham: Sociology Press.

Hakim, C. (1998) 'Developing a Sociology for the Twenty-first Century: Preference Theory', *British Journal of Sociology*, 49:1, 137–43.

Hakim, C. (2000) *Work-Lifestyle Choices in the 21st Century*, Oxford: Oxford University Press.

Hakim, C. (2005) 'Sex Differences in Work-Life Balance Goals' in D.M. Houston (ed.) (2005) *Work-Life Balance in the 21st Century*, Basingstoke: Palgrave Macmillan.

Hochschild, A.R. (1989) *The Second Shift*, New York: Viking.

Houston, D.M. (ed.) (2005) *Work-Life Balance in the 21st Century*, Basingstoke: Palgrave Macmillan.

Houston, D.M. and Marks, G. (2005) 'Working, Caring and Sharing: Work-Life Dilemmas in Early Motherhood' in D.M. Houston (ed.) (2005) *Work-Life Balance in the 21st Century*, Basingstoke: Palgrave Macmillan.

Irwin, S. (2003) 'Interdependencies, Values and the Reshaping of Difference: Gender and Generation at the Birth of Twentieth-century Modernity', *British Journal of Sociology*, 54:4, 565–84.

Le Feuvre, N. (1999) 'Gender, Occupational Feminisation, and Reflexivity: A Cross-national Perspective' in R. Crompton (ed.) *Restructuring Gender Relations and Employment: The Decline of the Male Breadwinner*, Oxford: Oxford University Press.

Lewis, S. (2003) 'The Integration of Paid Work and the Rest of Life. Is Post-leisure Work the New Leisure?', *Leisure Studies*, 22, 343–55.

Lister, R. (2002) 'The Dilemmas of Pendulum Politics: Balancing Paid Work, Care and Citizenship', *Economy and Society*, 31:4, 520–32.

▶

▶

Marks, G. and Houston, D.M. (2002) 'Attitudes Towards Work and Motherhood Held by Working and Non-working Mothers', *Work, Employment and Society*, 16:3, 523–36.

McDowell, L., Ray, K., Perrons, D., Fagan, C. and Ward, K. (2005) 'Women's Paid Work and Moral Economies of Care', *Social and Cultural Geography*, 6:2, 219–35.

McKie, L., Gregory, S. and Bowlby, S. (2002) 'Shadow Times: The Temporal and Spatial Frameworks and Experiences of Caring and Working', *Sociology*, 36:4, 897–924.

McRae, S. (2003) 'Constraints and Choices in Mothers' Employment Careers: A Consideration of Hakim's Preference Theory', *British Journal of Sociology*, 54:3, 317–38.

Pettinger, L., Parry, J., Taylor, R. and Glucksmann, M. (2005) *A New Sociology of Work?*, Oxford: Blackwell.

Ransome, P.E. (1996) *The Work Paradigm: A Theoretical Investigation of Concepts of Work*, Aldershot: Avebury.

Ransome, P.E. (2005) *Work, Consumption and Culture: Affluence and Social Change in the Twenty-first Century*, London: Sage.

Ransome, P.E. (2007) 'Conceptualizing Boundaries between "Life" and "Work"', *International Journal of Human Resource Management*, 18:3, 374–86.

Scourfield, J. and Drakeford, M. (2002) 'New Labour and the "Problem of Men"', *Critical Social Policy*, 22:4, 619–40.

Social Trends (2005) No. 35, London: ONS.

Taylor, R. (2002) *The Future of WLB?* Economic and Social Research Council, Future of Work Programme, Swindon.

Taylor, R.F. (2004) 'Extending Conceptual Boundaries: Work, Voluntary Work and Employment', *Work, Employment and Society*, 18:1, 29–49.

Taylor, R.F. (2005) 'Rethinking Voluntary Work' in L. Pettinger, J. Parry, R. Taylor and M. Glucksman (eds) (2005) *A New Sociology of Work?*, Oxford: Blackwell.

Ungerson, C. and Yeandle, S. (2005) 'Care Workers and Work-Life Balance: The Example of Domiciliary Careworkers' in D.M. Houston (ed.) (2005) *Work-Life Balance in the 21st Century*, Basingstoke: Palgrave Macmillan.

Walby, S. (1997) *Gender Transformations*, London: Routledge.

Walby, S. (2004) 'The European Union and Gender Equality: Emergent Varieties of Gender Regime', *Social Politics*, 11:1, 4–29.

Wallace, C. (2002) 'Household Strategies: Their Conceptual Relevance and Analytical Scope in Social Research', *Sociology*, 36:2, 275–92.

▶

▶

Warren, T. (2002) 'Gendered and Classed Working Time in Britain: Dual-employment Couples in the Higher/Lower-level Occupations' in G. Crow and S. Heath (eds) *Social Conceptions of Time: Structure and Process in Work and Everyday Life*, Basingstoke: Palgrave Macmillan.

Warren, T. (2004) 'Working Part-time: Achieving a Successful "Work-Life" Balance?', *British Journal of Sociology*, 55:1, 99–122.

Williams, F. (2001) 'In and Beyond New Labour: Towards a New Ethics of Care', *Critical Social Policy*, 21:4, 467–93.

Williams, F. (2002) 'The Presence of Feminism in the Future of Welfare', *Economy and Society*, 31:4, 502–19.

Windebank, J. (2001) 'Dual-earner Couples in Britain and France: Gender Divisions of Domestic Labour an Parenting Work in Different Welfare States', *Work, Employment and Society*, 15:2, 269–90.

5 On the Edge of the Time Bind: Time and Market Culture

Arlie Russell Hochschild

In *The Great Transformation*, Karl Polanyi argues that we have transitioned from being a society with islands of market life to a market with islands of society (2001 [1944]).[1] As the market has grown, so too, I would argue, has market *culture*. In this chapter I contend that the modern family is itself one such 'society' within the market, and that it is under pressure to incorporate aspects of market culture (Fevre 2003). It responds to this pressure by resisting, capitulating to, or simply playing with it through an ongoing process of symbolisation and re-symbolisation. The degree to which families resist or welcome market culture depends on the fit between individuals' embrace of market culture and their orientation to time. Temporal strategies preferred by employees at the top of the corporate ladders pose market culture's first port of entry into the home. Or to put it another way, market culture slips into the family through a crack on the edge of the time bind.

To illustrate market culture I describe a new consulting service, 'Family 360', organised by people trained to evaluate executives' work performance who now evaluate men's performance as fathers at home. To illustrate individuals' orientations towards time, I draw from my interviews with employees of a large multinational company, reported in my book, *The Time Bind* (1997).

First, what is market culture? I use the term here to refer to an 'ideal type' cluster of beliefs and practices that are based on the premise that the acts of buying and selling constitute an important source of identity. In truth, market culture is usually mixed with other sets of meanings too (Lasch 1977; Zelizer 2000). In various combinations it can appear with the culture of scientism (a value placed on objectivity, the scientific method, quantification), rationalism (a value on standardisation, bureaucracy efficiency), familism (a value on sacrifice for the sake of the family – including sacrifice of time), naturalism (a value on nature) and subjectivism (a value on acts – verbal or non-verbal – of interpersonal expression).

We are forever affirming and reaffirming our bonds with family, lovers and friends by drawing on a variety of sets of cultural meanings to say what we feel (Swidler 2001).[2] Throughout history, market culture as I define it here has been intermingled with family culture (Zelizer 1994, 2000). But in modern America, the market – as structure and culture – has been sundered from the family that has elaborated an identity fictively autonomous from it – a 'haven in a heartless world'. We are continually doing cultural work, choosing this symbol over that, or this combination of symbols over that combination in order to say 'I love you' or 'I would love you' or 'I tried to love you' or 'I'm trying to give up loving you'.

It is my argument that one set of cultural tools is gaining favour: those drawn from market culture (Hochschild 2003; Kuttner 1997). These tools, together with the salt and pepper of scientism and rationalism, draw into the home ways of being at work. In light of this rise of market culture, families become very busy resisting, playing with, or – as in the case I present here – embracing rationalism, scientism and market culture. This affects the way we conceive of time, and how we enact the way we see it – our temporal strategies. Contrariwise, our temporal strategies can form a 'port of entry' for market culture.

'Family 360': family as professional performance

One recent expression of market culture can be found in a new kind of service called Family 360. An issue of the *New York Times Magazine* devoted to the 99 most innovative ideas of 2002 described this new service. Designed by a management consulting firm called LeaderWorks based in Monument, Colorado, the programme offers 'personalised family assessments' to executives at corporations, such as General Motors, Honeywell and Dupont. Based on 'Management 360', a widely used programme for evaluating executives at the workplace, Family 360 offers, for $1000, to evaluate a client's performance as parent and spouse at home.[3] The journalist Paul Tough described how the service works:

> The Family 360 process starts with the executive's spouse, children and in some cases his parents and siblings filling out a detailed questionnaire in which they evaluate the subject both quantitatively – scoring him from 1 to 7 on, say, how well he 'helps create enjoyable family traditions' and 'uses a kind voice when speaking' – and qualitatively listing 'three to five positive attributes' and 'two things you want this person to do less'. The data are then analysed by Leader-Works, and the results are sent to the executive in a 'growth summary' report that presents his family's concerns in the form of bar graphs and pie charts and identifies 'focus areas' for such things as 'paying special attention to personal feelings ', and 'solving problems without getting angry'.
>
> (2002: 65)

The consultants interview the worker's spouse, children, other relatives, people who see him or her from every vantage point – hence the term '360'. Then LeaderWorks personnel meet with the family to create a 'Development Plan to Strengthen Family Relationships'. The company also provides, as Tough notes,

> ... an investment guide with hundreds of specific actions that let you connect with your family *as efficiently as possible* [emphasis added]: buy a speakerphone for the home so you can join in on family game night when you're on the road; go for a walk with your child every day, even if it's only to the end of the driveway; create 'communication opportunities' while doing the dishes with your spouse or waiting in line with your child at the store.
>
> (2002: 65)

The premise behind this service is that the executive can be as efficient at home as he is at work, with no loss – indeed, with a gain – to his or her family life. Indeed, as the web description for Family 360 notes, 'The Family 360 Process is a way to assess how you are doing with the precious time you have to build and strengthen your important personal relations. The Process can help you identify the "high leverage activities" that will mean the most to your important relationships.' In a web-based promise of a free, quick, report on work-life best practices, the applicant is asked to answer such questions as, 'If you have children, what specific actions have you taken to teach values, encourage contribution or create memories?' The process, the designers promise, is 'hard hitting' while also 'user friendly', and can be augmented by other offerings, such as the 'Family and Life Success Services'.

Clients' scores are totalled up and the evaluators appraise the impact of those scores on the client's desired 'individual legacy' and 'family legacy'. As is done in the business world, the executive can then compare his 'person practices' with those of 'other busy people' to see how the competition is doing.[4]

Family 360 suggests a remarkable contradiction. The service appeals to the executives' desire to be a participatory *dad* and this is a new ideal for highly placed businessmen in America. Even such busy men, the idea is, should share with women the task of raising children. Yet Family 360 invites men to do this in a *market kind of way*. Men are going home, so to speak, only to bring the marketplace with them. That is, Family 360 helps a time-starved father reconnect with his neglected family, and so reaffirms the moral sphere of the family. But the attitude of bureaucratic scientism, rational calculation and emotional detachment a client is asked to take towards his most intimate bonds also seems to undermine the moral sphere of the family. The ends affirm the family. The means affirm the marketplace. But as John Dewey once wisely noted, an idea is only as good as the means to achieve it.

The service seems to embody a number of cultural premises, one of which is that objectivity counts while subjectivity does not. A man's thoughts or feelings about his child remain unnoticed, while his outward behaviour is carefully monitored. The programme evaluates what it calls 'person practices' and advocates what it calls 'high leverage activities'. Behaviours, in turn, are quantified, lending them an aura of objectivity and science. What becomes most relevant is the amount of behaviour, not the *subjective quality* of it.

To the extent that the programme addresses a client's feelings towards his family, it treats them as a means, an instrument to some end. A father is not asked to find out how his son is doing today, but to cut to the chase and do something the son will remember – for there is a scale to quantify efforts to 'create memory'.

In the same spirit, through his fatherly good works, the client is asked to conceptualise a 'personal legacy' on the model of a personal portfolio. Finally, this service is offered as a 'starter' that is to be followed by a series of other paid services, proposing, in effect, the idea of the perpetually monitored family as a means towards the goal of 'adding value' to family life – much as through various stages of production, one adds value to a product.

Still, it is possible and even likely that the programme actually helps fathers turn their attention to their family, if only because it borrows from work the sense of serious urgency they associate with work. It may enable workaholic dads to snap out of their workaholism by speaking to them, so to speak, in 'workahol-ese'.

But the service also hides a contradiction. It helps fathers be fathers in a market kind of way. It helps them become market fathers. It helps them apply a speed-up to the very activities that most deeply symbolise fatherhood. It helps them *feel they are being a good father without sacrificing time*. Client and family are in this way prepared to live in a total market world.

Temporal strategies as ports of entry for market culture

The strong demands of work can make efficiency in the rest of life a useful and powerfully attractive idea. They can serve as an open portal to market culture. As a new service Family 360 has not yet entered the American mainstream. But there were small signs of the mentality it expresses in some of the interviews I conducted in the mid-1990s with employees in a Fortune 500 company. When I asked one hard-driving, ten-hour-a-day executive whether or not he regretted not having more time with his three daughters as they were growing up, he paused and said, 'Put it this way, I'm pleased with how my kids have turned out' (Hochschild 1997: 67). He spoke of his daughters very lovingly, but he also spoke of them as results, as a bottom line.

More generally, Americans often use the commercial element of market culture to describe personal relations. Americans might say, 'I don't want to mortgage our relationship.' Or 'If I keep going out with George, I face too many opportunity costs.' Or 'My mother-in-law is a liability.' As George Lakoff notes in *Metaphors We Live By*, the metaphor we apply to an experience determines how we see and feel about it. Metaphors guide feeling, and, of course, feelings also guide metaphors (Lakoff and Johnson 1980).

Closely linked to a market way of seeing human relations is a market way of seeing time. In the marketplace, time is money and money is a prime 'good'. In the film *Cheaper by the Dozen*, a humorous 1950s film, a father modelled on the efficiency expert Fredrick Taylor raises a large brood of children efficiently and does such things as time the children on household chores. Some spillover of the cult of efficiency from office to home has surely existed for at least as long as industrialism split the realm of work from home. But Family 360 represents a further development of this trend. *Cheaper by the Dozen* was, after all, a comedy, and the father devoted long hours to raising his children, however efficiency minded he was in doing it. In Family 360, the executive is advised in serious tones to get the same fatherhood value out of less time. He is told how to take time out of those activities that symbolise fatherhood. He learns to re-symbolise fatherhood. Now what symbolises fatherhood is the high-leverage activity, or even the act of hiring Family 360.

Cultural innovation often begins at the top of the social ladder, to be emulated later by those lower down, creating the so-called trickle down effect. Innovations also catch on when they appear as solutions to the problems people have. Several trends have increased the number of people for whom time is a problem. The first trend is the movement of women into paid work. Basically a very beneficial trend, the rising proportion of women in the workforce has helped develop the public sphere, allowed women opportunities, equalised the relations between men and women and, incidentally, lowered the birth rate. As an unintended consequence, however, it has removed the most powerful social anchor for the non-market world.

Many now also work longer hours than they did 30 years ago (Hinrichs et al. 1991; Thompson 1974).[5] And they spend more of their non-work hours watching television, which itself is a pipeline to the mall and increases people's need and desire to work (Putnam 2000; Schor 1998). With the recent erosion of state support for the non-working, the workplace has also become more essential to those who used to have alternative forms of social and cultural support.

To sum up, the movement of women into paid work, longer hours of work and the exposure to commercial culture, combined with the weakening of family culture, have increased the dominance of market culture. This unintended confluence of trends presents us with an important new challenge. The more of our lives we work and spend, the more we feel working and spending is all there is to life. The more working and spending become 'all there is to life', the more market culture presents itself as the filter through which to see.

All of this has important implications for how we experience time. Most obviously, market life encroaches on non-market life and it does so in various ways. In my interviews with 130 employees and others associated with the company I've called Amerco – the Fortune 500 company that I studied for *The Time Bind* – I discovered several temporal strategies that employees used to deal with overwork.[6]

Each temporal strategy determined the degree to which a person tries to maintain meaningful ties with family members or had abandoned or deferred the effort to do so. For those workers who kept trying, the issue arose: What shall symbolise my connection to my spouse or child? Can I change the symbol from here (an activity that takes a lot of time) to there (an activity that doesn't)? So a weekend getaway is replaced by a candlelit dinner, a camping trip with a game of ball. Some were more open to what we might call the *mobility of symbols* than were others.

Some of the temporal strategies I discovered – enduring, deferring, being a busy bee, outsourcing and resisting – were commonly used by any given worker at some point in their work life. So, over time, a worker would usually mix one strategy with another, though often one tended to dominate. Only some of these – and this is the main point – served as a 'port of entry' for market culture.

Endurers

Some workers simply endured. One assembly-line worker who worked a rotating seven-day schedule – different hours each week plus several hours a week of involuntary overtime – had this to say:

> I'm just getting through. The other day I was so tired that coming off the shift I bumped straight into my locker door. Last winter I was tired driving home, I ran into a mailbox. I'm not having a great time with my wife and kids. My wife and kids aren't having a great time with me, especially not my wife. We're just getting through. A lot of guys feel the way I do. We joke about it over break. 'Are we having fun yet ...?'

He wasn't trying to sustain meaningful bonds with his loved ones. His family was there. He loved them dearly. But he was in a state of siege. So he was putting his relationships with them on hold. To just get through what he was getting through, he lowered his expectations about having fun or meaningful times with his family. He did not focus on a future date after which he would engage with his family. For the time being, he renounced the wish to do that. As one young father of two, a night shift worker, told me:

> Who promised us a rose garden? Life isn't supposed to be like it is on *Lifestyles of the Rich and Famous*. The sooner a person recognises that, the better off he is. I'll be happy not to have this headache.

Another factory worker kept a lowered expectation of family life by comparing his fortunes to those of others still less fortunate:

> My wife is working overtime too, and we have the three kids between us. She has two from her first marriage and I have the one, Jessica, from my first. And I'll square with you. It's a challenge. But we're not as bad off as my brother [laughs ruefully]. He's working eight hours plus an hour commute each way, and my brother's wife has a half-hour commute. Theirs are older, mind you, but they've got five kids in the house. He has two and the three steps, and I don't think their marriage is going to last.

Endurance or 'just getting through' often turned out to be a temporary state but to people in that state it felt like it could go on forever. To the extent that they were able to detach themselves from the immediate pressures of work, drinking Cokes around the break-room table during a late night, they sometimes joked darkly about it: 'just three more brick walls to bump into [laughter]'.

Deferrers

While endurers renounced the joy of meaningful or fun times, the deferrers deferred them. Instead of telling themselves 'this is a hassle but this is life', they told themselves 'this is a hassle but it's just for now'. For example, one junior accountant seen by his superiors as a 'real up and comer' explained:

> Jennifer and I both dig in during the week and right now I'm working right through weekends, too. But we're planners and we make sure to get away once a month up to the lake. I always talk about that with my daughter, the fishing we'll do when we get up to the lake.

The deferrer could defer his wish for various lengths of time. 'Later' could be a day later ('we'll have quality time tonight') or a week later ('we'll go to the lake this weekend'). Or a production period later ('we'll relax after tax season'). As research by Rakel Heidmarsdottir (2002) shows, a number of workers who labour long hours keep themselves going by imagining their 'real life' after they retire. Indeed, for the early representatives of the Protestant Ethic, as Max

Weber (1958) noted, moments imagined to bring the greatest satisfaction came when God rewarded a person for good deeds after death.[7]

The busy bee

While both those workers who endure and those who defer temporarily gave up the idea of having meaningful connections with people outside of work for now, this was not the case for the 'busy bee'. The busy bee located meaning right where it always was supposed to be – in the daily activities of home life but condensed them so that they fit into smaller time slots. She did not renounce or postpone fun or meaning. She enjoyed it now, but in a busy, fast-paced way. She took pride in being efficient, effective, Type A. In essence, she absorbed the time bind *into her personal identity*. She absorbed rationalisation of time into her self. It fit her and she fit it. She was a busy, fast-paced-type of *person*. She identified with it. Furthermore, hurry was fun. What the endurers and deferrers saw as a hassle the busy bee saw as a challenge. She was energised by pressure. Working under pressure was, many workers told me, like a strenuous hike – good for you, hard, and something you're glad you did afterwards. She brought her image of family life close to the reality of it by saying, in effect, 'we *like* it this way'. Often she also persuaded other members of her family including her children that hurry was fun for them too: 'Come on kids. Let's see who'll get there first!'

Outsourcers

If endurers were doing without happy or meaningful time, deferrers were deferring them and busy bees were to some extent hollowing them out, then outsourcers were trying to find someone else to have some part of the happy and meaningful time for them. To be sure, nearly all of the two-job parents that I interviewed hired a day-care worker or nanny to look after their children while they worked. A few, in the so-called sandwich generation, also had elderly parents for whom they hired care workers or on whom they called and visited in nursing homes. Most wanted their children and elderly parents to receive excellent care from these care providers but to receive the most basic love from themselves. In other words, they wanted helpers, not substitutes for themselves, in these roles. Indeed, some nannies I interviewed reported that they had been fired when a mother became jealous of a child's love for the nanny. But other outsourcers sought very special caregivers with whom they hoped to share a central place in a child's heart. As one female top executive explained:

> We looked very carefully before we hired Karina, and I'm very glad we did. She is a dream come true. She's a widow, and lives alone. Her children live in Canada now, and she has no grandchildren. So she's alone here and she's fit

right into our lives and really clicked with Emily, who is two now. We include Karina at Thanksgiving and Christmas, just like family. And she loves Emily almost as a mother would, even better [laughs].

Resisters

Finally, instead of adapting themselves to a gruelling schedule, some workers altered the schedule itself, or tried to. Although deferrers and busy bees tended to be found at the top of the hierarchy – prominent examples to other workers of successful accommodation to intense work pressure – throughout the ranks of Amerco's workforce were some who sought to limit the source of pressure in the objective realities of the job or company. Such 'downshifters', as they have been called, tried to lead the life Todd Rakoff describes in his book, *A Time for Every Purpose* (2002). They envisioned and tried to allocate time so as to fit the purpose at hand to an optimum amount of time. As one mother of a nine-year-old girl described:

> I work 80 percent [*sic*] and for now this is just right. Like this afternoon I went out with Cheryl's Brownie troop [a girls activity club] on the bus. We were laughing at a dress I'd tried to make her that just didn't come out any which way. The sleeves were uneven, the neck was too small, and the skirt was too long. It was hilarious. And we were laughing, Cheryl and a bunch of her friends and me. A year ago, I would have tried to make one Brownie meeting a month, sneaking a look at my watch the whole time, not letting myself really relax and enjoy the occasion. It was a big deal for me just to let myself relax and enjoy it. I told my husband. Now I want him to get the same sort of into-it feeling too.[8]

Conclusions and implications

Those who simply endured their long hours were, virtually by definition, the least happy with their lives. Perhaps because they felt the most in control of their work lives, the resisters were the most happy. But it was most of all the busy bee and deferrer – generally the women and men of management – who neither changed their schedules nor felt a need to. And it was for them that market culture most seemed to offer itself as a solution to their work-family dilemma.

Busy bees and deferrers tended to be the professionals and executives at or near the top of the Amerco job ladder. Endurers were usually the assembly-line workers. Efficiency did not work for them and while they were not against it on principle, they did not think of it as a good thing. Staying cheerful was hard enough. Resisters did not believe in efficiency at home, and indeed a few actively disapproved of it, and so tried to change things so they could escape 'that trap'. Many such resisters were middle-level clerical and technical workers neither consumed by the career culture of the top nor overwhelmed by the financial hardships of the bottom. If the endurer succumbed to the pressure of work, the resister escaped it. Neither adjusted to intense work pressure or embraced the cult of efficiency as a happy or at least tolerable aspect of life. So they were less likely ports of entry for market culture.

Accepting a life of rush and pressure can both call for and become a covert form of emotion management. The deferrer and busy bee in particular could seem to be using over-busyness as a way of suppressing feeling. What each managed away could be a range of feelings – discouragement, anger, erotic interest or discontent.

In the age of the time bind, we might even say that, next to television, constant busyness is the most potent 'opiate of the masses' – a way of suppressing feelings and ideas that might challenge the status quo or the market culture into which we have unwittingly slid. Continual busyness by its nature inhibits the individual from thinking about such issues as why and how we get hooked into market culture.

In the end, the 'great transformation' from a society with markets to a market with societies is the basic story of modern history and it is likely there is no going back. But the daily lives of modern families reveal many clues to a muted but fierce ongoing struggle between market and family cultures. Each struggle determines whether market culture will move into the family or whether it will stay in the market. Similar struggles go on between the culture of the market and that of other independent moral worlds – the church, the school, the community.

At stake here is our ability to guard a critical space from which to ask of ourselves just how much market culture fits family life. The deferrer or busy bee who does not crack a smile at the terminology of Family 360 may have lost the critical space to ask: Are we increasingly seeing time, work, family and market culture only through the eyes of the market?

In the meantime, the Family 360 client may try to improve his 'person behaviours' in order to get a top-scoring '7' in 'memory creation'. But years later, when they are old and looking back, his children's most vivid memory may turn out to be that of those well-organised one-hour meetings around the dining room table when the experts tried to help dad love them efficiently.

Notes

1. This chapter is adapted from a talk given at the Danish Sociological Association, Aalborg University, 21 February 2003, and printed as 'Through the Crack in the Time Bind: From Market Management to Family Management' in Jacobsen and Tonboe (2004).
2. Here I apply Swidler's notion of a cultural 'tool kit' to the project of affirming social bonds (see Swidler 2001).

3. See Tough (2002).

4. Work trumps family – even in the rationale for using Family 360. The consultants offer two reasons. The first is to improve the busy executives' performance as a father and the second is to make him *a better employee – in his role as supervisor of working parents*. Worldwide Web, Family 360, LeaderWorks, Partners in Building Leadership Capability, Family 360 and Work-Life Coaching (http://www.family360.net).

5. Despite the promise of free time claimed by the early celebrants of industrialism and despite some early expansions in leisure earlier in the century, the US has seen – and many researchers have focused on – a recent rise in work hours, a trend that hits some groups harder than others (Schor 1992). Other theorists focus on particular cultural worlds that sustain a conception of time (Hochschild 1997) and still others focus on a general culture of *rush* – speed dials, remote controls, fast foods, ever-faster computers, email, answering machines – all so many products promising to save our time. As James Gleick notes in his book *Faster* (2000), film producers have increased the speed in cutting from scene to scene, and advertisers have done the same. The length of sound bites by presidential candidates has shrunk, he notes, from 40 seconds in 1968 to less than 10 in 1988. This cultural echo of speed would seem to emanate from the basic idea that time is money.

6. These strategies were not present in my first analysis of the material gathered for the book but are based on further reflections.

7. If endurers developed a work-entrenched self, the deferrer had developed what I call in *The Time Bind* a 'potential self'. This father resolved the contradiction between the demands of work and fatherhood by claiming to be an attuned dad now while doing what might earn him that identity later. He deferred (Hochschild 1997: 192–3, 235–7).

8. Each strategy has its light side. In a charming but telling story about his three-year-old daughter's life as a New York child, Adam Gopnik describes, in the *New Yorker*, overhearing Olivia talk to an imaginary friend she names Charlie Ravioli. Charlie is 'too busy' to play with her because he's working. In fact, Charlie hires an imaginary personal assistant to answer Charlie's calls because Charlie is too busy to say he's too busy (Gopnik 2002).

REFERENCES

Fevre, R. (2003) *The New Sociology of Economic Behaviour*, London: Sage.

Gleick, J. (2000) *Faster: The Acceleration of Just about Everything*, New York: Oxmoor House.

Gopnik, A. (2002) 'Bumping into Mr. Ravioli', *New Yorker*, 30 September, 80–4.

▶

Heidmarsdottir, R. (2002) 'Retirement Fantasies and Other Coping Strategies of Employees Experiencing Work-Life Conflicts', unpublished dissertation, University of Texas at Austin.

Hinrichs, K., Roche, W. and Sirianni, C. (eds) (1991) *Working Time in Transition: The Political Economy of Working Hours in Industrial Nations*, Philadelphia: Temple University Press.

Hochschild, A.R. (1997) *The Time Bind: When Work Becomes Home and Home Becomes Work*, New York: Metropolitan Books.

Hochschild, A.R. (2003) *The Commercialization of Intimate Life: Notes from Home and Work*, Berkeley: University of California Press.

Jacobsen, M.H. and Tonboe, J. (eds) (2004) *The New Work Society*, Copenhagen: Hans Reitzels.

Kuttner, R. (1997) *Everything for Sale*, New York: Knopf.

Lakoff, G. and Johnson, M. (1980) *Metaphors We Live By*, Chicago: University of Chicago Press.

Lasch, C. (1977) *Haven in a Heartless World*, New York: Basic Books.

Polanyi, K. (2001 [1944]) *The Great Transformation*, Boston: Beacon Press.

Putnam, R. (2000) *Bowling Alone: The Collapse and Revival of American Community*, New York: Simon and Schuster.

Rakoff, T. (2002) *A Time for Every Purpose: Law and the Balance of Life*, Cambridge: Harvard University Press.

Schor, J. (1992) *The Overworked American: The Unexpected Decline of Leisure*, New York: Basic Books.

Schor, J. (1998) *The Overspent American: Upscaling, Downshifting and the New Consumer*, New York: Basic Books.

Swidler, A. (2001) *Talk of Love: How Culture Matters*, Chicago: University of Chicago Press.

Thompson, E.P. (1974) 'Time, Work-Discipline, and Industrial Capitalism' in M.W. Flinn and T.C. Smout (eds) *Essays in Social History*, Oxford: Clarendon Press.

Tough, P. (2002) 'The Year in Ideas', *New York Times Magazine*, 15 December, 80–2.

Weber, M. (1958) *The Protestant Ethic and the Spirit of Capitalism*, New York: Charles Scribner.

Zelizer, V.A. (1994) *The Social Meaning of Money*, New York: Basic Books.

Zelizer, V.A. (2000) 'The Purchase of Intimacy', *Law and Social Inquiry*, 25:3, 817–848.

6 What Makes the Home Boundary Porous? The Influence of Work Characteristics on the Permeability of the Home Domain

Rozemarijn de Man, Jeanne de Bruijn and Sandra Groeneveld

Introduction

As a consequence of women (re-)entering the labour market and the increase of one-person households, more and more individuals now feel the pressure to fulfil the needs of both paid employment and home duties (Guest 2002; Van der Lippe et al. 2003). In scientific research, policy debates and in organisations, it is acknowledged that employees are better able to combine work and home with the help of the right supportive conditions (Kossek et al. 1999; Rau and Hyland 2002). Flexible work arrangements, such as telecommuting and flexitime, are developed as a solution to overcome the dilemmas of combining work and home life. These work arrangements are expected to enable employees to meet family demands by stretching regular work hours and places. The underlying rationale is that by integrating work and home it becomes possible to fulfil the demands of both domains whenever needed. These arrangements indeed appear beneficial, aside from being able to fulfil work and family duties and accommodating work-life balance (Hill et al. 2003; Ralston 1989), employees experience more autonomy and spend less time commuting (Kurland and Bailey 1999).

However, the need to nuance the benefits of flexible work arrangements is being recognised. One of the critical remarks is aimed at the very merits of flexible work arrangements: the integration of work and home. Research based on Boundary Theory – a relatively new strand within work-family research that addresses the linkage between work and home by focusing on the boundaries that divide them – points out that integration is not what employees always want (Ashforth et al. 2000; Nippert-Eng 1996a). Individuals differ in the extent to which they prefer work to integrate with their home lives, with some favouring integration and others favouring separation (Nippert-Eng 1996a). Individuals who prefer integration desire thin, permeable boundaries that help work and home to crossover easily. In contrast, individuals who prefer to separate work and home life often desire thick, impermeable boundaries to ensure that there is no crossover.

Access to and use of work arrangements do not necessarily correspond to the boundary preferences of individuals (Rothbard et al. 2005). If a work situation does not provide clear time and space markers, as is the case with telecommuting, individuals have to rely on their willpower and the success of their boundary management to separate work from home (Ahrentzen 1990). Individuals who want to profit from the benefits of flexible work arrangements but also wish to separate work from home will have to put in considerable effort to succeed in maintaining this separation. The 'democratisation' of flexible work arrangements and other less desired work characteristics that accommodate integration – such as pressure to work overtime or to take work home – have made the question salient as to whether employees have the opportunity to separate work and home if they wish to.

Although the impact that work characteristics may have on the work-home permeability is commonly acknowledged within Boundary Theory research, their effects have not been empirically measured. The research reported in this chapter fills this gap, examining the effect of various work characteristics on boundary permeability for 1065 employees of a Dutch multinational in the business sector. It examines if, and how, employees' own boundary preferences influence their boundary permeability. Moreover, the research examines if employees' boundary preferences moderate the influence of work characteristics. More specifically, the chapter addresses the following questions:

- What is the influence of work characteristics on the permeability of the home boundaries?
- What is the influence of boundary preferences on the permeability of the home boundaries?
- Do boundary preferences moderate the influence of the work characteristics on the permeability of the home boundaries? If so, in what way?

The following section provides a brief overview of Boundary Theory and previous research on boundary permeability, work characteristics and boundary preferences. The subsequent section provides a description of the research methods followed by the research findings. Finally, there is a discussion of the findings and a conclusion.

Theoretical considerations and research hypotheses

Boundary permeability

Individuals differ in the way that they combine work and home. As an example from the interviews, when Anton, a 53-year-old floor supervisor, comes home at six o'clock he forgets about his work. He changes his clothes and joins his wife for dinner. They talk about the children and whatever comes to mind but never about work. In the evening they watch television or engage in some other leisure activity. In contrast, Susan, a 28-year-old product manager, joins her co-workers for a drink after work. At seven or eight o'clock she meets her husband at home and they have a quick dinner and discuss their days. Often she works for an hour or two after dinner. Anton and Susan, each have their own style, their own habits in combining work and home.[1]

Boundary Theory provides a theoretical framework for understanding why and how individuals combine work and home in different ways (Ashforth et al. 2000; Nippert-Eng 1996a; Rau and Hyland 2002). The framework seeks to understand why some individuals perceive work and home as two separate worlds, while other individuals see the two domains as more fluid, overlapping realities. It does so by focusing on the boundaries that divide the two domains, the ease and frequency of crossing role boundaries (Ashforth et al. 2000) and the meanings that individuals assign to work and home (Nippert-Eng 1996a). Central to Boundary Theory is that the 'strength' of the boundary between work and home is seen as an indicator for the extent of integration of the two domains and the ease of transitioning between them. The theory distinguishes two boundary characteristics that generate the strength of the boundaries: *flexibility* and *permeability*.

Flexibility is the degree to which spatial and temporal boundaries are pliant to the needs of the domains (Hall and Richter 1988). For example, someone who has a flexible work schedule that permits him or her to adapt their working hours to the school-hours of their children has flexible temporal boundaries. *Permeability* is the degree to which a person physically located in one domain (for example the home domain) allows psychological and behavioural elements from another domain (for example the work domain) to enter (Ashforth et al. 2000; Hall and Richter 1988). This boundary characteristic refers to the extent to which boundaries are porous to intrusions, distractions or interruptions from other domains or domain members. Thus, permeability demonstrates individuals' actual behaviour in allowing or rejecting work to enter the home domain and vice versa (Eagle et al. 1997; Kossek et al. 1999; Pleck 1977).

Having a permeable home boundary does not imply that someone *wishes* to receive phone calls or to think about work. It might be that someone prefers not to perform work activities in the evening but that work characteristics trigger her to do so anyway. Therefore, permeability is to be differentiated from individuals' boundary preferences in that it defines what people actually do – not what they desire – and to what degree work actually enters the home domain (Eagle et al. 1997; Kossek et al. 1999; Pleck 1977).

Previous research on the determinants of home permeability is limited. However, demographical influences have been studied in some depth and there is contradictory evidence on gender differences. Some research found no significant correlations between gender and home permeability (Campbell Clark 2002) while other research found that men have more permeable home boundaries than women (Olson-Buchanan and Boswell 2005; Pleck 1977). On the other hand, Hall and Richter (1988) found that due to high demands of both work and home, women have more permeable home boundaries than men. Other research has indicated that when work and care must be combined – as is the case with working parents – individuals are likely to have permeable home boundaries (Kossek, et al. 1999; Staines 1980). Since women are more likely to take on the responsibility for household and childcare tasks than men, Kossek et al. (1999) propose that working mothers are more likely to have low separated, permeable boundaries between work and home compared to working fathers. Previous research found that the number of dependents does not correlate with home permeability for either men or women (Campbell Clark 2002; Olson-Buchanan and Boswell 2006).

Work characteristics and home permeability

For this study, work characteristics that tend to stretch regular work hours and places outside the traditional time and space markers were selected. Below are five work characteristics that may stretch regular work hours and places and their possible influence on home permeability. These five characteristics include telecommuting, flexitime, pressure to work overtime, opportunity to separate and boundary preferences.

Telecommuting

Telecommuting gives employees the opportunity to work at home on a regular – but not necessarily daily – basis (Kurland and Bailey 1999). Telecommuting implies an agreement between the employer and employee that work is done at home instead of the office during official work hours and is therefore differentiated from taking work home at the end of the work day.

Previous studies on work and home have placed work arrangements on a range from integration to separation[2] (Kossek et al. 1999; Rau and Hyland 2002).

In these studies, telecommuting was marked as the most integrating arrangement compared to flexitime, onsite childcare and a more standard work arrangement with strict working hours and a singular work place. Individuals who telecommute are available for home interruptions and distractions during business hours and for work distractions after business hours. Ahrentzen (1990) found role overlap for telecommuters in three dimensions: time, space and mind. Interestingly, Ahrentzen found telecommuters to have much less overlap with respect to space than to time and mind. Telecommuters are likely to combine paid work with domestic tasks and family caring during conventional working hours and push forward their work tasks into the evening, early morning or the weekend (Ahrentzen 1990; Kraut 1989). Telecommuting facilitates integration of work and home (Beach 1989) and enhances the perception of blurred boundaries (Kossek 2001). Consequently, it might be expected that

Hypothesis 1: The more that employees telecommute the more permeable are their home boundaries.

Flexitime

Flexitime can be defined as a work schedule that permits flexible starting and finishing times (Christensen and Staines 1990). Employees who have the opportunity of flexitime are often given a time range in which they can start and end their working day. For many individuals, flexitime is a highly valued work characteristic (Campbell Clark 2002) and previous studies have pointed out several benefits of flexitime. For example, research has found that flexitime has a positive influence on the ability to fulfil both work and home responsibilities (Ralston 1989) and on time spent with family members (Winett et al. 1982).

Elaborating on Boundary Theory, Rau and Hyland (2002) state that flexitime increases the flexibility of the temporal boundaries but maintains impermeable boundaries. Flexitime can therefore be a useful resource for managing work and home since it may offer employees control over temporal boundaries while ensuring that blurring and interruptions within domains are kept to a minimum. As such, flexitime may help to reinforce existing role distinctions and decrease boundary permeability. Therefore it might be expected that

Hypothesis 2: The more that employees can use flexitime the less permeable are their home boundaries.

Pressure to work overtime

The number of hours employees work is generally seen as an important source for work-home conflict (Frone et al. 1997; Greenhause and Beutell 1985; Pleck 1977), based on the rationale that hours worked cannot be dedicated to personal life. Managers often perceive the number of hours employees work as an indicator of their productivity (Perlow 1998). To increase productivity, managers try to influence and increase working hours. Perlow (1998: 329) describes this process of 'boundary control' as 'the various ways in which managers in organisations cajole, encourage, coerce or otherwise influence the amount of time employees physically spend in the workplace'. However, in a qualitative study on the combination of work and home that was part of this research project, respondents reported that co-workers act out most of the boundary control (De Man and De Bruijn 2004). Among co-workers in high level jobs there prevails a taboo on maintaining a '9 to 5 mentality' and whenever someone leaves at five o'clock, co-workers will joke and ask their colleague if he or she is taking the afternoon off.

Our qualitative study confirmed that many employees take their work home so that they are able to leave the office on time. Informal overtime – either by completing work at the office or by taking work home – has been found to intrude into the home domain and create practical and emotional difficulties for employees (Hyman et al. 2005). In a study on how individuals enact work-family balance by communication, Campbell Clark (2002) found positive correlations between the number of hours worked per week and home permeability. Based on the current literature, it therefore might be expected that

Hypothesis 3a: The more overtime hours that employees work the more are permeable their home boundaries.

Hypothesis 3b: The more that employees feel the pressure to work overtime the more permeable are their home boundaries.

Opportunity to separate

Paul is a mechanic who assists customers that have technical problems with their telecom system. In the morning he receives a long list with addresses that he has to visit. He fears that he will never be able to finish the list and as the day progresses he gets more stressed seeing the long list of remaining addresses. In order to improve efficiency his supervisors introduced new electronic systems and classified the mechanics in self-steering teams that deal with their own scheduling and administration. Paul fears he is losing ground because he has to learn the new systems and do his own administration in addition to his regular work. At the end of the workday he comes home exhausted and he still has to complete his administration. Twice a month he has to wear a beeper at the weekend in case of technical emergencies in the organisation.

His co-worker, An, works in the customer service department where she answers the telephone calls from people whose telecom system has malfunctioned. She starts her workday at 8.30 a.m. when the telephone lines open. An registers the name and address of the customer and gives a list of addresses to her supervisor at the end of the day. At 5.30 p.m. the telephone lines close and An knows her job is done.[3] For An, the boundaries around her work are clearly marked, she knows what work she has to do and where and when to do it. If she wishes to, she can forget about her work until the following morning. Paul on the contrary feels that his job stretches into his personal time; he is forced to work overtime and has to perform work tasks in the evening and feels stressed as a result.

The opportunity that organisations offer their employees to separate home from work is not an explicit work arrangement, yet separating these two spheres is a preferred work aspect for many employees (Pryor 1983). Previous research has indicated that separation can facilitate the combination of work and home if the work and home domain are very different (Campbell Clark 2000) and can diminish work-family conflict, role confusion and the perception of blurred boundaries (Ashforth et al. 2000; Desrocher and Sargent 2004).

Earlier research found that the home boundary is more porous for work intrusions than vice versa (Eagle et al. 1997; Frone et al. 1992; Hall and Richter 1988). Hall and Richter suggest that this difference in porosity may result from the fact that people have more control over interference stemming from home than over interference stemming from work. When employees' jobs do not allow them to separate work from home, they may see themselves forced to allow work to enter their home domain. In such a case, permeability is not a form of enactment of their boundary preferences but a prescription of the work situation. Based on existing literature it might be expected that

Hypothesis 4: The less a job allows separating work from home, the more permeable individuals' home boundaries will be.

Boundary preferences

Individuals differ in the extent to which they prefer to fence off their home life from their work life (Nippert-Eng 1996a). Permeable boundaries may be desired by some and undesired by others. Consciously and subconsciously individuals have preferences on the extent that work may or may not intermingle with their home lives, and where and when to draw the line. For example, someone may be willing to work from home during the week but may draw the line at working weekends.

Nippert-Eng (1996a) suggests that individuals develop their boundary preferences in interaction with their physical, temporal and cultural environments. Although previous research on the determinants of boundary preferences is limited, a handful of studies have addressed this subject. Kossek et al. (1999)

propose that those workers without extended family or care support, such as single parents, single children and dual households, are more likely to prefer the integration of work and home. Desrocher and Sargent (2004) found that employees who experienced significant blurring of the work and home boundary were more likely to prefer separation.

Boundary preferences are often enacted in more physical forms and decisions, such as keeping separate calendars for work and home or not discussing personal matters with co-workers. Kossek et al. (1999) propose that employees who prefer to integrate work in their home lives make themselves available to interruptions and distractions from work. By acting out their preferences, individuals can influence the permeability of the work and home boundaries. Therefore it might be expected that

Hypothesis 5: The more that employees prefer to separate work from their home lives, the less permeable are their home boundaries.

The interaction of boundary preferences and work characteristics on home permeability

Several work characteristics and their tenability to influence boundary permeability have been discussed above. Work characteristics that stretch traditional time and space markers lead to an increase in home permeability. Attention is now turned to the extent to which boundary preferences can moderate or increase the influence of these work characteristics on home permeability. Rothbard et al. (2005) indicate that previous research based on Boundary Theory started from the assumption that the actual boundaries of individuals match their boundary preferences. Rightly, they indicate that individuals' environments, such as their work situation, may cause a mismatch between preference and enactment.

If the requirements of a work situation contradict the preferences of the individual, it becomes salient whether the individual can reverse the impact of the work situation and thereby prevent a misfit between preferences and boundary enactment. Someone who prefers to keep impermeable home boundaries, but whose work situation does not provide strict time and space markers, as with telecommuting, must create the boundary markers. As such, separation is seen as the result of an active effort of individuals to attain impermeable home boundaries (Edwards and Rothbard 2000). Therefore it can be expected that

Hypothesis 6: Boundary preferences moderate the influence of the work characteristics on the permeability of the home boundaries.

Data, method and analytical framework

Data

The study used a sample of employees from a Dutch multinational company. Previous research has found a relationship between access to work arrangements that accommodate integration and the job level of employees (see for example Breedveld 1998). That is, most employees working in knowledge-based, high level jobs have the option to integrate work and home, whereas employees working in lower level, manual jobs are unlikely to have this option. Thus, an organisation that offered knowledge-based and manual work was selected for this research. A single case study enabled the analysis of boundary behaviour of employees with different opportunities to integrate and separate, while promoting comparability of other work and organisational characteristics.

The organisation is large and employs more than 20,000 people. Four departments were selected, varying with respect to access to and use of flexible work arrangements, job culture and work content, with a total of 8795 employees. For three departments it was possible to approach the whole working population because of their limited size (a total of 1270 employees). In the fourth and largest department – with a total working population of 7525 employees – respondents were selected by means of a singular stratified sample, whereby women and very low and very high job levels were over-sampled considering their under-representation in the multinational. In total 3711 questionnaires were distributed and 1252 were returned (33.7 per cent). After removing questionnaires that lacked demographic data, a total of 1065 completed questionnaires could be used in this study.

The final sample consisted of 67 per cent men and 33 per cent women ($M = 1.33$, $SD = .47$). Respondents ranged in age from 18 to 70 years, with a mean of 43 years ($SD = 8.72$). Most of the men and women (85 per cent) have a partner, with 64 per cent of this group being married ($SD = .94$). Most of the respondents had children (67 per cent, $SD = .46$) and 57 per cent of the respondents had one or more children living at home, varying in age from under-one to 27 years ($M = 9.37$, $SD = 7.06$). Company job levels ranged from 4 to 13 ($M = 9.25$, $SD = 2.47$) on a scale of 4 to 13. Employees working in job levels 4–8 (40 per cent) are primarily manual and administrative; employees working in job levels 9–13 (61 per cent) are mainly in management or other professional occupations and are often more highly educated ($r = .41$, $p < .01$). The average job tenure is 18 years; ranging from a few months to 43 years ($SD = 10.3$).

Operationalisation

Table 6.1 presents the operationalisations as used in this study (see appendix). The dependent variable *home boundary permeability* was measured using

Campbell Clarks' 6-item permeability scale (Campbell Clark 2002), and respondents rated their responses on a 5-point Likert scale ranging from 'never' to 'always'. Responses to the six items were averaged to form a total score ($\alpha = .80$), high scores indicating high home permeability. The work characteristics (independent variables) were measured as follows.

Whether respondents *telecommute* was assessed by the item 'How many of your working hours a week are spent working at home? (if none, write '0').' Higher scores indicate more hours of telecommuting at home.

Flexitime was measured by three items of Campbell Clark's flexibility boundary characteristics scale in Likert form ranging from 'never' to 'always' (Campbell Clark 2002). Respondents were asked whether they were free to come to work and leave when they wanted. The items were averaged in a total score ($\alpha = .82$).

Weekly hours of overtime were assessed by asking respondents how many working hours on average they worked in a week according to their contract, and how many hours they worked including overtime. In order to attain the average hours of overtime, for each respondent the contractual working hours were subtracted from the actual working hours including overtime.

Two different items measure *implicit pressure to work overtime*. One item asked for an implicit pressure to work overtime coming from co-workers: 'My co-workers regularly work overtime.' The second item addressed the implicit pressure to work overtime from the manager or supervisor: 'I have the feeling my boss expects me to work overtime regularly.'

Opportunity to separate was measured by a 4-item scale developed by Kreiner (2001). The scale addressed whether a workplace in general offers people the opportunity to leave work behind when entering the home domain. Respondents rated their response on a 5-point Likert scale ranging from 'strongly disagree' to 'strongly agree', coded such that 1 = strongly disagree and 5 = strongly agree. The items were recoded towards little opportunity to separate. Responses were averaged to form a total score ($\alpha = .89$). High scores indicate little opportunity to separate work from home.

Boundary preferences for the home domain favouring integration or separation were measured using a 5-item Likert scale, ranging from 'strongly disagree' to 'strongly agree'. Three items were used from Kreiner's (2001) scale on 'internal boundary permeability needs'. A Principal Component Analysis (PCA) and Cronbach's reliability analysis showed the additional value of two extra items of our own. The PCA showed a single component that explains the 68 per cent of the total variance. Factor loadings vary between .76 and .86 with an internal consistency reliability $\alpha = .88$. The responses to the five items were averaged to form a single score and high scores indicate a strong preference for separation.

A possible interaction effect of the boundary preferences on the relationship between work characteristics and home permeability was explored by constructing six *interaction terms*, one for each work characteristic: telecommuting, flexitime, the opportunity to separate, weekly hours of overtime, implicit pressure to work overtime coming from co-workers and implicit pressure to work overtime coming from managers.

In the theoretical section, discussions focused on research that suggested several variables that were related to home permeability or the opportunity to integrate work and the home environment (see for example Breedveld 1998; Hall and Richter 1988; Kossek et al. 1999). Therefore, sex, having a partner, having children and job level were adopted as *control variables* in this study. Bivariate correlations show the need for controlling for negative reorganisation experiences. A dummy variable is adopted indicating (strong) agreement with the item 'I had a negative feeling about this or other reorganisations.'

Analyses

Bivariate correlations were conducted to explore potentially confounding correlations and detect multi-collinearity (see Table 6.2 in the appendix). In order to prevent multi-collinearity between the interaction terms and their single components, the single components were first centred to their means and then multiplied to form interaction terms (Aiken and West 1991). However, bivariate correlations showed that the interaction variables – except the interaction between telecommuting and boundary preferences – were mutually highly correlated (between .89 and .93). Following guidelines on multi-collinearity (Lewis-Beck 1980) five out of the six interaction terms from the analysis were excluded. A preliminary regression analysis showed that there were no significant relationships between these interaction terms and the dependent variable 'permeability of the home domain' (non-significant β between –.05 and .11). Further bivariate correlations among the variables in this study and the interaction between telecommuting and boundary preferences were no higher than .53 and the variance inflation factor no higher than 2.42, so it can be assumed that multi-collinearity is no longer a problem (Lewis-Beck 1980; Myers 1990).

Multiple ordinary least squares (OLS) regression models were estimated to test the hypotheses as formulated in the previous section. In total, four regression analyses were conducted; in each step a new (group of) variable(s) was added. Initially the demographic control variables were entered and in the following step, the work characteristics were entered. Next the boundary preferences of the employees were entered so that it was possible to test the effect of boundary preferences controlled for the work situation. In the fourth and final step, the interaction effect between telecommuting and boundary preferences was added, predicting home permeability. The findings are presented below.

Results

Multiple hierarchical regression analysis was used to test the relationship of work characteristics and boundary preferences with the permeability of the home domain. Table 6.3 presents the results of the regression analyses and reports the non-standardised and standardised regression coefficient, the F-value and the adjusted R square.

After entering the demographic control variables in Model 1, results show that employees who have children have more permeable home boundaries. This more permeable home boundary applies as well for employees working in higher level jobs and for employees who contractually work (nearly) full-time. Experiencing a re-organisation as negative and having a partner do not show a significant effect on home permeability.

Model 2 introduces the work characteristics. Consistent with *hypothesis 1,* the number of hours employees telecommute is positively related to home permeability; the more hours that employees telecommute per week, the more permeable their home domain. This effect also applies to employees who only have 'seldom' or 'sometimes' the opportunity to telecommute (β = .20 at p <.01, not shown). When telecommuting is entered in the regression analysis, the earlier effects of having children, working in a high level job and weekly working hours by contract disappear.

Inconsistent with *hypothesis 2* that predicted a negative relationship between flexitime and home permeability, these findings suggest significant effects of flexitime on the extent of permeability. In other words, employees who have flexible time schedules report more permeable home boundaries than those who have little to no flexibility.

Hypothesis 3a proposed a positive effect of the number of hours worked overtime on home permeability. Inconsistent with *hypothesis 3a* the number of hours worked overtime was not related to boundary permeability. In *hypothesis 3b*, it was predicted that the more employees feel pressured to work overtime, the more permeable their home boundaries will be. Consistent with the hypothesis, both the implicit pressure from co-workers and that coming from management have a significant effect on home permeability, with pressure from management having the larger effect.

Hypothesis 4 stated that the less a job allows separation of work from home, the more permeable individuals' home boundaries will be. Results are in accordance with this hypothesis: employees who report that their jobs offer little opportunity to separate work from home life, report high levels of permeability.

Hypotheses 5 and *6* were formulated to test the influence of individuals' preferences on their home boundaries. Boundary preferences are added in Model 3.

Table 6.3 Results of hierarchal regression analysis predicting home permeability

Independent variables	Model 1		Model 2		Model 3		Model 4	
	B	β	B	β	B	β	B	β
Step 1: control variables								
Sex: man	-.01	-.00	-.03	-.02	-.04	-.04	-.04	-.04
Partner: yes	.04	.02	.04	.03	.06	.03	.05	.03
Child(ren): yes	.13	.10**	.01	.01	.00	.00	.01	.00
Job level	.01	.14**	-.00	-.02	-.00	-.02	-.00	-.02
Weekly hours by contract	.03	.22**	.01	.04	.01	.04	.01	.04
Negative re-organisation experience	-.02	-.03	-.02	-.03	.01	.02	.01	.02
Step 2:								
Telecommuting			.03	.24**	.03	.22**	.03	.25**
Temporal flexibility			.08	.12**	.06	.11**	.06	.10**
Overwork hours			.00	.04	.00	.03	.00	.02
Implicit pressure working overtime colleagues			.05	.09*	.04	.08*	.04	.08*
Implicit pressure working overtime supervisor			.10	.19**	.09	.19**	.09	.18**
Little opportunity to separate			.26	.39**	.26	.39**	.26	.39**
Step 3:								
Preference for separation					-.14	-.19**	-.18	-.23**
Step 4:								
Interaction between separation preference and telecommuting							.01	.09*
Adjusted R^2	.08		.43		.46		.47	
F	14.9		44.1		45.2		42.7	

Notes: *$p < .05$, **$p < .01$

Hypothesis 5 predicted that the boundary preferences of employees have a direct effect on home permeability. As hypothesised, employees who prefer to separate work from their home lives, seem able to do so. Regardless of any differences in their work situation, employees who prefer to separate work from home, have significantly less permeable home boundaries than employees with opposite preferences. The influential effect of telecommuting diminishes slightly, suggesting that employees who prefer separation telecommute less than those who prefer integration. A similar explanation can be given with respect to a small decrease of the effect of flexitime.

Model 4 combines all previous variables and adopts the interaction between telecommuting and boundary preferences in predicting the permeability of the home domain. As *hypothesis 6* proposed, there is an interaction effect of telecommuting and boundary preferences on permeability, though it is minor. The effect of telecommuting is stronger for employees who prefer to separate work from home than for those who prefer to integrate. In other words, the impact of telecommuting on home permeability increases if employees prefer separation. This finding suggests that employees who prefer to separate but who do bring their work home by telecommuting cannot avoid blurred boundaries.

Discussion

This research analyses the effects of both work characteristics and boundary preferences on the boundary permeability of the home domain. Drawing on Boundary Theory, it was first hypothesised that work characteristics that stretch the traditional time and space markers increase the home permeability. In particular, this research examined the influence of telecommuting, flexitime, pressure to work overtime and opportunity to separate work and home on the permeability of the home domain. Results indicate that work characteristics do account for a great amount of variance in home permeability. The main influence on home permeability comes from the opportunity to separate work from home life. Controlling for the effects of telecommuting, flexitime and (pressure to) work(ing) overtime, it was found that employees who report that their jobs allow little opportunity to separate, report more permeable home boundaries. It is possible however that the reverse is also true: having permeable boundaries leads to the perception that the job offers little or no opportunity to separate work and home. Future research should further examine the causalities in this relationship.

Telecommuting also increases home permeability. Surprisingly, even when employees telecommute on rare occasions, the home permeability increases.

Boundary Theory proposes that flexitime will increase the flexibility of boundaries, but not the permeability (Rau and Hyland 2002). Inconsistent with this proposition, this study found that flexitime is positively associated with an increase in boundary permeability. A small decrease of flexitime when boundary preferences are added to the analysis suggests that there is a self-selection mechanism at work: individuals who prefer integration have more temporal flexibility, possibly because they apply for jobs that match their preferences (Rau and Hyland 2002). A post-regression analysis, in which all variables were entered step by step, showed that the effect of flexitime disappears when 'pressure to work overtime' is added to the model, suggesting that an underlying pressure to work overtime may explain the effect of flexitime on home permeability. Brannen (2005: 113) argues that the flexibility of time generates feelings of control, but this control is rather of an 'illusionary nature'. It may not be easy to finish at three when most of your co-workers work until five or six o'clock and work is not completed. Employees may worry about this or could be tempted to continue working at home. This illusionary nature of control would be consistent with previous research by Mennino et al. (2005) who found that family-supportive workplace cultures reduce spillover rather than the availability of arrangements such as flexitime. Previous research has further suggested that the influence of flexitime may be moderated by additional work and family characteristics, such as the psychological experience of flexibility (Kossek et al. 2005). Future research must further examine the effect of flexitime on boundary permeability, taking into account additional work and family conditions.

Secondly, the influence of boundary preferences favouring integration or separation on home permeability was explored. Consistent with the hypothesis and the expectation of previous Boundary Theory research, this study found that boundary preferences are related to the actual enactment of boundaries (Rothbard et al. 2005). Employees who prefer to separate work from home report less permeability than employees with opposite preferences. By acting out their preferences, individuals influence the permeability of their home boundaries, regardless of their actual working conditions.

Thirdly, the research explored whether boundary preferences moderate the influence of the work characteristics on home permeability. This question is important since it indirectly asks whether employees have the opportunity to separate work from home if they wish to do so. Due to high multi-collinearity between most interaction terms and the other independent variables, the research was merely able to explore the interaction effect of telecommuting and boundary preferences on home permeability. The analysis suggests that boundary preferences do not serve as sufficient counter pressures to the conditions of telecommuting that enhance boundary permeability. Consequently, this lack of counter pressure may imply that employees who prefer separation but bring their work home by telecommuting cannot avoid home permeability. In fact, results indicate that telecommuting has a larger impact on boundary permeability for employees who prefer separation than for employees who prefer integration.

Some limitations in this study with respect to the data used and the operationalisations suggest guidelines for future research. A single case study – as used in this study – is advantageous since it generates knowledge on particularities, promotes comparability of work characteristics and synchronises the situational context for the respondents. However, examining the hypotheses tested in this chapter within other organisations would help to determining the generalisability of the results. Further, the operationalisation of permeability reflects the individual's perception of intrusions of the home domain. It is possible that these perceptions are influenced by their boundary preferences. Since this data was gathered at one point in time, assessing causality is difficult and results should be interpreted accordingly.

A central thrust of this chapter was to determine the specific effect of work characteristics on boundary permeability. Therefore it did not include more traditional work arrangements, such as strict time schedules. However for a thorough understanding of the determinants of permeability, these more traditional arrangements must be included. In addition, this study and previous studies have pointed out the importance of work-family friendly cultures. Unfortunately, it is not possible to know if the managers of the respondents in this study encouraged or discouraged the use of telecommuting or flexitime. A similar argument is at stake for the addition of individuals' power and resources to reverse the impact of the work situation and extra home variables, such as spousal support and family satisfaction.

Conclusion

Boundary Theory proposes that when domain roles are highly separated, out-of-role interruptions can have a large impact (Ashforth et al. 2000; Rau and Hyland 2002). Consistent with this proposition, the data presented here suggest that when boundary preferences of employees do not correspond to how they enact their boundary permeability, the impact of the work characteristics that endorse the misalignment increases. In line with Boundary Theory, two processes may trigger the impact of telecommuting for individuals favouring separation. Firstly, within a domain that is exclusively dedicated to one purpose, that is home, interruptions from another domain, that is work, attract much attention (Ashforth et al. 2000; Nippert-Eng 1996b). A person who prefers to integrate work with home does not think twice about answering a phone call about work after business hours. In contrast, someone who prefers separation notices the intrusion, is perhaps irritated and will debate whether to answer the call or not. For someone who prefers separation, work interruptions can be perceived as boundary violations, as infringements upon privacy. Secondly, separation increases the magnitude of change, making boundary crossing more difficult (Ashforth et al. 2000). As individuals who favour separation have a clear notion about where to draw the line between work and home, and of what belongs to work and home, they have to cross many borders. Each crossing may take effort and difficulty. An individual who prefers separation but receives a work-related phone call while at home may find it difficult to concentrate on the work-related phone call first and to forget about it afterwards. In contrast, for individuals who perceive work and home as 'one fluid world', crossings are easy and hardly noticed.

To conclude, this study has made a number of contributions to Boundary Theory. Firstly, it went beyond prior research since it empirically examined the influences of work characteristics and boundary preferences on home permeability, and the moderating effect of boundary preferences on the relationship between work characteristics and boundary permeability. Secondly, the data suggest that boundary permeability can be *the result of an active or inactive, involuntary process*. Boundary permeability can be actively formed by the enactment of boundary preferences. People may choose to make use of work arrangements that fit their preferences either by using the arrangements that are offered in their present job or by applying for another job. However, if workers do not have the opportunity to enact on their preferences, boundary permeability can be involuntary placed on workers by means of the characteristics of their jobs since boundary preferences do not serve as sufficient counter pressures. Future research should examine whether 'involuntary' permeability accounts more for work-family conflict than its active, voluntary counterpart.

Notes

1. These employees are two out of the 24 employees who participated in in-depth interviews on combining work and home (De Man and De Bruijn 2004). Names are pseudonyms.
2. The concepts 'segmentation' and 'separation' are both used in work-family research. We use the term 'separation' since it expresses more activity.
3. An and Paul participated in a previous study, see note 1.

Appendix

Table 6.1 Operationalisation of the scales used in this study

Scale	Alpha reliability	Factor analysis
Home permeability	.80	
I receive work-related phone calls when I am at home.		.80
I have work-related items at my home.		.63
I think about work-related concerns when I am at home.		.59
I hear from people related to my job when I am at home.		.79
I stop in the middle of my home activities to address a work issue.		.73
I take care of work-related business when I am at home.		.80
Flexitime	.82	
I am able to come to work and leave when I want.		.86
I am free to work the hours that are best for my schedule.		.83
I am able to go to work and come home when I want.		.87
Opportunity to separate	.89	
My job lets people forget about work when they're at home.		.86
Where I work, people can keep job matters at work.		.91
At my job, people are able to prevent work issues from creeping into their home life.		.78
At my job, people can leave work behind when they go home.		.92
Boundary preferences for the home domain	.88	
I don't like thinking about work when I'm home.		.76
I would prefer keeping my job and private life separate.		.84
I don't like work issues creeping into my home life.		.86
I like to be able to leave work behind when I go home.		.84
I would prefer to keep work life at work when I leave my work place.		.81

Table 6.2 Means, standard deviations and intercorrelations of the study

	M	SD	1	2	3	4	5	6	7	8	9	10	11	12	13	14
1. Sex (man)	.67	.47	—													
2. Partner (yes)	.86	.34	.09**													
3. Child(ren) (yes)	.68	.47	.11**	.33**												
4. Job level	8.48	3.60	.13**	.05*	.05											
5. Weekly working hours by contract	35.65	5.40	.52**	-.03	-.19**	.15**										
6. Negative re-organisation experience	.55	.49	-.07**	.01	.02	-.16**	-.11**									
7. Telecommuting	2.40	4.08	.13**	.08**	.10**	.19**	.16**	-.09**								
8. Flexitime	2.98	.98	.09**	.01	-.08*	.15**	.08**	-.12**	.21**							
9. Overwork hours	3.89	5.89	.09**	.01	-.03	.30**	.16**	-.08**	.34**	.10**						

	Mean	SD	1	2	3	4	5	6	7	8	9	10	11	12	13	14
10. Overtime pressure co-workers	2.94	1.06	.06*	.02	-.03	.19**	.14**	-.07*	.17**	.19**	.29**					
11. Overtime pressure management	2.94	1.12	.22**	.07*	.08*	.16**	.21**	-.04	.12**	.03	.21**	.30**				
12. Little opportunity to separate	3.06	.85	.12**	.02	-.10**	.10**	.17**	.00	.26**	-.02	.27**	.20**	.31**			
13. Boundary preference for separation	3.5	.75	-.11**	.01	-.06*	-.18**	-.10**	.33**	-.25**	-.23**	-.29**	-.12**	-.10**	-.14**		
14. Interaction preferences and telecommuting	-.76	4.02	-.08*	.01	-.08*	-.16**	-.06*	.17**	-.43**	-.13**	-.12**	-.06	-.01	-.10**	.55**	
15. Home permeability	2.67	.61	.16**	.06*	.07*	.17**	.23**	-.09**	.41**	.21**	.32**	.32**	.38**	.53**	-.34**	-.18**

Notes: Pearson correlations are significant at p < .01** or p < .05*

REFERENCES

Ahrentzen, S.B. (1990) 'Managing Conflict by Managing Boundaries: How Professional Home Workers Cope with Multiple Roles at Home', *Environment and Behavior*, 22, 723–52.

Aiken, L.S. and West, S.G. (1991) *Multiple Regression: Testing and Interpreting Interactions*, Thousand Oaks: Sage.

Ashforth, E., Kreiner, G. and Fugate, M. (2000) 'All in a Day's Work: Boundaries and Micro Role Transitions', *Academy of Management Review*, 25, 472–91.

Beach, B. (1989) *Integrating Work and Family Life*, Albany: State University of New York Press.

Brannen, J. (2005) 'Time and the Negotiations of Work-Family Boundaries: Autonomy or Illusion?', *Time and Society*, 14, 113–31.

Breedveld, K. (1998) 'The Double Myth of Flexibilization: Trends in Scattered Work Hours and Differences in Time Sovereignty', *Time and Society*, 7, 129–43.

Campbell Clark, S.C. (2000) 'Work/Family Border Theory: A New Theory of Work/Family Balance', *Human Relations*, 53, 747–60.

Campbell Clark, S.C. (2002) 'Communicating across the Work/Home Border', *Community, Work, and Family*, 5, 23–48.

Christensen, K.E. and Staines, G.L. (1990) 'Flextime: A Viable Solution to Work-Family Conflict?', *Journal of Family Issues*, 11, 455–76.

De Man, R. and De Bruijn, J. (2004) 'Integration of Work and Home in a Dutch Organization: An Exploratory Study on Boundary Preferences', paper presented at *the 22nd Annual International Labour Process Conference*, Amsterdam.

Desrocher, S. and Sargent, L.D. (2004) 'Validation Data on a Brief Measure of Work Family Integration and Blurred Boundaries', paper presented at the *2004 Academy of Management conference*, New Orleans.

Desrocher, S., Hilton, J.M. and Larwood, L. (2005) 'Preliminary Validation of the Work-Family Integration-Blurring Scale', *Journal of Family Issues*, 26, 442–66.

Eagle, B., Miles, E. and Icenogle, M. (1997) 'Interrole Conflicts and the Permeability of Work and Family Domains: Are There Gender Differences?', *Journal of Vocational Behavior*, 50, 168–84.

Edwards, J.R. and Rothbard, N.P. (2000) 'Mechanisms Linking Work and Family: Clarifying the Relationship between Work and Family Constructs', *Academy of Management Review*, 25, 178–99.

Frone, M.R., Russell, M. and Cooper, M.L. (1992) 'Prevalence of Work-Family Conflict: Are Work and Family Boundaries Asymmetrically Permeable?', *Journal of Organizational Behavior*, 13, 723–29.

▶

Frone, M.R., Yardley, J.K. and Markel, K.S. (1997) 'Developing and Testing an Integrative Model of the Work-Family Interface', *Journal of Vocational Behavior*, 50, 145–67.

Greenhause, H. and Beutell, N. (1985) 'Sources of Conflict between Work and Family Roles', *Academy of Management Review*, 10, 76–88.

Guest, D.E. (2002) 'Perspectives on the Study of Work-Life Balance', *Social Science Information*, London: Sage, 255–79.

Hall, D.T. and Richter, J. (1988) 'Balancing Work Life and Home Life: What Can Organizations Do to Help?', *Academy of Management Executive*, 2, 213–23.

Hill, E.J., Ferris, M. and Märtenson, V. (2003) 'Does It Matter Where You Work? A Comparison of How Three Work Venues (Traditional Office, Virtual Office and Home Office) Influence Aspects of Work and Personal/Family Life, *Journal of Vocational Behavior*, 63, 220–41.

Hyman, J., Scholarios, D. and Baldry, C. (2005) '"Daddy, I don't Like These Shifts You're Working on Because I Never See You": Coping Strategies for Home and Work' in D. Houston (ed.) *Work-Life Balance in the 21st Century*, Basingstoke: Palgrave Macmillan.

Kossek, E., Noe, R. and DeMarr, B. (1999) 'Work-Family Role Synthesis: Individual and Organizational Determinants', *International Journal of Conflict Management*, 10, 102–29.

Kossek, E.E. (2001) 'Telecommuting', available online: http://www.bc.edu./bc_org/avp/csom/cwf/wfnetwork/index.html.

Kossek, E.E., Lautsch, B.A. and Eaton, S.C. (2005) 'Flexibility Enactment Theory: Implications of Flexibility Type, Control, and Boundary Management for Work-Family Effectiveness' in E.E. Kossek and S.J. Lambert (eds) *Work-Life Integration*, Mahwah: Lawrence Erlbaum.

Kraut, R.E. (1989) 'Telecommuting: The Trade-offs of Home Work', *Journal of Communication*, 39, 19–47.

Kreiner, G.E. (2001) 'On the Edge of Identity: Boundary Conflict and Workplace Fit', unpublished doctoral dissertation, Arizona State University.

Kurland, N.B. and Bailey, D.E. (1999) 'The Advantages and Challenges of Working Here, There, Anywhere, and Anytime', *Organizational Dynamics*, 28, 53–68.

Lewis-Beck, M. (1980) *Applied Regression*, Beverly Hills: Sage.

Lippe, van der, T., Jager, A. and Kops, Y. (2003) 'In balans tussen werk en prive? De invloed van de arbeidssituatie en de thuissituatie op combinatiedruk van mannen en vrouwen', *Bevolking en Gezin*, 32, 3–24.

Mennino, S.F., Rubin, B.A. and Brayfield, A. (2005) 'Home to Job and Job to Home Spillover: The Impact of Company Policies and Workplace Culture', *The Sociological Quarterly*, 46, 107–35.

▶

▶

Myers, R. (1990) *Classical and Modern Regression with Applications*, Boston: Duxbury.

Nippert-Eng, C. (1996a) *Home and Work*, Chicago: University of Chicago Press.

Nippert-Eng, C. (1996b) 'Calendars and Keys: The Classification of "Home" and "Work"', *Sociological Forum*, 11, 535–82.

Olson-Buchanan, J.B. and Boswell, W.R. (2006) 'Blurring Boundaries: Correlates of Integration and Segmentation between Work and Non-work', *Journal of Vocational Behavior*, 68, 432–45.

Perlow, L. (1998) 'Boundary Control: The Social Ordering of Work and Family Time in a High-tech Corporation', *Administrative Science Quarterly*, 43, 328–57.

Pleck, J. (1977) 'The Work-Family Role System', *Social Problems*, 24, 417–27.

Pryor, R.G. (1983) *Manual for the Work Aspect Preference Scale*, Melbourne: Australian Council for Education Research.

Ralston, D.A. (1989) 'The Benefits of Flextime: Real or Imagined?', *Journal of Organizational Behavior*, 10, 369–73.

Rau, B.L. and Hyland, M.M. (2002) 'Role Conflict and Flexible Work Arrangements: The Effects on Applicant Attraction', *Personal Psychology*, 55, 111–36.

Rothbard, N.P., Phillips, K.W. and Dumas, T.L. (2005) 'Managing Multiple Roles: Work-Family Policies and Individual Desires for Segmentation', Philadelphia: University of Pennsylvania, http://www.management.wharton.upenn.edu/rothbard/documents/rothbard-phillips-dumas-2005.

Winett, R.A., Neale, M.S. and Williams, K.R. (1982) 'The Effects of Flexible Work Schedules on Urban Families with Young Children: Quasi-experimental Ecological Studies', *American Journal of Community Psychology*, 10, 49–64.

Work Relations and the Multiple Dimensions of the Work-Life Boundary: Hairstyling at Home

Rachel Lara Cohen

Introduction

The workers discussed in this chapter – hairstylists – appear to lack a work-life boundary. On the one hand, 'life' regularly intrudes into the world of work, with owners' friends and family assuming 'employee' roles (paid or unpaid); stylists' friends and family taking customer roles; others (children needing care, family or friends in search of a chat) spending time in the work-space for non-work reasons. Additionally, 'friendships' may grow from (and then impinge upon) workplace relationships. On the other hand, work may be taken outside of work-time and space, with stylists pursuing work-tasks for people with whom they have social or business relationships; in their or others' homes, hospitals or care-homes; for pay or gratis. Alternately, work can exceed given temporal schedules or work-hours can disrupt 'normal' social temporality. Lastly, affectations of 'cool' constructed as part of work-based aesthetic labour may spillover into workers' extra-work social and sartorial practices.

While the above suggests a relative absence of boundaries, most hairstylists desire, and feel they achieve, a work-life boundary. This anomaly is only explicable when the work-life boundary is understood as multi-dimensional, including (in a non-exhaustive list) dimensions of spatiality (dedicated workplaces versus non-workplaces), temporality (working times versus non-work times), rationality (instrumental versus value), task (job-related tasks versus processes demanded by extra-work tasks) and personnel (workplace social relations versus extra-work relationships) as well as aesthetics (commodified versus uncommodified self-presentation). The work-life boundary's multi-dimensionality means that when breaching appears to occur along one or more dimensions, symbolic restoration is possible by emphasising alternate dimensions' significance.

115

This chapter focuses on a specific type of multi-dimensional breaching – instances when work-tasks are performed outside the work-site (spatial breaching) and outside work-time (temporal breaching).

Sociology of the work-life boundary

While classical sociology says little about 'work-life boundary' per se, the separation of work from home life is central to most theories of modernity, albeit with varying foci: Marx's interest is in the temporal and physical dimensions of the boundary (workers moving into factories and under capitalist control for specified time periods); whereas bounded budgets and rationales are critical for Weber (the increasing separation of the household budget, and rationale, from that of the enterprise); and for Parsons role separation is central (different personnel, tasks and affect, belonging in each sphere). This range of foci suggests the possibility of theoretical and commonsense conceptualisations of the work-life boundary as multi-dimensional (which is not to suggest that all dimensions are equal). Meanwhile, after a century of acceptance, the proposition that modernity necessitates work-life separation has been challenged both by empirical research especially on workplace temporalities, homeworking and informal work, and by an emergent concern with conceptualising the work-life boundary.

Increased awareness of the temporal encroachment of work upon (and consequent disruption of) family life underpins growing interest among academics and policymakers in fostering 'work-life balance' (Hochschild 1997; Hogarth et al. 2000; Jacobs and Gerson 2004; Presser 2003; Schor 1991), but such research has generally focused on a single dimension (temporality) of the work-life relationship. In contrast, space is central to conceptualisations of homeworking or teleworking. Early advocates of telework (for instance Toffler 1980) predicted that workers' movement from spatially demarcated workplaces to the home would be liberating, with workers controlling their labour and becoming less alienated. However empirical studies have found that, instead of relishing their lack of boundaries, home-based workers constantly struggle to demarcate non-working time, spaces and relations (Boris and Daniels 1989; Felstead and Jewson 2000; Phizcklea and Wolkowitz 1995). Where they fail, the consequence is colonisation of the social realm by workplace tasks and rationales. Homeworking research has nicely revealed workers' desire for bounded spheres, concomitantly highlighting the extent of paid work at home which threatens these spheres. Another form of work that breaches boundaries is 'informal work' (also often performed in extra-'work' settings). Informal work may be done for friends or family and may be paid, unpaid, exchanged for favours or used to meet non-pecuniary needs (Nelson and Smith 1999; Pahl 1984). In the latter cases the rationales for and relationships within which work is organised are intertwined with workers' home lives – or, as Glucksmann suggests, there is an 'interconnectedness across boundaries between paid and unpaid work, market and non-market, formal and informal sectors' (2005: 29). While much informal work is performed by peripheral workers with few economic alternatives (Portes and Castells 1989; Williams and Windebank 1998), it is also performed by workers who additionally hold a formal job (Williams and Windebank 1998) who may use it to express identity (Snyder 2004), re-imposing 'life' (or value) rationales on 'work'.

Although the above research describes instances of porosity in work-life boundaries, it is mostly not framed this way. In contrast, Nippert-Eng's (1996) study of the ways in which individuals construct home-work boundaries directly addresses the task of conceptualising work-life boundary (re-)creation. She claims that everybody's sense of self is either continuous or realm-specific. Segmentation is produced by using 'different spatio-temporal places to support different ways of being' and is maintained by '[t]he ways we manage calendars, keys, clothes and appearances, eating and drinking, money and people' (Nippert-Eng 1996: 99). She argues that particular occupations, organisations, work groups, family ties and national contexts encourage the development of more 'integrated' or more 'segregated' lives. It is this argument that is developed here, with specific attention given not only to the role of work relations but also to socio-demographic factors, in determining which workers allow, or do not allow, their work life to spillover into or merge with the time, space, relations and rationalities of their home lives. This chapter also explores variation across workers in the dimension(s) of the work-life boundary that are salient. It develops three general claims:

(i)   the work-life boundary is multi-dimensional;
(ii) this multi-dimensionality enables workers' ideological reconstruction of boundaries where breaching occurs;
(iii) work relations need to be considered to understand work-life boundary(ies).

Empirical study

Hairstyling is a common occupation in Britain, with 171,347 people formally employed in hairdressing as their main job (ONS 2005b). Over 40 per cent of hairstylists are self-employed (Berry-Lound et al. 2000; HABIA 2001). Of these self-employed hairstylists approximately 40 per cent employ other workers, the remainder work alone (Berry-Lound et al. 2000). Chair-renting (a form of sub-contracting) is common. A 2000 survey found 14 per cent of salons 'renting out chairs' (Berry-Lound et al. 2000: 17–8). Women dominate the sector; the workforce is 83 per cent female (ONS 2005a). National Vocational

Qualifications (NVQs) in hairdressing have existed since 1987 (ECOTEC 2000: 38) requiring upwards of two years to complete, with training usually undertaken as an in-salon apprenticeship. Despite their training employees in hairstyling are poorly paid, ranking 335th out of 342 occupational groups in a 2004 survey (GMB 2005).

Research methods

Primary research was conducted in 'Northerncity', a city in the North of England. It took two forms: firstly, semi-structured interviews with hairdressers and barbers in a sample of the city's salons and barbershops; and secondly, a mail survey distributed to every salon/barbershop in the city. Salons were systematically sampled for interview from a geographically organised list. Supplementary interviews were conducted with stylists in salons with specified characteristics (barbershops, chains, salons with a primarily ethnic clientele, salons with 'chair-renting'). Interviews, ranging from 30 minutes to 2 hours, were carried out with at least one person in each selected salon and were taped. In total 71 workers in 52 salons or barbershops were interviewed. The mail survey included both open and closed questions about the salon and the respondent. The survey was hand-delivered and research aims were explained. The response rate was 40 per cent.

Research findings

Desire for boundaries

Most stylists expressed a preference for a bounded work-life: 82 per cent of respondents agreed or agreed strongly with the statement 'I like to leave work behind when I leave the salon' (see Table 7.1). Sex and work relations affect the strength of this preference. Neither male nor female stylists were likely to disagree but male stylists were significantly ($p < 0.1$) more likely to agree strongly. This result suggests that men see a work-life boundary as more essential than women, perhaps as a result of traditional gender roles wherein the 'home' constituted a workplace for women but a haven for men.

Statements of stylists in different work relations also vary significantly ($p < 0.05$). Half of trainees disagreed with the statement, suggesting a much weaker desire for a work-life boundary during the training period (although the low number of trainees surveyed requires that this finding be read cautiously). Owners and other qualified stylists overwhelmingly liked to leave their work behind when they left the salon but over half of stylists expressed strong agreement in contrast to under a third of owners. Perhaps stylists who achieved most inner

Table 7.1 Opinions about statement 'I like to leave work behind when I leave the salon', by sex and work relation

	Disagree or Disagree Strongly	Agree	Agree Strongly	Total % (N)
Men	14.7[+]	35.3	50.0	100 (34)
Women	18.8	54.1	27.1	100 (85)
Owners	16.1*	54.0	29.9	100 (87)
Trainees	50.0	37.5	12.5	100 (8)
Other stylists	12.0	36.0	52.0	100 (25)
All	17.6	48.7	33.6	100 (119)

Notes: Chi-square test for association: *($p < .05$); [+]($p < .1$)

reward from hairstyling became owners and this same inner reward accounted for their lesser desire to leave work behind at the end of the day or perhaps owners' less alienated labour process relationships transformed hairstyling from 'job' to 'identity', reducing their desire to shed it. Alternatively perhaps because owners did less extra-work styling (see below), their desire for boundaries was less burning. Anyhow, except for trainees, variation was in the *degree* (not existence) of a desire to relegate work to the workplace: just 16 per cent of owners and 12 per cent of other stylists stated that they did *not* want to leave work at work.[1]

Nonetheless, only a third of stylists introduced work-life boundaries as a concern during interviews. Most often the topic was broached in justifying a decision to restrict their extra-salon hairstyling. Emily, employed in an international hairstyling chain, is typical:

Q   Do you cut friends' and family's hair?

Emily: Family, close family, like my mum, dad and brothers. But I tend not to. I try to keep it separate. Otherwise you feel like all you're doing is hairdressing all the time. I like to, when I leave, switch off from it. And that's it. It's alright if you do family and stuff, but you're not going to charge them for doing it, so you're just doing it in your own free time, and a lot of time people who work full-time, don't get a lot of free time anyway ...

Later, notwithstanding her admission that she styles some family members' hair, Emily was more emphatic: 'I just don't cut hair at home. No. Not at all. I'd rather not.' Emily's focus on temporality in the separation – free and work time – was reiterated by other stylists: 'I think I just do enough. I wouldn't want to spend all my time ... of course I love doing it, I wouldn't want to spend all my time outside of work still doing it' (Jenny).

Emily and Jenny were commission-based stylists, so formally their incomes were less temporally dependent than stylists on hourly wages. Yet commission-based stylists were most likely to define the boundaries of their work, and to do so temporally. This temporal definition of work-life boundaries resulted from the fact that commission-based stylists work longer daily and weekly hours than workers in other work relations, with little ability to vary this (Cohen 2005). It gives their formal work rigid temporal boundaries, while leaving them little free time. Here work relations impact workers' at-work temporality, which in turn affects their desire to guard non-working time from further temporal encroachments, leading to temporal expression of the work-life boundary.

By contrast, where salon owners stated a preference for bounded home and work lives, they expressed this spatially, emphasising the salon/barbershop door as physical marker:

I do live quite a way away, so it's like, when I do shut the shop it is shut and forgot about, so I'm not on the doorstep.

(Tina)

When I need to shut this door at night I don't even think about work. I come here, I do me job. Away from work I don't want to think. And I can't even believe I cut hair for a living.

(Simon)

For neither Tina nor Simon did salon ownership diminish the desire for bounded spheres, but control over a physical space transforms understanding of the work-life boundary from temporal to spatial. Expression of boundaries in spatial rather than temporal terms made the flexibility and unpredictability (or unboundedness) of owners' at-work schedules commensurate with the desire (and understanding of) a bounded work-life (something especially salient for owners working alone, whose in-salon hours vary greatly).

Extra-salon styling

Despite stylists' overwhelming preference for leaving work at the work-place, half of those surveyed did some paid or unpaid extra-salon hairstyling (see Table 7.2) either in their own homes (43 per cent) or in others' homes (28 per cent). A quarter received payment, a rate of paid informal work much higher than the 2.9 per cent Williams and Windebank (1998) found in their study of an urban workforce. Thus hairstyling is an occupation in which boundaries – spatial, temporal, task and perhaps rationale – between work and

Table 7.2   Involvement of formally employed stylists in extra-salon styling

	Any styling	Any paid styling
Do hairstyling outside salon/ barbershop	49.6%	26.6%
In other people's homes only	6.4	13.6
In my home only	21.6	4.0
In both my and others' homes	21.6	8.0
Total (N)	100% (125)	100% (125)

home are remarkably frequently breached *despite* stylists' preferences for them to be maintained. This result highlights the importance of occupation: hairstyling skills are informally exchangeable and widely demanded, something true of many other occupations, especially craft and professional (such as masseur, doctor, plumber) but not all (such as policemen, production-line worker, receptionist).

Interviews with stylists bore out survey findings; approximately half did hairstyling outside of the salon. Notably, many who initially denied cutting hair at home, after prompting, admitted that there were particular people whose hair they did (or that they did some styling, 'but not for pay'). As with Emily (above), these stylists simultaneously perceive themselves not to undertake extra-work styling while allowing regular exceptions. The multidimensionality of the work-life boundary makes this possible. Stylists failed to immediately recognise certain acts of extra-salon styling work *as* styling work because they had constructed alternate boundaries in place of spatial-temporal or task boundaries. For instance, by defining styling work not just as a set of tasks but as those tasks performed for pay for people outside of social and/or reciprocal relationships, and to the extent that stylists limit the people whose hair they cut outside of the salon to immediate friends and family (those involved in ongoing reciprocal relationships), charging at most a nominal sum, the work-life boundary remains intact and stylists may assert they do not work at home.

The characteristics of stylists who do (paid or unpaid) extra-salon styling are shown in Table 7.3. The table reveals that the relationship between stylists' desire to leave work behind at the salon and the achievement of this end is complex. The most successful at aligning desire and practice were respondents who disagreed with the statement that they like to leave work behind when they leave the salon (implying desire to continue styling outside of the workplace/time); 83 per cent of this group did hairstyling outside the salon. Less successfully, 40 per cent of those who agreed that they like to leave work behind

Table 7.3 Whether stylists do extra-salon styling, by opinions on work-life separation, socio-demographic characteristics, work relations and workplace characteristics

	Do extra-salon styling	Do NO extra-salon styling	Total % (N)
'I like to leave work behind when I leave the salon.'	%	%	%
Agree Strongly	60.0*	40.0	100 (40)
Agree	39.7	60.3	100 (58)
Disagree	83.3	16.7	100 (18)
Gender	%	%	%
Men	50.0	50.0	100 (32)
Women	52.2	47.8	100 (92)
Main earner in family?	%	%	%
No. Someone else is.	61.7*	38.3	100 (47)
Hard to say; it's quite even.	34.5	65.5	100 (29)
Yes.	52.4	47.6	100 (42)
Work Relations	%	%	%
Owners	39.8**	60.2	100 (88)
Other qualified stylists	73.1	26.9	100 (26)
Trainees	88.9	11.1	100 (9)
Price of women's wash, cut and blow dry (in-salon):			
Mean (SD)	£14.87 (5.75)	£14.34 (5.44)	£14.61 (5.58)
Price of men's trim (in-salon):			
Mean (SD)	£7.00 (4.27)	£6.99 (3.91)	£7.00 (4.08)
Usual weekly (in-salon) hours:			
Mean (SD)	38.94 (8.39)	38.40 (7.80)	38.67 (8.07)

Notes: Chi-square tests for association of categorical variables; T-tests for equality of means: **(p < .001); *(p < .05).

when they leave the salon did hairstyling at home (failing to achieve their preference), while a huge 60 per cent of those who agreed strongly with the statement (and who might be expected to be the most determined to achieve strong boundaries) failed to align preference and practice and styled hair outside of the workplace/time. Thus while those who wanted to continue styling outside of the salon were able to do so, many others who would rather not do extra-salon work nevertheless also ended up doing it. It may be that the act of doing styling outside the salon reinforces a desire for bounded spheres, accounting for why a larger proportion of stylists who 'strongly agree' that they would like to leave work behind when they leave the salon (than those who 'agree') did work out of the salon.

Contrary to, for example, studies of the informal economy that have shown greater male than female participation (Williams and Windebank 1998) there was no significant gender difference in extra-salon styling. Fifty per cent of male stylists, as compared to 52 per cent of female stylists, did hairstyling outside of the salon (a similarity in gender practices that occurs irrespective of men's more strongly stated desire for a work-life boundary). This intra-occupational similarity highlights the importance of occupation; different labour force rates of male and female participation in the informal economy may be rooted in occupational sex segregation in the formal economy (and men's development of those occupational skills most demanded by informal networks).

Individual time pressure appears to be unrelated to the likelihood of extra-salon styling: mean in-salon work hours were virtually identical for workers who did hairstyling outside of the salon and those who did not (39.0 and 38.4 hours respectively). However, stylists' structural economic role vis-à-vis their household was consequential. Respondents who claimed that it was 'hard to say' whether they or another member of their family was the primary earner (that is those in the most economically egalitarian household relationships) are least likely to do extra-salon hairstyling: only 35 per cent did extra-salon hairstyling as compared to 52 per cent of main earners and 62 per cent of secondary earners. They were also least likely to do extra-salon styling for pay: 10 per cent versus 36 per cent (main earners) and 26 per cent (secondary earners). There was no significant gender variation in these proportions. Stylists stating that it is 'hard to say' if they or someone else was the primary earner were likely to be in households containing at least two full-time workers. This finding suggests that time-poverty at the household level affects participation in extra-work hairstyling – a reminder of the need to consider workers within the totality of their relationships and the constraints and compromises imposed by these relationships rather than as isolated individuals (see also Ransome's contribution to this volume).

A direct measure of income was not available because of seasonal variation in stylists' earnings and complexities produced by including workers in different work relations. Instead, the price of haircuts at the salon/barbershop where stylists work was taken as an (admittedly imperfect) proxy to investigate the relationship between income and extra-salon styling. Table 7.3 indicates that there was no significant difference in the mean prices of a woman's wash, cut and blow dry or a man's trim (the most widely available services) in workplaces where stylists were involved in extra-salon styling (£14.87 women's cut, wash and blow dry; £7.00 men's trim) and where they are not (£14.34 and £6.99). Therefore workers in low-cost salons/barbershops were no more likely than workers in high-cost salons/barbershops to engage in extra-work styling. On the other hand, stylists' work relations are important determinants of the likelihood of doing hairstyling outside the workplace. While only 41 per cent of salon-owners did extra-work hairstyling, 73 per cent of other qualified stylists and 89 per cent of trainees did it. These differences are striking (and significant, $p < 0.05$).

Logistic regression analysis with the dependent variable 'engagement in hairstyling outside of the salon'[2] was used to test the robustness of these bivariate relationships. Findings confirm that workers who did not seek a bounded working life were less likely to have one: although there was no significant difference between those who agreed (the reference category) and agreed strongly with the statement 'I like to leave work behind when I leave the salon', disagreeing (and thereby indicating a willingness to continue work outside of the salon) multiplies the odds of doing hairstyling outside the salon by a factor of nearly eight ($p < 0.05$). Socio-demographic variables had no effect: none of gender, age or family composition variables (marital status; household including school-age or pre-school children) were significant. However, membership of an equal-earner household reduced the odds of doing hairstyling outside of the salon by 70 per cent ($p < 0.1$). The distance of the salon from the stylist's home is also significant ($p < 0.05$): for every extra minute that the stylist takes getting to work, his or her odds of doing hairstyling at home increased by 4.7 per cent. Other workplace characteristics were insignificant. However the effect of work relations, found in bivariate analysis, persisted. Trainees were omitted since all but one did extra-salon styling (and so almost perfectly predicted the dependent variable). The analysis therefore considered qualified stylists only. Owners' odds of doing styling work outside of the salon are 84 per cent lower than non-owners' ($p < 0.1$). This difference was not a by-product of career stage since a variable measuring the years respondents had worked in hairstyling was included in the model and had no significant effect.

The following sections draw out these findings, using qualitative data to explore workers' rationales for doing hairstyling outside of the salon.

Rationales for extra-salon styling

Four rationales for styling at home can be identified. Each rationale is differently important for workers in different work relations. This means that *although workers in different work relations may act on the basis of similar rationales, the combination of rationales held by workers in one work relation tends to vary from that held by workers in another.* Additionally the connection between each rationale and the construction of particular types of boundaries between home and the work is drawn out.

Extra income

Since hairdressing is poorly paid and since stylists possess marketable skills, it is unsurprising that stylists frequently commented that 'others' (other stylists in their salon or stylists generally) did styling at home 'for that bit extra'. A couple of interviewees offered an economic rationale for their own extra-salon hairstyling:

> I mean, between you and not [the] taxman, you have to really, you have to do some at home because to make your money ... 'Cos relatives gives you so much for doing it and that. Because if you don't ... [shakes head] ... You probably know somebody who's doing haircutting on the side or something like that. The money [earned in-salon] is never ever, for the hours what hairdressers do, is not really good.
>
> (Tom)

Yet, despite the frequency of extra-salon hairstyling, very few interviewees mentioned income as a rationale for their own extra-salon styling. All who did worked in small salons earning an hourly wage for in-salon styling. Hourly paid stylists are detached from the value produced by their in-salon styling and may therefore be less perturbed by receiving lower rates for extra-salon work and more willing to sell their labour informally (stylists who charged for extra-salon styling generally agreed that it is 'impossible' to charge the same rates as in-salon).

Conversely some owners' rationale for not doing extra-salon styling was economic: 'It's not economically viable. For me to go out of the salon for two hours I would have to charge a hundred pounds at least. I mean, it's for weddings ... But it's just not worth it to me' (Martina). As an owner Martina received the total price for her in-salon work and so gained no advantage from out-of-salon work, which may be cash-in-hand but will not enable her to multi-task as is possible in the salon and will involve set-up and perhaps travel time on top of the styling itself. The 'hundred pounds' Martina quoted is over five times her rate for an in-salon haircut (and therefore an unrealistic amount to expect) but reflects a consideration of these issues.

While stylists may not do extra-salon styling 'for' income, many nonetheless received an income from it (as mentioned above, a quarter of survey respondents did paid extra-work hairstyling). Table 7.4 breaks down extra-salon styling, focusing on its recipients and stylists' work relations. Only 18 per cent of owners did paid work and they predominantly did it for 'other people' (that is people they class as neither friends nor family). On the other hand, 42 per cent of non-owner stylists received payment for extra-salon hairstyling[3] and although 30 per cent were paid by 'other people', 4 per cent received payments from immediate family members (partner, children, parents), a fifth were paid by wider family members, 8 per cent by their 'best friend(s)' and nearly a quarter by 'other friends'. Therefore, non-owner stylists were not only more likely to be paid for extra-work styling than owners but they were also in closer relationships to the people from whom they received payments. The small number of trainees in the sample makes it difficult to assess their responses but notably trainees' extra-salon paid work goes beyond styling friends and family. Unqualified trainees do not have in-salon clients, and therefore their extra-salon clients, who both pay for services and are not in proximate social relations, are their first encounters with 'real' clients. Thus for some trainees it is in extra-salon styling that they first fully embody the occupational identity of stylist.

Becoming a stylist – training and identity

A striking survey finding, reiterated in interviews, is that trainees almost universally did extra-salon hairstyling. Crystal made a general point: 'that's how you learn, isn't it', while Jenny described how doing her family's hair profited her at least as much as her family:

> It was a way of practicing. Which sounds bad, but I mean I never did anything on anybody if I didn't know what I was doing. I used to do it on me sister and she used to have a few unusual haircuts, but she didn't mind. But no, I did used to do a few people, a few more of me aunties.

Since extra-salon practice is a normal (albeit informal) requirement of apprenticeships, senior stylists expect juniors to do this alongside full-time commitments to the salon and/or college.

In addition, after-hours hairstyling facilitates trainees' construction of adult-worker identities. Hairstylist is an embodied identity; you cannot simply buy a hair salon (as you could a dry-cleaner's) and claim to be a stylist. Affiliation depends on the passage of tests and on the knowledge, experience and training embodied in the person of the stylist. It is underpinned by fellow stylists' positive assessments and by clients (including friends and family taking client roles). Clients are an especially important source of status legitimation

Table 7.4 Extra-salon styling, by work relation, form of compensation and relationship to client

Extra-salon styling for ...	Styling work done by:			All
	Owner	Qualified stylist	Trainees	
... pay	**18.2%****	**42.3%**	**55.6%**	**26.0%**
Immediate family	1.1	3.8	0.0	1.6
Wider family	0.0	19.2	1.1	4.9
Best friend(s)	2.3	7.7	22.2	4.9
Other friends	4.5	23.1	22.2	9.8
Other people	12.5	30.8	55.6	19.5
... favour/gift (no pay)	**9.1**	**15.4**	**22.2**	**11.4**
Immediate family	1.1	11.5	11.1	4.1
Wider family	2.3	0.0	11.1	2.4
Best friend(s)	4.5	11.5	11.1	6.5
Other friends	3.4	0.0	11.1	3.3
Other people	1.1	0.0	0.0	0.8
... nothing (not pay, nor favour/gift)	**30.7****	**61.5**	**66.7**	**39.8**
Immediate family	26.1	53.8	66.7	35.0
Wider family	6.8	3.8	0.0	5.7
Best friend(s)	6.8	19.2	11.1	9.8
Other friends	1.1	3.8	0.0	1.6
Other people	3.4	3.8	0.0	3.3
... pay OR not	**39.8*****	**73.1**	**88.9**	**50.4**
Totals (N)	100% (88)	100% (26)	100% (9)	100% (123)

Notes: Chi-square test of association: ***($p < .001$); **($p < .01$).
Percentages cannot be summed as, for example, stylists may do paid extra-salon styling for people in more than one type of relationship or for pay *and* for free.

for early-career stylists still *becoming* hairstylists. Trainees with their minimal desire for work-life boundaries and enthusiastic involvement in paid and unpaid extra-salon styling demonstrate the way that a work identity may be constructed inside *and outside* the workplace by increasing the number of interactions wherein this identity is central. To the extent that trainees' work identities are constructed outside of the wage-labour relation they are perhaps non-alienated. However, to the extent that trainees' extra-salon styling is performed *purely* for practice (rather than to express an identity) and to the extent that this extra-salon styling is necessitated by inadequate in-salon training, it represents a 'colonisation of home by work' like that found in homeworking (Felstead and Jewson 2000).

With training complete and hairstylist identity cemented, trainees' enthusiasm for extra-salon styling declines. Unfortunately, patterns of behaviour established while training are difficult to break and many stylists describe ongoing extra-work clients whom they would now prefer not to 'do', but from whom they find it hard to extricate themselves. This difficulty of changing established behavioural patterns exacerbates the demands made by relationships of social reciprocity.

Inter-personal reciprocity – rooted in social relations

Stylists and trainees most frequently rationalised styling outside the workplace as doing 'a favour'. This language was used irrespectively of whether payment was received and it was used to describe two different types of reciprocal relationships. The first interpersonal reciprocity rooted in extra-work social relations, is discussed here. The second reciprocity rooted in workplace relationships, will be discussed in the following section.

When explaining extra-work styling as 'favours' rooted in social relationships stylists focused on the closeness of particular relationships (friends and family). May, a young stylist, responded to a question about whether she cut friends' hair by first emphasising that she only does it as a favour. She then offered a 'checklist' of people whose hair she cuts: 'I do, like, my mum and dad, [x]'s boyfriend and that. But I don't really, do ... I've done my nana ...'. While the components of May's checklist are peculiar to her its character is not. Firstly, the list is organised by social (and familial) relationships. Secondly, it is limited. And thirdly, interspersed with a list of people whose hair May styles is a denial that she 'really' does extra-salon hairstyling. These three features are connected: by listing and employing recognisable extra-work social relations, denial is made to sit with the reality of extra-work styling; a work-life boundary is maintained by reference to personnel (and rationale) at a point at which it is breached spatially, temporally, and in terms of task. Janet's list contains the same three features: 'Mum and dad, boyfriend, one of me aunties, her daughter, my cousin, and her. No [I don't do it], not really. My best friend, I'll do her hair.' For Janet and May specific relationships (friends/family) underpin decisions to do extra-salon styling despite a more general 'decision' not to do so. For other stylists circumstances delimit those whose hair they style outside the salon, for example Denise insisted 'I don't' do extra-salon styling, and then admitted that 'I do some of me friends who have ... you know, kids and that ... at school, but I choose.'

Yet interviewees made it clear that 'choice' is difficult to exercise. Stylists found themselves pressed into work they prefer not to do by cajoling friends. Shana suggested that the only escape was to 'never let anyone know you're a hairdresser that doesn't need to know' as this was the only way to avoid the (irresistible) pressure to do styling out of the workplace. Even the closest of family (especially male family) were reported make demands that can generate resentment:

> You know what I do hate – when my husband asks me to cut his hair. I get home and he's always wanting me to do that. He's got hardly any hair, but still he always wants it cut.
>
> (Laura)

> Sometimes it's a pain in the backside ... I've got my son now, been on at me last two days, saying, 'Will you cut my hair, will you cut my hair?' and I get home and sorta ... you don't want to do it.
>
> (Tom)

One way to avoid the obligation of styling friends and family at home was to style them in-salon. Work relations affected this strategy. Owners (who are the least likely to work at home) emphasised that salon possession bestows the ability to choose not to do extra-salon styling: 'When we got the shop I was ... that was it. Got a salon: I'm not working on somebody's kitchen chair and breaking me back, am I?' (Simon).

Salon possession meant that owners were easily able to give friends and family free or discounted services in-salon. Perhaps as importantly, others were aware that the small business owners' earnings depended on in-salon take. This recognition may discourage friends and family from 'taking advantage' by demanding (usually discounted) out-of-salon services. Further, to the extent that ownership creates more identity between the salon and the stylist, the spatial demarcation of their place of work is reinforced. Lastly, a salon owned by a friend or family member may be felt to be an especially welcoming environment.

By contrast, stylists in corporate chains have little control over their workplaces and are unlikely to construct socialising spaces therein. These stylists assume that friends and family coming to the work-site *must* pay standard prices, an assumption not simply enforced from above but reinforced by pay systems based on personal take: 'Because you can't have friends coming in and doing them for nothing ... because at the end of the day you have figures to achieve'

(Carol). Where friends and family had to pay full price (which they may resist) and where any discounts would reduce stylists' 'figures' and therefore income, incentives existed to fulfil socially rooted styling obligations outside the salon.

Logistic regression analysis (above) showed that the further away from their workplaces stylists lived the more likely they were to do extra-work styling. Where distance makes it more difficult for friends and family to get to the salon (and unlikely that the salon is part of their 'community'), and to the extent that hairstyling is understood as social obligation, it is one that may only be met by hairstyling at home. Thus, paradoxically, where spatial boundaries between home and work are greatest (where work and home are at a distance) consistent maintenance of a spatial boundary is increasingly difficult, with work-tasks seeping into the life-world.

Social reciprocity is a rationale for paid as well as unpaid extra-salon hairstyling. Some stylists stated frankly: 'you can't charge family [and/or friends]', and Table 7.4 shows that few stylists charged immediate family members while many styled them gratis. However stylists generally received payment from more distant relatives: 19 per cent of non-owner stylists styled their wider family's hair for pay, whereas only four per cent did so for free. Stylists' 'best friend(s)' were most likely (after immediate family) to be styled for free (by 19 per cent of stylists and seven percent of owners). However, they were also styled for pay (by eight per cent of non-owners and two per cent of owners) or for tangible reciprocal goods: 'a favour/ gift in return' (12 per cent of non-owners and five per cent of owners). Acceptance of payment may be phrased in terms of succumbing to the demands of relatives (rather than economic requirement): 'My brother and his wife, they won't let me do their hair for nothing 'cos at the end of the day it's my time, so they always buy me a present or something' (Carol). Where stylists received money or gifts from friends/family at the latter's insistence rather than as payment due to their work, their styling remained unrecognised as work and their obligation to do it can be framed in terms of social rather than economic rationales.

Work relations influence whether payment is received for out-of-salon styling work performed in a context of social relationships. Chair-renting and commission-based stylists (with income directly related to 'take') understood the value of their labour and consistently expressed the expectation that they were paid for extra-salon work. Furthermore, statistically, workers with in-salon employment in more expensive salons (where they may also earn more) were more likely to be paid if they did styling outside the salon (despite being no more likely to do it). The mean price of an in-salon wash, cut and blow dry was significantly higher ($p < 0.05$) where stylists were paid for extra-salon styling (£16.43) than where they did unpaid extra-salon styling (£13.10). This result contrasts with findings (above) that stylists explicitly mentioning pay as a rationale worked in less-expensive, wage-only salons. It suggests that well-paid chair-renting or commission-based stylists may not do extra-work hairstyling *for* pay but nevertheless valorise their work and are more likely to be paid when they do extra-salon hairstyling to meet social obligations.

It was noted above that stylists who were secondary earners in their households did more extra-salon styling than 'main' earners but when *paid* out-of-salon work was examined this relationship was reversed: being paid for extra-salon work was most likely where stylists' incomes were more important to their family. Given that much extra-salon styling is for people in close social relationships, it is probable that the decision to compensate stylists (or not) sometimes reflects others' assessment of how critical a stylist's income is to their household. This assessment roots compensation (or its absence) in a substantive, rather than formal, determination of value. Thus even the exchange of labour services for money may neither signify that such practices are ruled by workplace rationalities nor that they constitute a breach of the work-life boundary.

Inter-personal reciprocity – rooted in the salon

In addition to friends and family members, extra-salon styling may be a 'favour' for in-salon clients. This situation is most common when clients are injured, lose mobility with age or when special occasions (namely weddings) necessitate out-of-hours styling. Most often stylists described favours as reciprocation for long-standing clients' 'good' custom.

> I have been to people's houses who have had major operations. When clients have been: 'Oh I can't ... can you come round? I've had hysterectomy or mastectomy, or whatever.' I will; I'll go to their house and do it. Because if they could come in they would; but they can't.
>
> (Jenny)

Jenny implied that a condition of her extra-salon styling was that the people for whom she did it 'would come in if they could'. As a chair-renting stylist dependent on maintaining a steady clientele regular clients were at a premium for her and acknowledging particular loyalty was worthwhile. Owners of small salons, especially sole owner-operators, were in an equivalent situation and Oona drew a similar line:

> It's only regular ones. I wouldn't do a mobile service for anybody who wasn't a regular customer, because it's their loyalty that makes you do it you see. So they've been here for a long time ... Like last Christmas, I had a customer who broke her ankle between Christmas and New Year. And she was incapacitated for about six months and in that six months I used to go up and do her hair every couple of weeks. To keep her feeling happy with herself.

Although Oona initially focused on her client's length of custom, and it is clear that her extra-work styling was a reward/inducement for repeat custom, at the end she reframed the relationship – taking responsibility for the client's happiness. As relationships are reframed in non-work terms, breaching of owners' strong spatially demarcated work-life boundaries can be accommodated by reconstituting styling as necessary for well-being, an extra-work social good.

Conclusions

Boundaries are used to conceptually demarcate our lives (Lamont and Molnár 2002: 168). The work-life boundary is both a product of the alienated nature of work and a potential defence against further alienation in our home lives. Therefore it is hardly surprising that unboundedness may represent either the re-socialising of productive labour (wherein the performance of work-tasks in extra-work surroundings produces an uncommodified or social identification with the work) or, alternatively, the commodification of social relationships (wherein workers' awareness of the value of their own labour-power may mean that even labour performed as a favour for a sibling is given a price). Although the existence and form of a workers' work-life boundary cannot be directly read off his or her work relations, this chapter has shown that without knowledge of the latter it is difficult to understand the former or its repercussions. Work relations affect both whether and how work-life boundaries are drawn because they affect the rationales for drawing boundaries and the dimensions along which they can be drawn. Moreover, they have this effect to an extent that workplace and social-demographic characteristics (gender, age, marital status, having children) do not.

Among hairstylists, trainees were found to have the most malleable work-life boundaries both in terms of intent and practice. Work identity is created outside the workplace and work-skills are honed at home. However, early-career unboundedness constructs or exacerbates social obligations that over time are decreasingly welcome. Owners' boundaries were more concrete and were conceptualised spatially. Breaches were rooted in long-term work-based economic interests (maintaining a clientele) and understood as occasional favours. To the extent this extra-salon styling was conceptualised using extra-economic language ('making someone happy' rather than 'keeping clients'), it was made commensurate with strong spatial boundaries. Non-owner stylists had greater disjuncture between their desire for boundaries and actual practice. Usually conceived temporally, their boundaries were frequently transgressed under economic pressure (the need to keep clients, earn extra income) and social pressure (reciprocity demanded by extra-work relationships).

To account for transgressions stylists constructed boundaries using alternate markers – social relations, tasks performed and receipt (or not) of financial compensation. Where work-tasks were performed for pay for people who were not otherwise socially related to the stylist these three markers corresponded, marking activities as work (even when performed after-hours and outside the salon). However, only stylists who explicitly stated that they did extra-work styling for pay found this correspondence. More often lines drawn around out of work styling were messy. For instance, where stylists did styling 'as a favour' for friends or family, even receipt of pay for work-tasks may not be enough to constitute the activities as work. However a boundary that differentiates between work and non-work activities on the basis of the 'closeness' of particular social relationships will be slippery over the long run (as people move in and out of stylists' immediate social circle) and over the short run (as friends-of-friends become increasingly hard to define as part of either the work- or home-sphere). Therefore despite the symbolic potential offered by the multi-dimensionality of the work-life boundary, increased extra-work-site work in circumstances where different types of boundary cease to correspond may eventually present insurmountable obstacles to a coherently constructed work-life boundary. What the social and psychological implications of this are requires further exploration.

The man who left his suburban home and family and went to work on the production line had separate and bounded temporality, spatiality, personnel, task and rationality. But most workers are (and indeed were) not like this man. Accountants, homeopaths, academics, bicycle repair mechanics along with many others resemble hairstylists, possessing work-skills that they can and that many do employ outside of the time, space, rationality and social relations of the workplace. To the extent that workers desire a bounded work-life, and this chapter has suggested that most do, their ability to achieve this will depend on their ability to consistently employ one or more dimensions of the work-life boundary as a symbolic marker. In fulfilling this task not all boundaries are equal or equally stable. For instance, while spatiality is relatively time-invariant, social relations may be a more inconstant marker. Investigation of these differences and of the ways in which different dimensions of the boundary are breached or symbolically and practically maintained is a necessary ingredient of future conceptual and empirical analysis of the work-life boundary, as must be consideration of the consequence of variation in work relations.

Notes

1. In exploratory multinomial logistic regression with this question as dependent variable both owner and gender were significant predictors.
2. Analysis not shown. Available from author on request.
3. Given, firstly, higher rates of paid extra-salon styling among non-owner stylists and, secondly, a national hairstylist population with fewer owners than within this study survey, the actual proportion of salon-employed stylists engaged in paid extra-salon styling will be *greater* than found here.

REFERENCES

Berry-Lound, D., Cocks, N., Parsons, D.J. and Sauve, E. (2000) *An Occupational Analysis of the Hairdressing Sector*, Doncaster: HABIA (Hairdressing and Beauty Industry Authority).

Boris, E. and Daniels, C.R. (eds) (1989) *Homework,* Urbana and Chicago: University of Illinois Press.

Cohen, R.L. (2005) 'Styling Labor: Work Relations and the Labor Process in Hairstyling', unpublished doctoral thesis, UCLA, Los Angeles.

ECOTEC (2000) *New Trends and Developments in the European Hairdressing Sector*, CIC-Europe and Uni-Europa, Birmingham.

Felstead, A. and Jewson, N. (eds) (2000) *In Work, at Home*, London: Routledge.

Glucksmann, M. (2005) 'Shifting Boundaries and Interconnections: Extending the "Total Social Organisation of Labour"' in L. Pettinger, J. Parry, J. R. Taylor and M. Glucksmann (eds) *A New Sociology of Work?*, Oxford: Blackwell.

GMB (2005) *GMB Publish New National Pay League by Occupation*, available online: http://www.gmb.org.uk/Templates/Internal.asp?NodeID=91819, accessed 7th July 2005.

HABIA (2001) *Sector Workforce Development Plan*, Hairdressing and Beauty Industry Authority, Doncaster.

Hochschild, A.R. (1997) *The Time Bind*, New York: Metropolitan.

Hogarth, T., Hasluck, C. and Pierre, G. (2000) *Work-Life Balance 2000*, Institute for Employment Research, Department for Education and Employment, London.

Jacobs, J.A. and Gerson, K. (2004) *The Time Divide*, Cambridge: Harvard University Press.

Lamont, M. and Molnár, V. (2002) 'The Study of Boundaries in the Social Sciences', *Annual Review of Sociology*, 28, 167–95.

Nelson, M.K. and Smith, J. (1999) *Working Hard and Making Do*, Berkeley: University of California Press.

Nippert-Eng, C.E. (1996) *Home and Work*, Chicago: University of Chicago Press.

Office for National Statistics (ONS) (2005a) 2001 Census: Specially Commissioned Table C0229, London.

Office for National Statistics (ONS) (2005b) 2001 Census: Specially Commissioned Table C0427, London.

Pahl, R.E. (1984) *Divisions of Labour*, Oxford: Blackwell.

Phizcklea, A. and Wolkowitz, C. (1995) *Homeworking Women*, London: Sage.

Portes, A. and Castells, M. (1989) *The Informal Economy*, Baltimore: Johns Hopkins University Press.

Presser, H.B. (2003) *Working in a 24/7 Economy*, New York: Russell Sage Foundation.

Schor, J. (1991) *The Overworked American*, New York: Basic Books.

▶

▶

Snyder, K.A. (2004) 'Routes to the Informal Economy in New York's East Village: Crisis, Economics, and Identity', *Sociological Perspectives*, 47, 215–40.

Toffler, A. (1980) *The Third Wave: The Classic Study of Tomorrow*, New York: Bantam Books.

Williams, C.C. and Windebank, J. (1998) *Informal Employment in the Advanced Economies*, London: Routledge.

8 Getting the Job Done: The Impact of Employees' Conception of Work on Work-Life Balance

Anne Bøgh Fangel and Stinne Aaløkke

Introduction

In recent years flexible working has been a rising trend; particularly within the Danish context, where many organisations are now providing their employees with computers and Internet connections to support working from home (Bjerrum and Nielsen 2003). Denmark now has the largest rate in Europe of individuals working from home on a regular basis (Danmarks Statistik 2005). Thus, for many workers in Denmark, the boundary between work and home is becoming increasingly blurred.

From an employee perspective, flexible working has clear liberating potentials. For instance, flexibility in working hours as well as the possibility to work from home provides new opportunities to manage the balance between work and home (Bjerrum and Nielsen 2003; Gottlieb et al. 1998; Hildebrandt and Rishøj 2003; Hutchinson and Brewster 1994; Hyman et al. 2002). This is particularly important in Denmark because men and women participate equally in the workforce. However, the increased blurring of the boundary between home and work also carries the risk of work taking over non-work life. Temporal and spatial boundaries between work and home dissolve, so that work seems continuous (Hildebrandt and Rishøj 2003).

In the Danish debate there has been a tendency to focus on the negative effects of the loss of a clear boundary between work and private life. Maintaining a clear boundary between work and home is often considered as a mechanism against becoming over-worked (Jensen et al. 2003). Unions, authorities and private organisations in Denmark are joining up to demand initiatives that will ensure a better work-life balance for workers in the future. There are two questions that arise in this respect. Firstly, what constitutes a good work-life balance? Secondly, what influences the balance between work and private life? Answers to these questions are mostly taken for granted, but, as Guest (2002: 4) indicates, many of the discussions 'about work-life balance occur without any clear and consistent definitions of what we mean by work-life balance'. Much research and debate tries to suggest objective criteria for keeping a balance, for instance a certain maximum number of working hours and maintaining strict boundaries between home and work. However, such suggestions are often based on simplistic conceptions of the relationship between work and private life and do not consider the subjective variations in the understanding of what constitutes a good work-life balance (see for example Crosbie and Moore 2004).

As part of a broader study of flexible work, we analysed whether the way in which individuals enact the boundary between work and non-work has an influence on work-life balance. The study indicated that a 'good work-life balance' is neither achieved by creating and maintaining clear boundaries between home and work nor is it just a matter of governments and employers establishing regulations and family-friendly initiatives to secure and support employee work-life balance. It also found that the blurring of the boundary between work and home in itself is not problematic. After briefly outlining the theoretical framework and the empirical study, these findings will be discussed in more detail. The chapter then investigates another possible factors impacting on work-life balance: the individual's conception of work. Evidence from a series of Danish case studies suggests that an individual's own conception of work is more important for achieving work-life balance than the flexibility and permeability of the work-life boundary. Therefore, with flexible ways of working becoming more prominent, the work-life balance debate needs to focus more on individual perceptions of work.

Creating boundaries and balance

Early work-life studies take the dissimilarity of the two domains 'work' and 'home' as a starting point (Edwards 1979; Landes 1983; Mills 1956; Owen 1979). More recent studies have focused on the loss of boundaries between work and home (Barley and Kunda 1992; Ouchi 1980; Van Maanen and Kunda 1989; Wilkins and Ouchi 1983). In this respect, Nippert-Eng's (1996) analysis demonstrates how boundaries between work and home are continuously constructed and crossed. By deconstructing the dichotomy between the two domains, she provides an analytical tool that this chapter draws upon to examine the boundary work of employees.

According to Nippert-Eng, social scientists generally work from a set of underlying assumptions of what work is and when it takes place: '[they] have written about home and work as if we all know what these terms mean and as if the territories they encompass and the ways they are related are the same for everyone' (1996: 4). Home and work are often described as fixed categories that are both spatially and ideologically separate. Work is associated with the negative connotations of tedious activities whereas home is linked to positive images of fun and relaxation. Nippert-Eng argues that such an understanding of work and life is a highly inadequate interpretation that does not capture the 'rich variations on these themes composed by real people living real lives' (ibid.). Moreover, assumptions about the relationship between home and work do not only shape the way this relationship is understood but they also influence the interpretation of the development and dissemination of new working styles that affect and (re-)shape the boundaries between work and life.

Nippert-Eng suggests that the notions of work and home carry a wide range of different meanings depending on, for example, cultural, organisational and personal circumstances. In order to understand the full complexity of the relationship between the categories of home and work, this relationship needs to be conceptualised as a continuum ranging from full integration to complete segmentation. Integration and segmentation denote ideal-types of work-life boundary enactment that can be understood as two ends of a continuum. Integrators maintain none or highly flexible and permeable boundaries between work and private life whereas segmentors establish clearly defined, rigid and impermeable boundaries between home and work. Both ideal-types represent extreme forms of work-life boundary enactment. In reality, boundaries are constantly (re-)constructed, maintained and crossed (Nippert-Eng 1996), with some professions allowing for more or less integration between home and work than others. Therefore, experiences and behaviour of real people will fall somewhere between integration and segmentation on the continuum.

Nippert-Eng's distinction provides a fruitful starting point for analysing different forms of work-life boundary enactment. However, she is primarily concerned with how boundaries between home and work are maintained according to specific socio-cultural constraints and re-negotiated through objects, habits and social practices. The aim of this chapter is to extend the analysis by linking her distinction between integrators and segmentors to the prerequisites and solutions for obtaining good work-life balance discussed in the work-life balance literature.

Essential to the work-life balance literature is the assumption that the balance between the two domains of working life and home life can either be supported or obstructed (see also Eikhof et al. 2007). The literature is extensive and varied with many different thematic strands focusing on structural and organisational constraints as well as individual, cultural and gender barriers (Caproni 2004;

Gambles 2006 et al.; Kossek and Lambert 2006). Illustratively, Hochschild's (1997) analysis of the work-life balance includes many of these perspectives. Hochschild investigates how modern families maintain a balance between work and private life and examines a company that has set up an extensive family-friendly work initiative that nevertheless fails to create good work-life balance among its employees. From the company's perspective, all appropriate structures are in place. Hochschild analyses why the employees are still not obtaining a good balance between home and private life and finds the answer in a reversal of the categories of home and work: the workplace has become an environment for personal fulfilment with many employees experiencing work as fun and rewarding. By contrast, life at home has become a place for thankless duties and chores. As a consequence, women and two-job families still struggle to find the right balance between work and family life.

Within a Danish context, Hochschild's descriptions seem ever more relevant. Despite increased focus on family-friendly initiatives and regulations both from the government and employers, many Danish workers find it increasingly hard to obtain a good work-life balance (Lund et al. 2007). While it is debatable whether this inability is caused by socio-structural mechanisms or by the seductive nature of work, setting clear boundaries between work and private life is often proposed in Danish public debate as the best way to protect the home from becoming invaded by work. The same attitude towards the relationship between home and work is prevalent in much literature and academic debate. Kunda provides an indicative description of how organisational members perceive the relationship between work and private life:

> ... most members find that work, by its nature, is not limited to a time or place. Consequently, the construction of time boundaries for an organisational self is essential. In the recurring imagery, work is impure and crazy; nonwork is pure and sane. Work is at once seductive and repulsive; nonwork must be protected. Maintaining a time boundary between the two is considered important and difficult.
>
> (1992: 167)

The work-life balance debate suggests such clearly defined boundaries between work and non-work, in Nipper-Eng's (1996) terms a segmentation-type of work-life boundary enactment, as a prerequisite for good work-life balance. Starting from the assumption that a 'good' work-life balance is what the individual worker perceives as such, we analyse the relationship between boundary enactment and work-life balance through the study of individuals working in new, flexible working arrangements such as telework or flexiwork.

Case studies and research methods

The analysis presented in this chapter draws on a series of case studies conducted as part of a Nordic research project, DEKAR,[1] on the relationship between innovation, collaboration and workplace design. The purpose of these case studies was to examine new ways of working within Danish workplaces in order to find out how conditions for knowledge-sharing and innovation are influenced by the physical design of the workplace. However, since an explorative approach with a broad set of issues concerning work and collaboration within organisations was chosen, data from these studies also offered insight into the work-life balance experienced and conceptions of work of the organisations' employees. The case studies were carried out over a period of three years and encompassed a major law firm, a large IT company and a media company. The three companies were selected because they had all implemented strategies for the development of flexible forms of work.

The law firm is one of the largest law firms in Scandinavia with more than 200 employees. It had recently introduced team working in order to increase collaboration and knowledge-sharing between employees. As part of this new way of working the company had also introduced family-friendly initiatives, such as alternative career paths, options for part-time working and increased opportunities for telework. The IT company is a major Danish IT company with more than 500 employees. It had recently created a new office environment for its development teams, mixing development, sales and support in order to encourage knowledge-sharing between different parts of the organisation. The company is generally known for its family-friendly culture. The research centred on the company's development teams, studying collaboration and new working styles in all parts of the new office environment. The media company is a Danish regional news provider with 200 employees, producing content for newspapers, radio, TV and the Internet. To support this cross-media production the company had recently introduced a new organisational structure and office layout, resulting in entirely new ways of working for journalists and production staff.

In all three case studies different research methods, such as interviews, observation and work logs, were combined, each of which studied the research issue from a different angle. This triangulation of methods enabled in-depth analysis and understanding of the research themes (Denzin and Lincoln 1994; Tashakkori and Teddlie 2000). Furthermore, the variety of different methods can uncover differences between what respondents say they do and what they actually do (Holy and Stuchlik 1983; Schensul and Lecompte 1999).

The research team observed and logged specific features of working patterns to see what working activities were carried out when the individuals were working in the office and when they worked from home or undertook mobile work.[2] In total, around 400 hours of observation was carried out at the companies. Based on the observations in each company, interviews with both managers and employees in the organisations were conducted. Across the three case studies a total of 150 respondents were interviewed. In the law firm these interviews comprised 40 partners, lawyers, trainees and personal assistants as well as the managing director, HR director and knowledge manager. In the IT company 60 programmers, sales and support staff, team leaders, managers and secretaries were interviewed and from the media company 50 media editors, group leaders, journalists and senior managers. The interview questions were semi-structured and open ended, and each interview lasted for approximately one and a half hours. They focused on the individuals' work processes and working patterns, the flexibility and mobility in their work and how they experience the balance between work and private life.

Work-life boundaries and keeping balance

Investigating the work-life boundary enactments and work-life balance perceptions of employees, the three case studies revealed a range of variations in how workers dealt with the relationship between home and work. Applying Nippert-Eng's (1996) distinction between segmentation and integration to this data uncovered that both integrators and segmentors were existed in all three companies. Some workers would maintain a very clear boundary between home and work whereas others would have a much more integrated understanding of the relationship between work and private life. At the same time, some employees felt they had found a good balance between home and work, while others were frustrated and experienced a conflict in their work-life balance. These variations of both work-life boundary enactment and work-life balance experience occurred not only between the three companies, but notably also within a single company and within the same profession. Consequently, neither work-life boundary enactment nor work-life balance experience could be solely determined by organisational structures, specifically by the flexible working arrangements put in place. The following section uses Nippert-Eng's concepts of segmentation and integration to explore whether, as suggested by the literature, rigid work-life boundaries promote work-life balance.

Segmentation and the work-life balance

In all three companies many workers enacted the work-life boundary in the way that Nippert-Eng describes as segmentation; they tried to keep work and private life strictly separate and saw such segmentation as ideal. These workers typically described the relationship between life or home on the one hand and work on the other in the following way: 'When I go home, I am off' (male technical trainer, IT company) or 'I try not to work from home. It is my ambition not to do it' (male lawyer, law firm) or 'I have become better at separating my two lives' (male manager, IT company). In some cases the workers were extremely aware of keeping a sharp distinction between work and private life:

> I don't have a work station at home because I'm afraid that my work would spread. It's ok to do little things at home. I have a computer at home, but it is slow and runs on a modem. Previously I checked e-mail from my house, but it took up much time. I prefer to be off duty when I'm home. I'd rather stay a bit longer at work to finish up [than to take work home with me].
>
> (female secretary, media company)

Workers who chose to maintain a rigid boundary between life and work often used this boundary as a shield against work taking over. According to Ashforth et al. (2000) employees who keep work confined in time and space have often suffered from asymmetrical work-life balance experiences. They deliberately disconnect work and home by creating and maintaining both temporal and spatial boundaries. Ashforth et al.'s findings were mirrored in our research, for instance in the account from the previously quoted secretary. One of her colleagues reported similar experiences: 'I have a good balance now. I don't work from home because I am afraid it will take over' (male journalist, media company).

However, keeping home and work strictly separate did not necessarily lead to an improved work-life balance. A substantial share of respondents recounted how segmentation can lead to the worker being at work all the time, rendering little time for private life and thus distorting the work-life balance. A partner in the law firm who was married with three children described his work-life relationship as follows:

> I try not to work at home. My ambition is not to work at home. But it's nice to have the opportunity to communicate if you're home sick or have a sick child. It is probably one of the three most difficult challenges as a lawyer: That you have to let your private life give way to our work. My private life is very flexible in relation to my work. You have to marry well – it takes enormous family support … Last November I was gone for three months without coming home.
>
> (male partner, law firm)

What makes this account indicative of many is the combination of regret that work had a tendency of taking over life, thus distorting work-life balance, and conscious efforts to reach a better work-life balance by separating work and private life. Overall, the case studies showed no evidence that workers who maintain a strict segmentation of work and private life experience a better work-life balance than workers with an integrated approach to work and life.

Integration and the work-life balance

Between the three case studies, a considerable number of respondents integrated or mixed work and private activities, living a life as integrators in Nippert-Eng's sense. These workers maintained virtually no boundary between work and private life. A project manager from the IT company provided an indicative example of these employees:

> Everything blurs together. I work all the time – I'm connected and answer e-mails in the evening, but on the other hand I can leave early. I love it. I leave whenever it suits me. It's completely up to me. And I have no problem shutting off/disconnecting. It's a great liberty and my family doesn't suffer. Some people might experience it as a pressure. But as long as I enjoy the work ...
>
> (female project manager, IT company)

In many cases this integration of work and life was experienced as liberating, providing individuals with the opportunity to maintain a good balance between work and family life. Young parents would leave work early to pick up children from kindergarten, spend time with their family and resume work after having put the children to bed. Other young parents would choose to work from home occasionally, turning commuting time into quality time spent with the family.

Moreover, resembling the workers in Hochschild's (1997) case study, many lawyers in the law firm found their work so exciting and stimulating that they continued to work all the time. Their attraction to work resulted in lawyers frequently taking work home: 'Generally, we use our home offices to work more. We work from home when we need to do overtime' (male trainee, law firm). However, as several respondents also recounted, working from home generally meant they would work even more.

However, for a considerable number of workers the integration of home and work did not work to their advantage. In these cases it seems more applicable to talk of an invasion of work on private life rather than a mutual integration:

> There's way too little family life. We have dinner at 7 p.m. My daughter says to me on Sundays – Dad, I'll see you on Friday! It's nice with a summer cabin

without cellular coverage, network – I'm pretty good at taking my vacation. But when I'm at home I have a work-rhythm on the weekends. There're performance demands that make you work too much. If you're a partner then you have to give, work a lot – it's not a lifetime position, job … It's difficult to disconnect, go home and actually be off duty. It's that habit of slipping in and working at the computer.

(male partner, law firm)

Taking advantage of the technological possibilities for working at home, this employee allowed boundaries between work and life to blur with respect to space and time at weekends, but kept work and family life separated during vacations. But as this quote illustrates, integrating work and life does not necessarily ensure good work-life balance. In this case, the hours put into work, regardless of where and when, leave little time for family life.

While an integrated work style was liberating for some workers, for others it was quite the contrary. As with the segmentation approach, the integration of work and life, too, allowed for different experiences of work-life balance rather than leading to a single work-life balance quality.

Conception of work and the impact on the work-life balance

Overall, all workers studied had a very clear attitude towards the relationship between work and home. Some explicitly preferred to keep them completely separate; others would have a more integrated approach. But as demonstrated in the previous section, neither way of managing the relationship between work and life turned out to be a recipe for good work-life balance. The position on Nippert-Eng's (1996) continuum did not determine the work-life balance; employees at either end of the continuum had both balanced and unbalanced work-life experiences. To understand why some workers managed to make flexible ways of working work to their advantage while for others work took over their private life, the data were analysed for other potential influence factors. Possible and plausible causes for these differences comprised gender, occupations, corporate culture or the different socio-structural expectations within the companies. However, even within one organisation, there are examples of integrators as well as segmentors, with some employees struggling to maintain a good balance between home and work while others experienced no problems in maintaining a balance. Likewise, gender or occupation did not seem to have an impact either.

One influential factor that emerged from the data was the worker's partner. In particular for male workers, the experience of balance was not so much determined by the hours of work or by the work-life boundary enactment as by their partner's willingness to accept their working style. As one employee recounts: 'It is difficult to keep a balance. To keep a good balance you have to be married with someone who thinks it is okay that you come home late or bring work home with you' (male group leader, media company). While accounts of how the partner's ability and willingness to cope with one's work-life boundaries enactment influences work-life balance were mostly given by male employees, this perception was not restricted to men. A female journalist describes how she depends on her husband:

> I don't work much from home. I might write a bit from home or check my e-mail ... I have a good balance because my husband works steady hours. Otherwise it probably wouldn't work. It's not so much the long shifts but more that I don't leave once they end ... I think it's fun and I want to finish things myself.
>
> (female journalist, media company)

But while the support workers receive from their spouses certainly contributes to positive work-life balance experience, it did not feature prominently enough in the data to be the sole influencing factor. Further analysis of the case study data uncovered another, seemingly more influential factor; individuals' understanding or concept of work. This aspect emerged as a key new finding from the research. The comparison of observation data with data from interviews and work logs revealed a systematic gap between how the workers said they were working and actual working patterns. Throughout all three case studies, workers would record fewer work practices than were logged by the observers. A more detailed analysis of this gap uncovered that workers and observers differed in their understanding of work and consequently would record different activities. The remainder of this chapter focuses primarily on the IT company and the law firm as these two case studies most clearly illustrate the influence of conceptions of work on the work-life balance.

Throughout the day employees are involved in a range of different activities, such as reading email, informal and formal meetings, making telephone calls, and reading reports, newspapers and mail. However, at the IT company and the law firm, employees acknowledged only few of these activities as work. They employed a specific conception of work; understanding it as an individually undertaken and attributed activity. When asked to describe their work, they focused almost exclusively on personal work tasks and underlined the individual nature of activities, such as casework, programming or administration, discarding, for instance, discussions with colleagues regarding cases or programmes. A typical description of work at the IT company was given by a system developer: 'I'm the kind of person who spends all my time at my desk doing concentrated work' (male system developer, IT company). Likewise, law firm respondents placed great emphasis on individual casework with many of them subscribing to the idea that legal work was primarily individual work, as this quote from a female lawyer illustrates: 'I work on very big cases. It is a very long process where I alternately do research on the case, write indictments and make pleas' (female lawyer, law firm).

As part of the case studies, the workers were asked to record their working pattern over a period of five weeks. Comparison of these records with the observation logs showed that many workers had not recorded what observers considered to be the full working pattern. They often omitted hours spent on certain activities in the workplace; most notably informal meetings, or failed to include hours worked at home. Observation data showed that lawyers spent a considerable amount of time in small, ad hoc meetings and that there was a constant traffic in and out of each other's offices. Such activities, however, were not recorded in the work logs as the respondents did not consider them to be part of the 'real' casework. Rather, these activities were regarded as a luxury and several respondents reported compensating for the time they spent on informal discussions by doing extra work in the evening, either in the office or at home: 'I spoke to several people – almost an hour with my boss. Then I had to work until late' (male trainee, law firm). In short, the lawyers only included what they considered 'real' work in their work logs, the work for which they could debit clients, and this was generally individual casework:

> I was at the office all day from half past eight. I worked on two major cases – I stayed until eight o'clock. We share an office so sometimes I stay a bit longer. I only write down the hours I can debit. I talked a bit with different people – 15 minutes with my boss. I often finish a bit late because I appreciate the social aspects and then you have to stay a bit longer.
>
> (male trainee, law firm)

Likewise, at the IT company, observations showed that IT workers spent a lot of time away from their desks although they described their work as primarily individual and desk-bound. Mostly, the work space would be half empty. It was only when asked to describe their previous workday in detail that respondents from the IT company actually described a variety of working activities carried out during that day, including work activities away from the desk and in collaboration with colleagues. Generally, IT workers understood 'real' work as that which is individual and focused on production.

Contrary to the accounts from workers at both the IT company and the law firm claiming their work to be individual, observation logs showed that individual, autonomous work was anything but dominant. Supplemented by a more holistic analysis of the interviews, the observation logs provided a rather different picture. Most workers would have a great variety of working tasks every day, including phone calls and meetings with customers. Colleagues would stop by to ask questions and workers would have numerous small ad hoc meetings and discussions throughout the day. However, such collective activities were not considered as 'real' work by the respondents themselves. As a result of these observations, the research developed the framework of the 'conception of work':

> The conception of work is what you consider 'real' work. At each workplace employees carry out a lot of different tasks everyday, but they only consider some of them as being work activities, others are disturbances or even directly obstructing the 'real' work. So it is the 'work mindset' of the employees we are exploring when talking about conception of work.
>
> (Bjerrum and Aaløkke 2005a: 1)

Many factors play a role in the construction of specific conceptions of work, ranging from structures in society and traditions within different professions to incentive structures at the workplace, such as reward systems, management behaviour and constructions of corporate culture. However, such structures are not deterministic but intertwine with the agency of the individual and the individual's preferences and choices. This allows for variation in conceptions of work, even within a given profession or a specific workplace. However, this chapter focuses on the consequences of conceptions of work rather than on processes of social construction.

Firstly, the understanding of work as individual had obvious effects on work in the office. Workers focusing on individual work as 'real' work felt disturbed when colleagues walked by, talked on the phone nearby or had informal meetings: 'People show too little consideration for the ones who are trying to work' (male system developer, IT company).

Secondly, the conception of work as individualised practices greatly affected how workers perceived working from home (Bjerrum and Aaløkke 2005b). Several respondents described how home had become a sanctuary for work where it is possible to concentrate on one's own, individual work. Working from home was considered an escape from the noisy workplace and its manifold interruptions: 'You are not disturbed when you work from home. It is more efficient' (male system developer, IT company). In this sense, working from home provided an opportunity to focus on the 'real' work, to be efficient and productive: 'I work from home on Fridays – that's when I do on-duty schedules and budgets. It's faster to do planning tasks from home' (male group leader, media company). However, while working alone, focused and undisturbed is of course crucial at times, interruptions, questions and quick ad hoc meetings are becoming increasingly important and functional for the successful fulfilment of one's job – and to help others fulfil theirs. The conflict between these two modes of working was noticeably pronounced in the IT company. During the time of this research, office escapism had reached a stage whereby managers considered limiting the possibilities of working from home in order to support the development of a more interactive and collaborative working style.

Thirdly and most interestingly, the conception of work seems to be connected to the work-life balance experience. Workers who saw their work as individual were often dissatisfied and frustrated with their work-life balance. They were ambitious and commonly overworked. However, the prevailing conception of 'real' work as individual was adding increased pressure on their work-life balance. Workers actually tried to balance three different activities: 'real', that is individual work on which they based their career progress; work that they did not consider 'real' work, that is collaboration with colleagues and interactions with other work-related persons; and non-work or life activities. This triple-bind was particularly noticeable in the law firm that tried to promote team organisation and collaboration in the company. As one of the female lawyers expressed: 'it is difficult to find time to collaborate'. At the end of the day, workers in the law firm often felt they were yet to get the 'real' job done, either by staying late or doing extra work at home in the evenings. Either of the latter solutions for balancing 'real' work and 'non-real' work would inevitably disturb their work-life balance. The following account of a female lawyer provides a typical example for such a situation:

> I can leave early – there's an incredible flexibility and I like that freedom. It's up to you to keep the balance. I think it's great to get in at 8.30 a.m. and leave at 15.30 p.m. That means that I can be flexible. It's important to be there for your kids. But it can also be like burning your candle at both ends. It's tough to debit 7 hours a day. That means that you have to work more or be under pressure the whole time. It would be nice to feel that you were on top of it. It kills collaboration because that isn't something you debit. I don't want to live that way. It can be a large pressure to work under. Some evenings I just don't want to work.
>
> (female lawyer, law firm)

This lawyer had an integrated approach towards the boundary between work and home and still felt that she was under pressure to keep the balance because she only considered some of her work activities 'real' work. Other necessary tasks, such as discussions and collaboration with colleagues, only added to the workload and had a negative influence on the work-life balance since she had to put in extra hours in the evening to make up for time lost in non-individual work.

Findings from the IT company further highlighted how the conception of work as individual affected work-life balance for workers with an integrated work-life approach. Interview data from the IT company suggest that office escapists risk frustration about achieving the triple balance. They retreat to home as a sanctuary for real work, but still experience disturbances, both by telephone calls from colleagues or by calls or visits from family and friends. Working from home could have been experienced as liberating and even contributing to work-life balance, enabling workers to adjust their work to the general rhythms of their lives. Yet workers would end up frustrated because they would still be disturbed and prevented from getting the 'real' job done.

The above findings indicate that the individualistic conception of work may have a powerful and problematic influence on work-life balance: if, firstly, only work that is undertaken by oneself, at the desk, in concentration and solitude is perceived as real work, and, secondly, (IT-mediated) collaboration and communication with colleagues, customers and others takes up an increasing amount of time, the only way to 'get the job done' is to work during times and in spaces previously reserved for private life. A more holistic perception of work that encompasses not only individual work but also meetings, communication or networking tasks allows for a different perception: 'getting the job done' by engaging in these tasks for a full working day. Particularly at the media company, where such a holistic concept of work was more widespread, respondents were more likely to feel satisfied about the work that they had accomplished in a day.

Concluding discussion

In recent years there has been increasing debate among academics and in the wider public sphere about the challenges of obtaining a satisfactory balance between work and private life. Indeed, quite a number of the workers interviewed as part of the case studies experienced difficulty in maintaining a good work-life balance. Some workers spent a considerable amount of time at work as well as working from home because they enjoyed work, which is in line with Hochschild's (1997) findings. However, the research also found examples of how this dedication to work is experienced as an unstable work-life balance. Equally, the issue of maintaining boundaries between the two spheres, as described by Kunda (1992), emerged as a central theme. Indeed, one line of argument in the work-life balance debate has been that family life must be shielded and protected from work by keeping a firm boundary between work and private life. However, this chapter has demonstrated that the blurring of boundaries is not per se problematic. Drawing on Nippert-Eng's (1996) notion of work-life boundaries and her deconstruction of the dichotomy between home and work, this study has shown that maintaining rigid boundaries between work and private life does not in itself provide workers with the experience of a good work-life balance.

Rather, this research proposes that the experience of a good work-life balance is influenced by the individual's conception of work. The case studies suggest that new, flexible forms of work may be problematic when they are coupled with certain conceptions of work. Many of the workers studied considered only individual work as 'real' work; the remaining activities were regarded as interfering and as obstacles for carrying out 'real' work. Not only did this have implications for how workers took on new forms of working, it also influenced how workers experienced their work-life balance. Where flexible forms of working could have been experienced as liberating, providing them with the opportunity to adjust their work to the general rhythm of their lives, for some workers the opposite was true. Working from home became an escape from disturbances or a place to catch up on unfinished work. Either way, the choice of working from home was not taken so much out of preference as it was taken out of necessity: with 'non-real' work taking over time needed for 'real' work, 'real' work took over time and space reserved for private life. The feeling of having to surrender home/private life to 'real' work in order to 'get the job done' influenced the general experience of work-life balance.

These findings suggest that the perception of an appropriate work-life balance is strongly influenced by employees' conceptualisation of work. In contrast to what was suggested by the literature, the permeability of the boundary between work and life as such appeared to have no causal relationship to the quality of work-life balance. The workers studied at the IT company, the law firm and the media company can be seen as indicative for a larger number of professional workers who are struggling to come to terms with the growing importance of collaboration and communication within occupations that have traditionally depended on individualised work practices. This study suggests that as collaboration and communication increases, the pressure of 'real' work on private life is likely to become more widespread. As work-life balance has become a central issue for these professionals (see also Warhurst et al.'s contribution to this volume), further research is needed to fully explore the notion of conceptions of work and its influence on workers' experience of their work-life balance. This study suggests that it may be the individual conception of work that more than anything constitutes a major (mental) boundary for striking a balance between work and a private life.

Acknowledgements

We want to thank Susanne Bødker and Eva Bjerrum at the Centre for New Ways of Working and Leysia Palen of the University of Colorado for discussions as well as comments on our research. We are also grateful to Nordic Innovation for funding the DEKAR project.

Notes

1. The DEKAR project was partly funded by the Nordic Industrial Fund. Partners in the DEKAR project were Telenor Research and Development (Norway), Alexandra Institute (Denmark), Helsinki University of Technology (Finland), School of Architecture at Royal Institute of Technology in Stockholm (Sweden) and Iceland Telecom/Siminn (Iceland).
2. One method that was used to log workplace activities consisted of taking snapshots. We used two variations: the first way to do this was to walk through the building recording on paper what people were doing at the specific time that we passed them. The second way of taking 'snapshots' spanned over longer periods of time as we sat in a given area of the building logging peoples' activities throughout the day.

REFERENCES

Ashforth, B.E., Kreiner, G.E. and Fugate, M. (2000) 'All in a Day's Work: Boundaries and Micro Role Transitions', *Academy of Management Review*, 25:3, 472–92.

Barley, S.R. and Kunda, G. (1992) 'Design and Devotion: Surges of Rational and Normative Ideologies of Control in Managerial Discourse', *Administrative Science Quarterly*, 37, 363–99.

Bjerrum, E. and Aaløkke, S. (2005a) 'The Office as a Strategic Artefact for Knowledge Sharing?', Proceedings from the 6th *International Learning and Knowledge Conference*, Trento, 446–71.

Bjerrum, E. and Aaløkke, S. (2005b) 'Working Together: Work Space, Organization and Conception of Work', *International Telework Conference & Workshop*, Preston.

Bjerrum, E. and Nielsen, O. (2003) *Bliver man småsær af at have sit eget kontor*, Århus: JP Bøger.

Caproni, P.J. (2004) 'Work/Life Balance: You Can't There from Here', *Journal of Applied Behavioural Science*, 40:2, 208–28.

Crosbie, T. and Moore, J. (2004) 'Work-life Balance and Working from Home', *Social Policy and Society*, 3:3, 223–33.

Danmarks Statistik (2005) *Nyt fra Danmarks Statistik*, 359:19, København: Danmarks Statistik.

Denzin, N.K. and Lincoln, Y.S. (eds) (1994) *Handbook of Qualitative Research*, Thousand Oaks: Sage.

Edwards, R.C. (1979) *Contested Terrain*, New York: Basic Books.

Eikhof, D.R., Warhurst, C. and Haunschild, A. (2007) 'What Work? What Life? What Balance? Critical Reflections on the Work-Life Balance Debate', *Employee Relations*, 29:4, 325–33.

▶

▶

Gambles, R., Lewis, S. and Rapoport, R. (2006) *The Myth of WLB: The Challenge of Our Time for Men, Women and Societies*, Chichester: Wiley.

Gottlieb, B.H., Kelloway, E.K. and Barham, E. (1998) *Flexible Work Arrangements: Managing the Work-Life Boundary*, Chichester: Wiley.

Guest, D. (2002) 'Perspectives on the Study of Work-Life Balance', *Social Science Information*, 41:2, 255–79.

Hildebrandt, S. and Rishøj, S. (2003) *Familien på arbejde*, Copenhagen: Gyldendal.

Hochschild, A.R. (1997) *The Time Bind*, New York: Metropolitan Books.

Holy, L. and Stuchlik, M. (1983) *Actions, Norms and Representations: Foundations of Anthropological Inquiry*, Cambridge: Cambridge University Press.

Hutchinson, S. and Brewster, C. (1994) *Flexibility at Work in Europe*, London: Institute of Personnel and Development.

Hyman, J., Baldry, C., Scholarios, D. and Bunzel, D. (2002) 'Balancing Work and Life: Not Just a Matter of Time Flexibility', *British Journal of Industrial Relations*, 41:2, 215–39.

Jensen, B.C., Netterstrøm, B. and Borg, V. (2003) *Arbejdsmiljøet indenfor IT branchen*, Copenhagen: Arbejdsmiljøinstituttet.

Kossek, E. and Lambert, S. (eds) (2006) *Work and Life Integration: Organisational, Cultural and Individual Perspectives*, Mahwah: Lawrence Erlbaum Associates.

Kunda, G. (1992) *Engineering Culture: Control and Commitment in a High-Tech Corporation*, Philadelphia: Temple University Press.

Landes, D.S. (1983) *Revolution in Time*, Cambridge: Harvard University Press.

Lund, H., Tanggaard Andersen, P., Lond Grosen, S. and Kold, V. (2007) 'Arbejdsliv – Familieliv', *Tidsskrift for Arbejdsliv*, 1, 5–10.

Mills, C.W. (1956) *White Collar*, New York: Oxford University Press.

Nippert-Eng, C.E. (1996) *Home and Work: Negotiating Boundaries through Everyday Life*, Chicago: The University of Chicago Press.

Ouchi, W.G. (1980) 'Markets, Bureaucracies, and Clans', *Administrative Science Quarterly*, 25, 129–41.

Owen, J.D. (1979) *Working Hours*, Lexington: Lexington Books.

Schensul, J. and LeCompte, M. (1999) *Designing and Conducting Ethnographic Research*, Walnut Creek: AltaMira Press.

Tashakkori, A. and Teddlie, C. (2000) *Mixed Methodology: Combining Qualitative and Quantitative Approaches*, Thousand Oaks: Sage.

Van Maanen, J. and Kunda, G. (1989) 'Real Feelings: Emotional Expression and Organizational Culture' in L.L. Cummings and B.M. Staw (eds), *Research in Organizational Behavior*, 11, Greenwich: JAI Press.

Wilkins, A.L. and Ouchi, W. (1983) 'Efficient Cultures: Exploring the Relationship between Culture and Organizational Performance', *Administrative Science Quarterly*, 28, 468–81.

Occupation Matters – Blurring Work-Life Boundaries in Mobile Care and the Media Industry

9

Annette Henninger and Ulrike Papouschek

Introduction

There is no doubt that increasingly flexible working practices have affected the relationship between paid work and other spheres of life in most industrialised countries. However, similar social and economic changes are framed differently in academic discourse. While there is a discourse on work-life balance in the UK and the US, debates in Germany and Austria focus on the 'dis-enclosure' of work that leads to a blurring of boundaries of work and life.

As Fleetwood (2007a, 2007b) states, discourses on flexible working practices and work-life balance emanated from the neo-liberal economies, such as the UK and the US. It is argued that this boom has its origins in long-term social and economic transformations: changes such as the erosion of standard employment contracts and organisational efforts to increase flexibility and to lower labour costs coincide with changes of individual values and aspirations, changes in families and households, a decline of the male breadwinner model and an erosion of support structures for care work that were formerly provided by extended families or communities. These changes lead to increasing tensions for individuals when they try to integrate different activities, such as paid employment, unpaid care and domestic work, social interactions and leisure. While solutions for the resulting problems are mainly sought at the individual or household level, a range of new policies at company and state levels also address issues of work-life balance (see for example Blyton et al. 2006; Fleetwood 2007a; Houston 2005).

By contrast, against the backdrop of a strong regulation of work in Germany and Austria, growing de-standardisation and flexibilisation are interpreted

as a deep transformation in the configuration of wage labour that has consequences for work-life boundaries. It is assumed that recent social and economic
changes may result in a blurring or even a dissolution of established boundaries
between paid work and other spheres of life that is labelled 'dis-enclosure' or
'de-limitation' of work. It is assumed that the phenomenon of dis-enclosure
affects working times and places, the organisation of work at company level,
employment contracts and the relationship between individuals and their
labour power and puts new demands on workers that contain opportunities as
well as risks (see for example Eichmann et al. 2004; Gottschall and Wolf 2007;
Pongratz and Voß 2003). Empirical studies investigating the dis-enclosure
thesis primarily focus on white-collar workers in the putative knowledge
economy, such as workers in the IT and media industries (Gottschall and Wolf
2007), as well as on tele-homeworking and freelance work in various sectors
(Gottschall and Voß 2003a). Comparative studies are still rare and there is a
tendency to generalise the impact of flexible working conditions.

This chapter tests the assumptions of the dis-enclosure debate using empirical
data drawn from two case studies in contrasting occupational fields: mobile care
workers in Austria and freelance journalists, designers and software developers
in Germany. It will examine whether, and how, the boundaries between paid
work and other spheres of life shift in these two fields as a result of flexible working, as well as how workers deal with these changes. The first part of the chapter
refers to the dis-enclosure debate in more detail, highlighting its differences and
commonalities with the work-life balance discourse. Following this debate, the
comparative dimensions that serve as a framework for the analysis of the two
occupational fields are addressed. Following the presentation of the case studies, the influence of occupational fields on work-life balance is discussed and it is
argued that dis-enclosure phenomena, as well as workers' strategies to cope with
blurring boundaries between work and private life, differ considerably due to
particular (labour) market conditions, work assignments and levels of qualification. The final part of the chapter discusses the lessons learnt from the findings
for the theoretical debate on work-life balance and 'dis-enclosure'.

The dis-enclosure debate

In the German-speaking media, as well as in public and company policies, the
Anglicism 'work-life balance' has become a fashionable new term. However,
the academic discourse has remained critical about the analytical potential of
the term as well as the possibilities of putting work-life balance policies into
practice (Hildebrandt and Littig 2006; Metz-Göckel 2004).

Instead, in the sociology of work in Germany as well as in Austria, there is an
ongoing discussion on the 'dis-enclosure' of work. In this debate it is assumed

that dis-enclosure is a general trend in the course of which there is a deep-going transformation in the configuration of wage labour (Gottschall and Wolf 2007; Kratzer and Sauer 2003). The starting point of this diagnosis is the weakening of established norms and standards of the utilisation of labour. In international comparison, Germany as well as Austria still show a high degree of labour market regulation and were therefore classified as coordinated market economies (Hall and Soskice 2001). At the same time, due to the relatively high welfare-state support of waged labour, the two countries can be regarded as conservative welfare states (Esping-Andersen 1998) and their gender regime is oriented on a modernised model of a strong male breadwinner and a female part-time earner/caregiver (Crompton 2001). The growing de-standardisation and flexibilisation of work lead social scientists to the interpretation that the utilisation of labour has reached a new, post-Fordist stage. Whereas a separation of paid work and private life was characteristic of an ideal-type standard working contract during the Fordist period, it is assumed that the dis-enclosure of work may result in a dissolution of the boundaries between both spheres.

'Dis-enclosure' is not a precise term or a fully developed analytical concept (Kratzer and Sauer 2003). Rather, it is used as an umbrella term to analyse various developments in the organisation of work in several dimensions. These dimensions include organisational forms, the division of labour, work spaces, working time, employment contracts and the relationship between individuals and their labour power (Eichmann et al. 2004; Pongratz and Voß 2003). Gottschall and Voß (2003b: 18) understand dis-enclosure as the 'guiding tendency in the current changes in employer-employee relationships as a whole ... which potentially affects all social levels of the make-up of work and earning'. This suggests that growing flexibility and the subsequent erosion of traditional standards of work and employment result in a blurring of the boundaries between work and private life, which, at least for the male dominated industrial workforce of the Fordist period, had seemed clear-cut.

The dis-enclosure process is closely connected to the overall aim of improving organisational and individual flexibility. As such it is expected to place new demands on workers that contain opportunities as well as risks. In particular, the changing nature of the relationship between individuals and their labour power, which in the Taylorist version of work organisation resulted in a strict separation between intellectual and manual work and a suppression of the subjectivity of non-managerial labour, can imply not only meaningful improvements but also real dangers. While improvements are also discussed under the broader notion of 'subjectivisation of work' (Baethge 1991), dangers are seen in the commercial utilisation of the 'whole person' including workers' physical, cognitive, psychic and emotional potentials, which for those affected make it difficult to draw a line between work and personal life. Critics have emphasised the risks of this development that can be summarised in the slogan 'more pressure through more freedom' (Kratzer and Sauer 2003).

The dis-enclosure debate has a strong analytical focus on changes in the social organisation of work that are traced in different dimensions. Changes in the relationship of work and non-work activities are analysed as historical trends due to the development of new forms of production, for example the transition from the Fordist to a post-Fordist type of capitalism. The constraints and options this transition implies for individual subjectivity and agency are analysed with a critical impetus. However, the dis-enclosure debate tends to underrate individual choice and to confound organisational demands and individual dispositions.

On the contrary, with a low degree of work regulation in liberal economies, the work-life balance debate tends to focus on individual choice and therefore has been criticised for obscuring structural and relational constraints (Lewis et al. 2007). Moreover, the debate has a strong normative strand – it is often assumed that there can be an ideal 'balance' between 'work' and 'life', while neglecting historical shifts as well as questions of gender and culture (Lewis et al. 2007). 'Work-life balance' has also been criticised for being a more descriptive rather than an analytical term (Hildebrandt and Littig 2006), respectively for being a 'slippery concept' (Fleetwood 2007a: 354).

Whereas both discourses share a certain fuzziness, the analytical potential of the dis-enclosure debate seems to be developed somewhat further. While the work-life balance discourse focuses mainly on time allocation and individual preference, the debate on 'dis-enclosure' aims at the development of analytical tools to investigate a broader range of work-related changes. While avoiding some of the problems of the work-life balance discourse, such as the focus on individual choice and its normative impetus, the dis-enclosure debate also shares some of its flaws. It tends to neglect questions of context, such as national regimes and policies as well as differences between sectors of the economy and occupations. Also, as it is the case for work-life balance, comparative studies are still rare[1] and there is a tendency to generalise the impact of flexible working conditions.

The research in this chapter attempts to overcome some of these shortcomings. Using empirical data drawn from two case studies in contrasting occupational fields – mobile care workers and freelance journalists, designers and software developers – the assumptions of the dis-enclosure debate are tested by asking whether and how the boundaries between paid work and other spheres of life shift in these two fields, as well as how workers deal with these changes. For the comparative framework, the research draws on the analytical dimensions that are discussed in the dis-enclosure debate, focusing on work-related changes in the dimensions of time, space, the organisation of work and workers' personal and professional aspirations. However, while changes in a temporal as well as in a spatial dimension can also be identified within the fields of investigation, the last two dimensions have to be adapted for purpose of this research.

There is widespread agreement that in a *temporal* dimension dis-enclosure can be understood as a flexibilisation of the positioning and duration of working hours. The *spatial* dimension of dis-enclosure refers to increasing demands for mobility and changing places of work (Eichmann et al. 2004; Pongratz and Voss 2003). However, whether workers can benefit from the options linked with this flexibilisation or whether they are instead driven by market forces or by the demands of 'greedy organisations' presumably depends on their ability to plan their work.

In the dis-enclosure debate, special emphasis is placed on changes in the *organisation of work* at company level. Some authors understand dis-enclosure as the result of new rationalisation strategies with the aim of extended access to the subjectivity, personal resources and temporal availability of employees. In addition, the blurring of the boundaries of companies and markets and the emergence of new organisational forms has been identified as a dimension for analysis (Kratzer and Sauer 2003; Manning and Sydow 2007). However, while these might be relevant changes in other industries, for mobile care as well as for freelancers in the media industry a company-type organisation of work has never been a central feature. To investigate dis-enclosure as well as countervailing tendencies, it was therefore decided to incorporate the dimension of *cooperative relationships*. This analytical category allows the analysis of various forms of work, the specific competencies or areas of responsibility that the workers have and the social context in which work is carried out.

Dis-enclosure of work is also regarded as a new trend towards a commercial utilisation of the workers' 'whole person', with their physical, cognitive, psychological and emotional potentials (Kratzer and Sauer 2003; Pongratz and Voß 2003). Here, the category *worker/subject* is applied as an analytical dimension to analyse possible tensions between the aspects of subjectivity that are required in the labour process respectively desired by workers (Baethge 1991), their subjective understanding of their work and their chances of demarcating their role as workers and their private lives.

In summary, these comparative dimensions are well-known analytical tools to sociologists of work. However, what is innovative in this work is their application to fields of activity and forms of work that have not been previously investigated in depth, as well as their extension beyond the immediate company context, taking into account the (labour) market conditions, work assignments and qualification structures in contrasting occupational fields.

Methodology

This chapter presents a secondary analysis of two empirical studies exploring the impact of flexible working conditions on work-life arrangements: an Austrian study on mobile care work with a high degree of part-time and atypical employment (Krenn and Papouschek 2006) and a study on freelance journalists, designers and software developers in Germany (Henninger and Gottschall 2007).[2] The comparison of data from different national contexts is justified since Germany and Austria have similar gender regimes and regulatory conditions regarding the labour market and social security. In both countries, employment contracts that do not correspond to the standard working contract, such as self-employment, part-time work and atypical employment, permit the acquisition of only a marginal claim to benefits and show a comparatively weak regulation of work by employer and employee associations or professional organisations. Thus, the fields of activity investigated are on the margins of the regulatory regime.

At the same time, mobile care and knowledge-based services in the media industry represent contrasting extremes of the service economy. Both fields differ in terms of (labour) market conditions, employment structure and some details on the regulation of labour. Mobile care workers are mostly dependent workers with a low or medium level of qualification but hold a strong market position due to labour shortages, while the self-employed media and IT workers are predominantly academically qualified and many of them choose self-employment due to a difficult labour market situation. Moreover, in contrast to the media industry, activities in mobile care are heavily regulated by government institutions. Thus, a comparision of both fields may help to answer the question of whether the dis-enclosure of work is a general trend, as it is presumed in theoretical debates. It also allows for a closer investigation of the opportunities and risks that flexible working conditions entail as well as the strategies that workers develop to cope with the postulated changes.

Both studies used quantitative as well as qualitative data. In order to gather information on the respective fields, existing statistical data and expert interviews were evaluated. In mobile care the main survey encompassed four company case studies, including document analyses and 33 problem-centred interviews at all levels of the organisation (management, works council, employees with various employment contracts and at differing hierarchical positions).[3] For freelancers in the German media industry a questionnaire survey (N = 185) was carried out among the members of professional organisations in three main clusters of the industry (Berlin, Köln and Hamburg) in order to collect socio-demographical data. This design made it possible to select 39 freelancers for semi-structured interviews according to pre-established sampling criteria (gender, household type, age and income).[4]

After a short introduction into the employment structure, (labour) market conditions and the regulation of work in both fields, the empirical findings on mobile care and freelance workers in the media industry are presented on the basis of the analytical dimensions developed in the previous section.

Work-life boundaries in mobile care

With qualified nurses, mobile care includes an employment segment with a medium qualification level as well as poorly qualified care auxiliaries and home helps who provide services such as housework and caring for clients' social needs. Women comprise 90 per cent of these workers. Mobile care is dominated by direct employment in open contracts that are often part-time. The number of self-employed workers is rising but they still form the exception in Austria. There is also an increase in atypical employment and a considerable proportion of moonlighting.

Through the introduction of a tax-financed nursing allowance in Austria in 1993, a new legally regulated market for person-related services has emerged. The expansion of outpatient care led to a high demand in the labour market for experienced carers, for whom there are alternative employment opportunities in inpatient care. Approximately 90 per cent of outpatient care in Austria is provided by non-profit organisations. The providers have to meet certain criteria and receive a contract with the provincial government that pays for the services if clients cannot afford them and that also establishes quotas of clients. This narrow regulatory corset allows little room for market-type processes. Currently, cost-cutting measures in the public sector are exerting increasing pressure on the providers, who are reacting with rationalisation and efforts to downgrade skills.

In Austria, incomes in mobile care vary between occupational groups, though they are generally low and below the income level of inpatient care institutions. Since 2004, a collective agreement has been in place that aims to standardise wages; however, the regulatory effect of this agreement is weak. At the same time, training and access to the caring occupations are legally regulated and self-employment is only possible for qualified nurses.

Working hours

Formally, with regard to the agreed working hours, mobile care workers have a high degree of influence and as a rule they can change the number of working hours stipulated in their employment contract. However, the actual situation is characterised by high flexibility demands and overtime with little planning.

Working times in care organisations range from 6.00 a.m. to 9.00 p.m. Qualified care workers can divide their duties more freely as medical home-care is mostly not dependent on the time of day. However, for auxiliary care workers and home helps, working time is greatly affected by split duties, with a first shift in the morning followed by a break of two to four hours and then a second shift in the evening. As a rule, weekend work occurs twice a month. Moreover, workers' schedules change from day to day and from week to week, often at short notice. The flexible working hours result from care requirements as well as the short-term absence of clients, for example due to hospitalisation. At the same time, absent staff cover is kept to a minimum for cost reasons. Thus, if a colleague calls in sick, more clients have to be looked after by the remaining staff. In the four care organisations studied, significant overtime had been worked for some months.

Together with staff shortages and working overtime, this pressure for short-term flexibility leads to problems reconciling the paid work and private lives of care workers. The overwhelming majority reported that they had to adapt their private life to the requirements of the job. Short-term flexibility is experienced as a significant burden on private life. The reconciliation of paid work and private life is particularly problematic for workers with care obligations of their own. Moreover, due to traditional divisions of labour, female care workers also bore the main burden of household and care work in their families.

Workplaces

In mobile care, the place of work is prescribed by the duty roster. Individual field-work in clients' homes makes up to almost 95 per cent of activities. Thus, care workers are confronted with the problem of isolation despite the company structure of care organisations. In addition, their workplace is not only outside the company but in the private sphere of the client. Whereas in IT services, for example, crossing the boundaries of the company means working in company-type surroundings of the customer, in mobile care the boundary of the world of work is also crossed when the private home becomes the workplace. As a result, care workers face specific demands for the constant, active re-establishment of working-type boundaries, for example resisting 'encroachments' and impositions by clients or their family members. These demarcation strategies can be more or less successful.

Cooperative relationships

In mobile care, the range of services, tasks and competencies is legally regulated. Moreover, mobile care is organised in company form. Employees are subject to directives and are embedded in company hierarchies. Teams of qualified nurses, care auxiliaries and home helps are responsible for particular territories. For care workers, the mutual support among colleagues in this team is extremely important as it compensates for the negative effects of their isolated field-work. Traditionally, regular team discussions in care organisations took place weekly but more recently, team meetings have been lessened – from weekly to monthly – inorder to reduce indirect working hours. Careworkers' exchange of knowledge and support with colleagues therefore becomes more difficult.

In mobile care, the relationships with customers have a special character. Firstly, many clients have limited resources as the majority are financially dependent on public allowances to pay for the services. Most are elderly, sick people who are frequently dependent on the nursing staff. Secondly, customers do not enter directly into negotiations with care workers; instead the provider acts as a mediator between them. Requests regarding duty times must be registered with the central office and are decided according to coordination necessities. The clients, however, have a significant influence on the working methods of the caring staff. Despite guidelines regarding hours and content of care, the activity has to be attuned to the requirements of the client and to special situations. In mobile care, control by superiors primarily means controlling the working hours by counterchecking workers' records and the duty sheets signed by the client. Quality control is limited to spot checks. At the same time, a certain degree of mutual supervision (by peers) is provided by the care workers themselves.

Worker/Subject

Care work consists of an encounter between two subjects. The working process can be understood as an interaction between the carer and the client in which both sides actively contribute to the result. Indeed, recent analytical concepts understand care as interactive work (Dunkel and Rieder 2001). In order to take into account the subjectivity of the clients, care workers have to bring their own subjectivity into the working process (Böhle 2002). Emotions, empathy and experience are central for care work and affect the well-being of the client.

The interactive and emotional character of care work resurfaces in the care workers' professional self-conceptions. For most interviewees, the response to clients – as an intuitive involvement – is a central feature of their work. This involvement is important in order to achieve good quality care work and the well-being of the client but also it is a source of workers' satisfaction, as positive feedback from the client is a visible signal of the meaningfulness of their efforts. At the same time, a failure to maintain emotional boundaries entails considerable risk for the emotional stability of care workers.

The care organisations exploit this understanding of care work in a contradictory way. On the one hand, they argue in favour of stricter demarcations for time-saving reasons. Thus, the client orientation of the care workers can contradict the organisations' rationalisation objectives. On the other hand, organisations appeal to their workers' client orientation to impose higher workloads. The prospect of potentially 'uncared for' clients is used as an implicit threat to ensure that carers accept increased pressure resulting from staff shortages and the reduction of indirect working times.

Care workers' possibilities to develop strategies for establishing emotional boundaries against the demands of clients and organisations imposed on them are contingent on the level of their professionalism. Home helps are the most strongly affected owing to their low professional and social status. In this occupational group, images of self-sacrifices of 'doing a good turn' – that is, female role attributes and a traditionally gendered subjectivity – are widespread, which makes boundary-drawing difficult. Qualified care workers are better equipped to develop counter strategies: emotional distancing, specialist training and reflexivity are important elements of professionalisation in the caring professions (Friese and Thiessen 2003). In addition, for qualified workers, their higher social status and range of tasks means that they are less exposed to interference from clients and their family members.

Work-life boundaries in the media industry

In contrast to mobile care, journalism, design and software development are highly skilled occupations. The numbers of workers with higher educational qualifications have increased considerably over the last few decades, however, professional titles are not protected by state regulation. The barriers for market entry are low and in all three occupational fields the workforce has increased significantly over the last decade. Women comprise about 50 per cent of employees in design, about 40 per cent in journalism and around 20 per cent in the IT sector (for details see Henninger and Gottschall 2007).

In the media industry product markets are highly dynamic and there is a consolidation process in some parts of the industry. Private companies dominate and the public sector is only involved in public radio and television. Cost pressure emerges through intense competition and the high speed of innovation. The companies react to these circumstances with outsourcing and a differentiation of core and peripheral staff. Freelancers are used as a flexible reserve to complement the in-house workforce. In journalism and design there has been a reduction in direct employment in recent years and because of the difficult labour market situation, freelance activity is now the only opportunity for many journalists and designers to enter the market or to avoid unemployment.

By contrast, with labour shortages and a growing workforce in the computer professions, there were no major employment problems until the 2001 crisis. The different labour market conditions are reflected in the different ratios of freelancers. At the end of the 1990s, freelancers comprised 45.4 per cent of workers in the artistic professions (including journalism and design) and 10.6 per cent in the computer professions (Dostal 2002).

There is no legal regulation of work and the bargaining power of collective actors is weak in the media industry. Although the professional organisations have made attempts at collective employment regulation, their influence on the setting of price and quality standards is generally small – with the exception of the public media, where a collective agreement also includes regulations for freelance work. Moreover, these professions lack the monopoly position or a protected market that according to Lane et al. (2000) are characteristic of classic professions, such as doctors and lawyers. The dominant form of employment regulation in this field is described as 'informal governance' (Baumann 2002). The result is an individualisation of market risks combined with a weak market position. In combination with the over-supply of labour in journalism and design this leads to a broad field of lower and middle incomes, with only a small elite earning top incomes. Against the background of greater demand in the labour market, software freelancers can achieve significantly higher incomes (Henninger and Gottschall 2007).

Working hours

Flexibility of hours is common practice among freelancers in the media professions. However, while deadlines are fixed, the place and length of working hours are generally not prescribed by the customer, allowing freelancers to have much room for manoeuvre. Their organisation of work is determined by the demands arising from paid work as well as from private life. Parents of small children prefer to work when the children are being cared for elsewhere; evening and night-time hours serving as an additional time buffer.

The strategies that freelancers develop to deal with the occasional contradictory demands from paid work and private life are greatly influenced by their market position and their own priorities:

- A *dis-enclosure of work and life*, in which the boundaries between working time and leisure become blurred, was observed in about a third of the sample. This group included some freelancers in the upper income brackets who were highly committed to their job and had extensive working hours. Generally, they felt compensated by their highly interesting and rewarding jobs. A female journalist who worked long hours when travelling to gather the material for her stories explained, 'I am even paid for it, that I can experience all this'. However, dis-enclosure tendencies were also observed in the lowest income bracket. These respondents experienced the negative consequences of the economic insecurity connected to their status as freelancers. They report 'bulimic careers' (Pratt 2000: 432), working long hours when a job comes in, followed by periods of unwanted idleness.

- Almost a third of the respondents drew *clear boundaries* with regard to time. They worked regularly at the same times. For them, work and leisure time were clearly separate from each other. In some cases, working hours were structured through incorporation into the client company, which was frequently the case for software freelancers. For others, the local opening hours of small companies or the standard working day offered structure or working hours were structured around their children's schedule.

- The remaining respondents showed a *flexible balance* of the demands of paid work, family life and their own needs. When there was a large amount of work they worked longer hours but they also took time off when there was less to do. These interviewees described the opportunities to choose their working time as essential to their motivation, although some critically reflected that it could lead to the extension of working hours and an intensification of work.

It is possible to discern learning processes that can shift arrangements of paid work and private life. Some of the respondents who were young and at the beginning of their careers regarded their high commitment to work as temporarily necessary while they build up their businesses. Some middle-aged respondents wanted to impose stricter limits on their working hours after a phase of intensive professional commitment in order to maintain their working ability in the long term and to have more private life. However, the precondition was a secure market position, otherwise older freelancers could also experience market-driven dis-enclosure.

Workplaces

Due to the fact that they are self-employed, most media freelancers are not integrated into organisational work processes. All the same, there are considerable differences concerning the place of work between software developers on the one hand, who work predominantly or even exclusively at their client's companies, and the journalists and designers on the other hand, who are typically not tied to one place of work. Also, workplaces vary according to individual strategies. Approximately half of the freelancers interviewed had an office or studio separate from their residence, which some of them shared with colleagues. The remaining respondents worked primarily at home, either to avoid additional costs for office rent and overheads or to be able to reconcile paid work and childcare.

Cooperative relationships

In contrast to mobile care, for freelancers in the media professions integration into the market does not take place through an organisation and the range of services, tasks and responsibilities are not legally regulated. Instead, cooperation with clients and colleagues is actively produced and reflexively managed.

For most freelancers, personal contacts and the reputation acquired in a particular field are crucial for the acquisition of contracts (Henninger and Gottschall 2007). The quality of work and the quality of the cooperation are decisive in the continuity of the cooperation. Successful cooperation produces mutual trust and creates loyalties that also bind individuals together for future projects (Manning and Sydow 2007). Most of the respondents worked for regular customers which made the handling of contracts easier but at the same time created dependencies.

As the characteristics of a project can be difficult to define in advance, negotiations between the contractor and contractee are necessary. Freelancers attempted to negotiate room for manoeuvre, for example the compliance to conceptions of quality and professional standards gained in professional training. While freelance journalists generally enjoy a high degree of autonomy in carrying out contracts, the activity of the designers and software developers is characterised by a higher demand for cooperation with customers due to a high degree of consultancy. External control is exercised mainly in the form of results controlled by the client. As software freelancers are usually paid on an hourly basis, customers also attempt to control their working time by making them work on site. In journalism and design a fixed price tends to be paid and the freelancers themselves carry the risk of miscalculation.

Freelancers risked isolation due to the fact that they are self-employed. Contacts with colleagues provide an opportunity to overcome this isolation, and drawing on Gold and Fraser (2002), this research describes contacts with other freelancers that are not based on direct cooperation as a professional network. Professional networks provided a feeling of community and offered support through the sharing of information or job offers. In addition, they facilitated communication on quality and price standards. To develop such networks, freelancers used professional association events, mailing lists or newsgroups on the internet and personal contacts of a professional or private nature. However, the utilisation of private social contacts to compete in the market place observed in other research (Manske 2003) could not generally be confirmed for the freelancers studied. While approximately half of the respondents saw overlaps between professional contacts and private circles of friends and acquaintances, others separated their private and professional contacts. The incorporation of family members in paid work was not common, presumably due to the high level of specialisation among the occupational groups surveyed.

Worker/Subject

Among the freelancers in the media industry, subjectivity in the form of creativity or intuition is necessary for many activities. However, freelancers' wishes may clash with the demands of their clients. This is particularly true of the desire for creative self-realisation which can be observed among designers and journalists, as well as the ethical standards held by some journalists. Other demands are more compatible with market conditions, such as the wish for variation or for opportunities to learn something new. Some of the respondents saw their professional career as a personal development process while others saw working on projects as a confirmation of their skills or as coping with challenges. The strategies that freelancers developed to balance their own demands of their work and the requirements of the contractors were heavily influenced by their professional self-conceptions.

A small part of the sample strove primarily for recognition within their professional community on the basis of *professional innovation*. These respondents identified very strongly with their profession and thereby indicated similarities with the professional ethos characteristic of the classical professions. Contracts that did not permit the realisation of their quality standards were refused. This group included a number of respondents who were very successful in terms of income and reputation. Some designers and journalists were also prepared to dispense with a secure income in favour of artistic self-realisation. Such a professional ethic can lead to dissolution of the boundaries between paid work and private life. Some respondents from this group were aware of this risk and developed strategies to draw boundaries, arguing for example that being overworked can lead to serious errors and thus impair the quality of work.

The majority of the freelancers interviewed wanted to offer *professional services that fulfil the demands of the customer*. Reliability and meeting deadlines were central to them in order to acquire a good reputation in the market. They saw varying opportunities to realise their own quality standards and claims to self-realisation in different projects. Some combined contracts that primarily served as a secure income with other projects with greater room for manoeuvre but which offered only poor or no income. For some respondents this service orientation was the result of a learning process in which they acquired a greater distance from their activity.

Discussion: the impact of occupational fields

As the comparison of both occupational fields shows, the dis-enclosure phenomena in the analytical dimensions studied as well as workers' strategies to cope with blurring boundaries between work and private life differed considerably.

In general, freelancers in the media industry have greater room for manoeuvre than mobile care workers and thus are in a better position to cope with flexible working conditions.

What makes flexible *working hours* and *workplaces* outside of organisational boundaries highly problematic for mobile care workers is their lack of influence on where, when and how long they have to work. Thus, the flexible working practices in mobile care constrain the reconciliation of paid work with other spheres of life. By contrast, self-employed workers in the media professions have more room to develop their own working schedules – as long as they keep to their deadlines. Also, freelance journalists and designers can, for the most part, choose their workplaces. This greater room for manoeuvre creates new opportunities to combine paid work and caring responsibilities. Thus care as a 'female' occupation offers worse preconditions for reconciling paid work and family responsibilities than independent self-employment in the media professions, although freelancers in these professions are generally considered to be pioneers of dis-enclosure.

In the *cooperative relationships* dimension it becomes clear that being integrated into a company structure does not in itself facilitate cooperation, as the opportunities for communication and exchange among the mobile care workers are limited by the predominance of isolated field work. The reduction of team discussions due to rationalisation strategies made contacts with colleagues even more difficult. In contrast, the conditions for the development of cooperative relationships with colleagues – either in the form of professional networks, office or studio associations – were more favourable among the freelancers in the media professions.

In the *worker/subject* dimension, there are contradictions between organisational demands on and workers' wishes for subjectivity. In mobile care, the difficulty for workers lies primarily in distancing themselves from excessive demands of the clients and the care organisations. According to Friese and Thiessen (2003), the fluid boundaries between qualified and supposedly female private care work are an important obstacle for the professionalisation of person-related service work. The blurring of boundaries between paid work and private life thus proves to be the old problem of insufficient professionalisation in the caring occupations. However, workers' opportunities for drawing boundaries rise with the level of qualification, as a professional formation promotes the ability to develop a professional distance. Thus, for care workers, professionalisation is a potential resource for boundary-drawing, at least in the higher qualified segments of this occupational field. By contrast, freelancers in the media industries face a different problem. They have to negotiate professional standards and their personal demands on their work with the requirements of their customers. In this group, the respondents who were subject to the danger of dis-enclosure in the worker/subject dimension were primarily those approaching the professional ethos of the traditional professions. Thus, professionalisation, following the example of the traditional professions, can lead highly qualified media freelancers into a situation with blurred work-life boundaries but not necessarily with the beneficial assets of this model, such as a high income and a secure market position.

The greater room for manoeuvre for the media freelancers in the dimensions of work hours, workplaces and cooperative relationships is partly due to their occupational status as independent contractors, while the mobile care workers are employees that are embedded in organisational hierarchies. However, the different employment status of both groups result at least partly from the different labour market situations in both occupational fields – labour shortages and a heavy regulation of self-employment in mobile care versus a reduction in direct employment and low barriers for market entry as a freelancer in the media industry.

But the differences between both groups are also clearly determined by the work assignments and levels of qualification that are specific to the occupational fields studied. In mobile care, the division of tasks as well as the work activities themselves are meticulously regulated by legal norms that also constitute hierarchies among the different professional groups involved (nurses, care auxiliaries and home helps), leaving little scope for individual decisions. Organisational rationalisation strategies put additional pressure on workers and the special character of care work as interactive work as well as the worker's gendered self-concepts based on the ethic of care make it even more difficult for them to block the demands of their 'greedy organisations'. By contrast, journalism, design and software development are professional activities that require a certain level of qualification and allow more individual decisions, and the freelancers in these fields contract work packages that were outsourced by media companies. They have to deliver a product that meets the expectations of their clients, professional standards and also their personal demands but the working process itself is not at all predetermined by legal or organisational regulations and prescriptions.

To put it more pointedly, the central problem of care workers is the lack of control over their working hours and thus also over their time in general. In this group, those with the lowest qualifications (home helps) are also in the worst position to develop counter strategies. In contrast, freelancers in the media industry demonstrate a greater room for manoeuvre. The ability to take advantage of flexible working conditions, however, requires a market income or the financial support from a partnership that provides security. There is an internal differentiation in the sample according to market position: if a secure livelihood is at risk, the private sphere is called upon to survive in the market. The main problem for the freelancers studied is thereby the availability of a secure livelihood in view of the unpredictability of the market.

Concluding remarks

What can be learned from the comparative empirical findings for the debate on dis-enclosure and on work-life balance? Firstly, dis-enclosure in the sense of a divergence from standard contracts of employment is by no means a new phenomenon in the fields of activity studied. However, tighter market conditions and consolidation of the media industry as well as growing cost constraints in mobile care are putting additional pressure on the companies which react with flexibilisation strategies. These strategies entail greater efforts for workers to 'balance' paid work and other spheres of life. However, the opportunities to do so are spread unevenly between occupational groups, between workers with different qualifications and according to gendered self-conceptions and norms. Not surprisingly, it is those workers who have the least resources, particularly the low-qualified home helps who are in the worst position to balance work and life, while flexible working conditions increase work-life balance opportunities in the high-qualified segments of the service economy, for example freelancers in the media industry. But even in this latter group, which seems privileged in comparison to mobile care workers, the 'balance' between paid work and private life is in constant danger of tipping towards work due to the demands of the market.

Secondly, the findings emphasise the importance of distinguishing between 'employee-friendly' flexible working practices and 'employer-friendly' practices (Fleetwood 2007b). While the first form of flexibility has the potential to enhance workers' work-life balance, the second form is sought by employers to increase workers' availability and as a result constrains the reconciliation of paid work with other spheres of life. Thus, it is not flexible working conditions per se that are problematic but their combination with the lack of influence on the part of the workers. As shown above, the different occupational fields studied here offer different room for manoeuvre in this respect.

Thirdly, in comparing mobile care work and freelancing in the media professions the chapter linked an analysis of the constraints and opportunities that are influenced by structural features of the respective occupational fields. These features included (labour) market conditions, work assignments and qualification structures, with a focus on workers' individual strategies to cope with these conditions. As highlighted, these coping strategies do not necessarily imply a high degree of choice. Consequently, the research tried to overcome the tendency of the dis-enclosure debate to focus mainly on structures as well as the tendency of the work-life balance discourse to focus mainly on individual strategies; structure and agency are heavily intertwined and should both be taken into account when analysing flexible working.

However, the findings are limited to two occupational groups from two countries with a similar regulatory setting. To explore further the limits and opportunities of flexible work, more comparative research is necessary to investigate not only different occupational backgrounds but also different national contexts, including countries with diverse regulatory and gender regimes.

Notes

1. For empirical studies on the so-called knowledge economy in the UK that focus on work-life balance, see for example Dex et al. (2000) and Perrons (2003); for empirical evidence from the US, see Pratt (2000). For comparisons of different occupational groups cf. Eichmann et al. (2004). For comparisons at the organisational level see Charles and James (2004); Lewis and Cooper (2005).

2. Both studies ran from 2003 to 2005. The Austrian project was carried out at the Forschungs- und Beratungsstelle Arbeitswelt (FORBA) in Vienna by Manfred Krenn, Jörg Flecker, Christoph Herrmann, Hubert Eichmann and Ulrike Papouschek and was supported by the Federal Ministry for Education, Science and Art. The German study was conducted by Karin Gottschall and Annette Henninger at the Center for Social Policy Research/ University of Bremen and was supported by the Federal Ministry for Education and Research.

3. The size of the care companies studied varied from 135 to 450 workers. One team generally consisted of 25 to 30 care workers.

4. Half of the respondents were women, one third were parents, two thirds lived with partners. Middle-aged freelancers (35–55 years of age) accounted for two thirds of the sample. Precarious incomes (under 20,000 € p.a.), middle (20,000–50,000 € p.a.) and top incomes (over 50,000 € p.a.) were evenly represented.

REFERENCES

Baethge, M. (1991) 'Arbeit, Vergesellschaftung, Identität – Zur zunehmenden normativen Subjektivierung der Arbeit', *Soziale Welt*, 42:1, 6–19.
Baumann, A. (2002) 'Informal Labour Market Governance: The Case of the British and German Media Production Industries', *Work, Employment and Society*, 16:1, 27–46.

▶

▶

Blyton, P., Blunsdon, B., Reed, K. and Dastmalchian, A. (eds) (2006) *Work-Life Integration*, Basingstoke: Palgrave Macmillan.

Böhle, F. (2002) 'Vom Objekt zum gespaltenen Subjekt' in M. Moldaschl and G. Voß (eds) *Subjektivierung von Arbeit*, München/Mehring: Hampp.

Charles, N. and James, E. (2004) 'Gender, Job Insecurity and the Work-Life Balance' in D. Houston (ed.) *Work-Life Balance in the 21st Century*, Basingstoke: Palgrave Macmillan.

Crompton, R. (2001) 'Gender Restructuring, Employment, and Caring', *Social Politics*, 8:3, 266–91.

Dex, S., Willis, J., Paterson, R. and Sheppard, E. (2000) 'Freelance Workers and Contract Uncertainty: The Effects of Contractual Changes in the Television Industry', *Work, Employment and Society*, 14:2, 283–05.

Dostal, W. (2002) 'Berufe im Wandel: Anforderungen an die Entwicklung von Berufen im Kultur- und Medienbereich aufgrund des Einsatzes neuer Technologien' in O. Zimmermann and G. Schulz (eds) *Kulturelle Bildung in der Wissensgesellschaft – Zukunft der Kulturberufe*, Berlin/Bonn: Deutscher Kulturrat e.V.

Dunkel, W. and Rieder, K. (2001) 'Interaktionsarbeit zwischen Konflikt und Kooperation' in A. Büssing, A. and J. Glaser (eds) *Dienstleistungsqualität und Qualität des Arbeitslebens im Krankenhaus*, Göttingen: Hogrefe.

Eichmann, H., Flecker, J., Hermann, C., Krenn, M. and Papouschek, U. (2004) *Entgrenzung von Arbeit und Chancen zur Partizipation*, first report, Wien: Forschungs- und Beratungsstelle Arbeitswelt (FORBA).

Esping-Andersen, G. (1998) *Social Foundations of Postindustrial Economies*, Oxford: Oxford University Press.

Fleetwood, S. (2007a) 'Re-thinking Work-Life Balance: Editor's Introduction', *International Journal of Human Resource Management*, 18:3, 351–9.

Fleetwood, S. (2007b) 'Why Work-Life Balance Now?', *International Journal of Human Resource Management*, 18:3, 387–400.

Friese, M. and Thiessen, B. (2003) 'Kompetenzentwicklung im personenbezogenen Dienstleistungsbereich – Aufwertung und Entgendering-Prozesse' in E. Kuhlmann and S. Betzelt (eds) *Geschlechterverhältnisse im Dienstleistungssektor*, Baden-Baden: Nomos.

Gold, M. and Fraser, J. (2002) 'Managing Self-management: Successful Transitions to Portfolio Careers', *Work, Employment and Society*, 16:4, 579–97.

Gottschall, K. and Voß, G. (eds) (2003a) *Entgrenzung von Arbeit und Leben*, München/Mehring: Hampp.

Gottschall, K. and Voß, G. (2003b) 'Entgrenzung von Arbeit und Leben: Zur Einleitung' in K. Gottschall and G. Voß (eds) *Entgrenzung von Arbeit und Leben*, München/Mehring: Hampp.

▶

▶

Gottschall, K. and Wolf, H. (eds) (2007) 'Work Unbound? Patterns of Work and Organization in German Media and Cultural Industries', *Critical Sociology*, 33:1–2, 11–18.

Hall, A. and Soskice, D. (eds) (2001) *Varieties of Capitalism,* Oxford: Oxford University Press.

Henninger, A. and Gottschall, K. (2007) 'Freelancers in the German New Media Industry: Beyond Standard Patterns of Work and Life', *Critical Sociology*, 33:1–2, 43–71.

Hildebrandt, E. and Littig, B. (2006) 'Concepts, Approaches and Problems of Work-Life Balance', *European Societies*, 8:2, 215–22.

Houston, D. (ed.) (2005) *Work-Life Balance in the 21st Century*, Basingstoke: Palgrave Macmillan.

Kratzer, N. and Sauer, D. (2003) 'Entgrenzung von Arbeit: Konzept, Thesen, Befunde' in K. Gottschall and G. Voß (eds) *Entgrenzung von Arbeit und Leben*, München/Mehring: Hampp.

Krenn, M. and Papouschek, U. (2006) '… ja, was willst du viel mitbestimmen? – Partizipationschancen im entgrenzten Arbeitsfeld mobile Pflege', *Österreich-ische Zeitschrift für Soziologie*, 31:2, 6–28.

Lane, C., Potton, M. and Littek, W. (2000) *The Professions between State and Market*, Cambridge: University of Cambridge.

Lewis, S. and Cooper, C. (2005) *Work-Life Integration: Case Studies of Organisational Change*, Chichester: John Wiley & Sons.

Lewis, S., Gambles, R. and Rapoport, R. (2007) 'The Constraints of a "Work-Life Balance" Approach: An International Perspective', *International Journal of Human Resource Management*, 18:3, 360–73.

Manning, S. and Sydow, J. (2007) 'Transforming Creative Potential in Project Networks: How TV Movies are Produced Under Network-based Control', *Critical Sociology*, 33:1–2, 19–42.

Manske, A. (2003) 'Arbeits- und Lebensarrangements in der Multimedia-branche unter Vermarktlichungsdruck – Rationalisierungspotenzial für den Markterfolg?' in E. Kuhlmann, and S. Betzelt (eds) *Geschlechterverhältnisse im Dienstleistungssektor*, Baden-Baden: Nomos.

Metz-Göckel, S. (2004) 'Wenn die Arbeit die Familie frisst' in M. Kastner (ed.) *Die Zukunft der Work Life Balance*, Kröning: Assanger.

Perrons, D. (2003) 'The New Economy and the Work-Life Balance: Conceptual Explorations and a Case Study of New Media', *Gender, Work and Organization*, 10:1, 65–93.

Pongratz, H.J. and Voß, G.G. (2003) 'From Employee to "Entreployee": Towards a "Self-Entrepreneurial" Work Force?', *Concepts and Transformation*, 8:3, 239–54.

Pratt, A. (2000) 'New Media, the New Economy and New Spaces', *Geoforum*, 31, 425–36.

Re-Establishing Boundaries in Home-Based Telework

10

Camilla Kylin and
Jan Ch. Karlsson

> Separating entities from their surroundings is what allows us to perceive them in the first place ... It is boundaries that help us separate one entity from another ... Examining how we draw them is therefore critical to any effort to understand our social order.
>
> (Zerubavel 1991: 1–2)

Introduction – the need for boundaries

Boundaries, and their relevance, have been the subject of many disciplines. The act of creating boundaries is crucial for several reasons. Firstly, on a basic and individual level, detachment from our surroundings is essential for the development of self and identity (Zerubavel 1991). Furthermore, people create and maintain boundaries in order to simplify and order their environment. 'Mental fences' (Zerubavel 1991: 2) are built around areas, events, ideas and so on that seem to be similar, functionally related or associated in some other way (Ashforth et al. 2000).

'Home' and 'work' are two examples of domains created by boundaries (cf. Larsson-Sjöberg 2003). The home plays an important role for individuals, families and societies. Beside the physical locality including its functions, home is further a place of ontological security, understood as 'confidence or trust that the world is as it appears' (Giddens 1984: 375). People perform basic personal and household activities, for example cooking, eating, cleaning and caring for others in their homes. The home is also the environment where individuals satisfy their basic and intimate needs, for example for physical comfort, love and affection (cf. Stokols 1976). Thus, the home is a crucial place for individuals regarding residential, personal, social and restorative aspects. Work is another important social domain and there is extensive research showing the relevance of waged work to individuals and the importance of their conditions of work

(Eriksson 1998; Johansson et al. 1996). Jahoda (1979) suggests that employment – apart from making it possible to earn a living – provides employees
with a time structure, shared experiences with people outside the immediate family, links to purposes that transcend their own goals, personal status
and identity as well as motivation for activity. The process of negotiating and
maintaining boundaries between work and non-work is the concern of a body
of literature that can be termed 'Boundary Theory' (Ashforth et al. 2000; Mirchandani 1998; Nippert-Eng 1996; Zerubavel 1991) and includes the cognitive
process of social classification in individuals (Ashforth et al. 2000; Frone 2003;
Zerubavel 1991).

The overall aim of this chapter is to investigate the interaction between work
and non-work life in home-based telework and to analyse different types of
boundaries involved. In home-based telework, work is relocated from a traditional workplace to the private sphere. When work is located in the home, the
domains of work and home overlap and new situations for both the employees
and their co-residents arise. In addition, traditional boundaries in time and
space become blurred and control systems modified. As a result, teleworkers are forced to arrange and construct their workplace within the domestic
domain (Felstead and Jewson 2000). By relating to Boundary Theory, and with
a Grounded Theory approach, the aim of this chapter is to shed light on the
phenomenon of work-life boundaries per se and the dynamics involved in the
process of establishing them.

An outline of the research

The study is based on interviews conducted with 14 employees in a Swedish
municipality. These employees had an agreement with their employer whereby
they could carry out home-based telework. The policy document for the
telework agreements contained the following conditions: telework must not
decrease the level of service provided to the citizens; the period of teleworking should not exceed two weeks each month and the teleworking employee
should be present at the telework workplace at certain times if needed and if
agreed on by the employer and employee (these times differed, depending on
the working tasks and related responsibility) (Policy document, Home-based
Telework 1997). Although a maximum of two weeks a month (and an average
of one day a week) might be considered a short time when analysing telework,
it is not necessarily a disadvantage. If processes of establishing boundaries are
discovered, the implication is that these processes will also exist in cases where
teleworking is more extensive.

Since the number of teleworkers in the municipality was limited, no definite criteria concerning specific occupational characteristics could be followed

when selecting participants. A range of professions were included, such as reme-dial educationalist, principal, IT-specialist and headmaster. Although the occu-pations differed, many of their work activities were of a similar nature and in their regular work they all had to carry out some form of evaluation or documen-tation. These tasks were typically the ones that they chose to perform at home. The remedial educationalist, for example, wrote reports on the results of different psychological and pedagogical tests on children, the principal carried out prepa-ration, organising and administrative work at home, the IT-specialist worked with support from the telephone or computer and the headmaster worked on certain administrative tasks. Thus, none of the employees had changed work tasks due to the home-based telework arrangement but rather it was an implicit condition of the contract that their regular work included tasks that could be performed at home.

Since the aim of the study was to obtain information about how people han-dle the interaction between work and non-work life while working from home, the research involved minimal structure for the interviews. Following a reflexive interview approach (Thomsson 2002), the respondents were asked to speak freely about six topics which included telework, family, home, work, leisure and health. Some general questions were also asked to obtain as much detailed infor-mation as possible about how a typical telework day would proceed. The inter-views were recorded and then transcribed.

The process of analysis was based on techniques used within Grounded Theory (Glaser and Strauss 1967). During the process of open coding, this research found several codes for different topics. The process of analysing continued with comparing and re-comparing, relating and re-relating codes and writing and re-writing research notes. As the research proceeded, two theoretical codes (Glaser 1978), 'boundary' and 'boundaryless', emerged. Where it was applicable, analytical techniques such as fourfold tables were used (Starrin et al. 1991). Finally, one main category emerged as providing the basis as to why boundaries were created and re-established in this otherwise boundaryless work arrange-ment, namely the process of legitimising work.

Home-based telework as a modified trust relationship

Home-based telework has been portrayed as a privileged working arrangement (Rifkin 1995; Toffler, cited in Forester 1989). However, there are findings that contradict the 'myth of autonomy' (Allen and Wolkowitz 1987) – that is the image of homeworkers as a privileged group who have flexible and autono-mous working conditions. Instead, the traditional management control system (which mainly consists of control through time and space) is modified and replaced by other control mechanisms, such as the nature of the work tasks and deadlines. The situation for many teleworkers also constitutes an 'autonomy paradox' (Huws et al. 1990: 72) in the sense that they often seem to be caught between management control strategies and the demands of domestic labour (Armstrong 1999; Felstead et al. 2003).

Nevertheless, through the location of work in the home and the weakening of traditional control mechanisms, this work arrangement creates an idea of an extended trust relationship between the employer and employee. One respondent described it as:

> It's not really so common that people work at home, and it is regarded as a privilege by many that you are sort of trusted. And from that point of view, I really think that people around me think: 'Oh! Allowed to work at home!'
>
> (Human Resource Manager, female)

When the employee is out of sight, control must be complemented with something else and in this context, arguably by trust (Aronsson and Karlsson 2001) as closely related to self-discipline and work morality (Foucault 1977; cf. Büssing and Broome 1999). Trust can be defined as 'a bet about the future contingent actions of others', while distrust is 'the negative mirror-image of trust' (Sztompka 1999: 25–6). The importance of trust for home-based telework arrangements does not mean that employers only rely on trust. In this study, they did not go as far as exercising direct control by making visits to the homes of the teleworkers, as has been reported in the UK (Felstead and Jewson 2000), but there were other means of control. As the contract for working at home had to be authorised by the manager, the initial process involved a control acts and demands of deadlines and reports were other control mechanisms. Still, the possibility of working at home seems to convey the idea of trustworthiness, an extended trust relationship based on moral obligations which puts pressure on the employee to be 'worthily' trusted (cf. Felstead et al. 2003). A further indication of this view is the finding that none of the interviewees in the study charged their employer for expenses incurred as a result of teleworking, for example telephone calls, computer equipment or electricity. As an explanation of not charging for expenses, many mentioned the privilege aspect of this home-based working arrangement. Reflecting on the disadvantages of teleworking, one interviewee explained:

> I certainly see this as a major privilege and that also makes me want to handle it very, very well. And that results in my putting in a lot of work on those days to make it work. ... Well, it costs a bit; of course, I use my own phone and my own mobile.
>
> I: Can't you claim expenses for that?

No, I've never done that [laughs]. I think it's so nice to have these days at home, but that could perhaps be regarded as a drawback.

(Remedial Educationalist 2, female)

These are indications of the consequences of some kind of experienced 'gratitude' which employees want to pay back. That is, the employees feel they have to pay for the privilege of this apparent extended trust relationship. In this case the teleworkers seemed to dissolve the traditional boundary between work and non-work by using private equipment in their work without claiming the expenses for this from their employers. They regarded this use of private equipment as a cost to be paid for the advantage of being trusted by the employer. Although the use of private equipment may occur among employees without home-based telework agreements, it is arguably of greater impact among home-based teleworkers. This is because of the extra costs due to longer periods of working at home and through the contract of working at home per se (including the need for equipment).

The trust relationship with the employer was an important mechanism for re-establishing boundaries between waged work and other activities at home. The teleworkers felt that trust would be recognised through not allowing other things to intrude upon their telework. But how does the relocation of work from a regular workplace to the home affect these employees's closer social environment, for example the family, neighbours and colleagues? Interestingly this issue seemed to be one of the main concerns and struggles identified by the respondents:

All the time I have to point out that I'm actually not off work. And that gets a bit tiresome after a while – that people do not accept and understand what this is all about. ... I feel that I can't let it go even once, but I have to point out that 'no, I'm not off work, I work at home.' Otherwise it's so easy for them to get the idea I'm off. In the beginning it happened sometimes that a neighbour phoned and then I had to be very clear and say that I was working and expecting a phone call so I couldn't talk.

(Remedial Educationalist 2, female)

There were teething problems when they asked 'Are you off work?' And I didn't like that. But they [family members] have stopped that now, because I'm far from off work ... So now they say: 'Do you work at home? Which days do you work at home?' But it took time, because somehow, if you are at home it's a bit difficult for them to understand that you work.

(Remedial Educationalist 1, female)

Contrary to the feeling of enjoying extended trust from the employer, the trust of the teleworkers' social surrounding seems to be reduced or even turned into distrust. In a study of the meaning of the workplace as a physical place, Österåker (2003) found that home-based teleworkers encountered or felt that they were being questioned and often doubted their capability of performing paid work at home. In this case, several respondents reported similar doubts in that they felt distrusted and questioned by their family, friends and neighbours as to whether they were doing any work at all for their employers when at home. This perception created a strong incentive to re-establish boundaries between their waged labour and their home work and leisure activities in order to legitimise being at home during the working day. Perhaps paradoxically then, the distrust of the teleworkers' close social surroundings produced the same tendency as the trust of the employers of re-establishing boundaries. The following section examines the type of boundaries that were re-established.

Spatial, temporal and activity boundaries

How do employees construct their working day and workplace within their homes? Apart from rare occasions, the employees studied had their homes to themselves during their teleworking day. Households with small children had arranged childcare, which is a common feature of Sweden's welfare system. Older children were at school and if grown-up children lived at home they would be out at work, as would the employee's partners. Nevertheless, spatial boundaries were created in the form of, for instance, a specially arranged workroom or a corner of a room. More specifically, a boundary could be a wall or a door that divided the workplace from other parts of the home (cf. Ahrentzen 1990). Some employees did occasionally shift from the workroom to, for example, the living room where they could use a comfortable chair for reading tasks. It is possible to say that there was a core boundary consisting of an arranged place or room and an outer spatial boundary consisting of the apartment, house and garden.

> Because I have a special room that I can use, and which I used in the beginning. But somehow, it has, it suits me better this way. I have some problems with my back and I have a good chair in the living room and so on. But if someone should be at home, the boy is sick or so, then I have to lock myself in.
>
> (IT-specialist, female)

Temporal boundaries were created in the form of time schedules for the work day at home. These time schedules were often similar to the ones used on regular working days, that is, they followed the time patterns of the regular workplace. This pattern appeared to be due in part to the conditions in the agreement that the teleworkers had to be available to colleagues and possible clients for part of the day. Furthermore, it reflected the opportunities and restrictions of the environment, for example, family members away from the home during certain hours. However, there were also indications that while working at home many had flexible working hours and that they worked longer hours. These longer hours appeared to result from the nature of the work tasks, in that many of them had work that had to be completed the same day. Moreover, these employees seemed to count work time in relation to optimally productive hours. This corresponds with findings from a study on the meaning and use of time in teleworking by Steward (2000). For instance, most of them would take coffee breaks when appropriate, particularly in relation to the work tasks or when they needed a break mentally. Some would occasionally work during their lunch breaks. Mirchandani (1998: 175) found that teleworkers even seemed to reduce 'the meaning of work to include only a small group of activities directly related to measurable work goals' (see also Fangel and Aaløkke's contribution to this volume).

When working at a regular workplace (that is not the home), the work day is temporally scheduled in accordance with coffee and lunch breaks (Zerubavel 1981). This segmentation allows the opportunity for employees to deal with private matters. It is not unusual that the degree of tolerance of these other activities can be quite high. For example, employees may browse the Internet on private business, read newspapers, chat with colleagues and make personal appointments (Österåker 2003). When people work at home, it is likely that people will deal with household activities during break times and this issue is often regarded as one of the advantages of home-based telework (Distansarbetsutredningen 1998; Huws 1990). This possibility results in a positive attitude towards home-based working and some respondents appreciated the opportunity of fitting waged work and household work together. However, the same issue also created problems for some teleworkers regarding what was considered appropriate or inappropriate.

> I talk to a lot of people who say 'But how can you do that work, I would vacuum or do this and that', but I say 'Heavens, then I couldn't have this deal, I couldn't work in this way.' The job doesn't do itself, the tasks don't disappear, they're still there.
>
> (Remedial Educationalist 1, female)

Although many saw the possibility of dovetailing household and professional activities, some respondents rejected participating in any kind of household activity while others mentioned only some selected activities. The most commonly mentioned activity was doing the laundry while other activities included doing the dishes, walking the dog, picking up the children from the day-care centre or school and then continuing to work later.

While the procedure of demarcation in space and time seemed quite unproblematic, there were indications that the procedure of creating boundaries for activities was more associated with emotional concerns. In her study, Steward (2000: 70) also found that 'flexible working involving synchronous work and domestic activity was particularly associated with guilt'. Arguably, this relates to the fact that there are standards and norms for time and space that were implemented during industrialisation (Thompson 1991; Stenbeck 1983). Even though there are different time schedules for different categories of occupations, and a 'normal working day' can differ considerably (cf. Harvey 1999), the majority of the population still work during the daytime and in Sweden from about 8.00 a.m. until 5.00 p.m. (Holm et al. 2004). Consequently, standards and norms exist for time and space. However, in contrast to space and time, there are no clear standards or established norms for which certain activities may be appropriate and legitimate during a teleworking day. Particularly when people are uncertain about their own situation (including their emotional responses to it), they will compare these responses with others in similar situations in order to evaluate their reactions (Buunk et al. 1998; Steward 2000). Hence, the lack of comparability of activities, in particular, during a work day at home appears to give rise to uncertainty and problems among home-based teleworkers.

Mental boundaries versus mental aspects of boundaries

Some studies on teleworkers research psychological or mental boundaries (Ashforth et al. 2000; Clark 2000; Hall and Richter 1988). Clark (2000: 756) defines psychological boundaries as 'rules created by individuals that dictate when thinking patterns, behaviour patterns and emotions are appropriate for one domain and not the other'. To some extent this definition of psychological boundaries seems reasonable as there are different socialisation processes that create norms with regard to when special thoughts, behaviours and emotions are appropriate and these norms can be very dominant, such as work discipline (cf. Steward 2000). However, it is also reasonable that rules governing thinking patterns and emotions can only be controlled to a certain degree. For instance, it can be hard to perform work tasks that demand full mental concentration after a certain length of time or after interruptions from individuals or elements in the surrounding environment (cf. Kahneman 1973). One of our respondents recounted.

> Maybe I make some coffee and hang up a load of washing and things like that and then I go in and have some coffee. Then I can go back to work again.

Because it can become too much – too many numbers. And the same thing when you're making an assessment, you have to think it through, and sometimes it'll grind to a halt.

(Administrator of environmental issues, male)

Hall and Richter (1988) make a physical and psychological distinction between home and work. The physical separation is understood as a territorial matter, while the psychological separation is achieved when individuals are mentally preoccupied with the domain within which they are located. Mirchandani (1999: 93) relates this distinction to telework, 'physical boundaries are created in terms of space and schedules, and these allow teleworkers to maintain a corresponding psychological boundary'. Consequently, although mental boundaries in terms of rules governing thinking and behavioural patterns may exist, it is reasonable that they have limits. Rather, it seems reasonable that boundaries in space, time and activities, besides a physical aspect, also consist of a *mental aspect*. Applied to the three identified boundaries, the related mental processes when working at home include the following. Firstly, the spatial movement from a workroom to a leisure room (crossing a boundary physically) may lead to mentally 'switching' from work thoughts to home thoughts. However, the parallel shift, physically and mentally, is not always the case as thoughts of work might linger in the non-work domain. Secondly, looking at a clock (time boundary) or hearing a ringing bell signalling the end of a working day may similarly bring about a changed mental focus but thoughts about work can occur even after crossing that boundary. Finally, the shift in activity can lead to a shift in mental focus. There are several studies showing that people are often preoccupied with thoughts of work while at home, outside scheduled working times (Frone 2003). In contrast to the above separation by means of boundaries between two domains, it is important to deal with an *overlap* of the two (Hartig et al. 2007).

It is reasonable to assume that the robustness of mental boundaries is related to the degree of concentration needed for the performance of a certain activity. That is, depending on the nature of the activity in terms of the need of concentration, a shift in activity may or may not lead to a mental shift. For instance, shifting from an activity within the work domain that involves great demands on concentration (for example writing evaluations of children's problems) to a highly concentrative household activity (for example planning an important purchase) is more likely to result in a mental shift as both activities need concentration. A corresponding shift to a monotonous activity at home (for example washing up) may not require a mental shift. For some individuals in this study, monotonous work even helped them to continue dealing with their work tasks mentally while performing unpaid repetitive routine work.

> I'm happy to do monotonous jobs sometimes. It's so restful. Besides, you think so well when sawing wood, or with a wood-splitter for instance that runs really slow. And doing the same thing umpteen times, right. Then I don't, sort of think about the machine, I think about other, more creative things. I get many good ideas when sawing and chopping wood.
>
> (Strategist of health issues, male)

Here, the situation of teleworkers and the establishment of boundaries during activities seem particularly interesting. Similar to previous findings (Hultén 2000; Mirchandani 1999), the participants in this study revealed that they undertake special activities during their work breaks. Thus, 'despite the fact that these activities (household activities) are seen as 'breaks', they actually help teleworkers to do their paid work more effectively' (Mirchandani 1999: 95).

Considering the discussion in the previous section on boundaries for activities, it seems reasonable to assume that whether or not a household activity is perceived as appropriate will depend on the nature of the activity in terms of the mental concentration level. Household temporalities, in comparison with waged work temporalities, are more often characterised by strong cyclical structuring of the activities and sequencing and synchronisation of different tasks (Harvey 1999). Furthermore, they seem to consist, to a considerable extent, of repetitive and routine activities for which less mental concentration is generally needed. Consequently, this feature of household activities is arguably one of the reasons why many studies show the spillover effects from the work domain to the life domain (family, home and household), or, in other words, why work seems to be the dominant sphere for most individuals (Frone 2003; Grzywacz and Marks 2000; Hochschild 2001; O´Driscoll et al. 1992).

Returning to the problems experienced by home-based teleworkers when creating a mental separation between the domains of home and work, including their activities, another phenomenon emerges with the creation and effect of rituals, or rites of passage (van Gennep 1965). Several respondents described a procedure for easing the start of their teleworking day. Typical procedures mentioned included reading the newspaper, making and drinking coffee, opening the mail, entering the workroom and checking emails. One respondent described his day:

> I can start the day by hanging up the washing or sorting out the dishes that I didn't have time to earlier ... You have that moment also when you go to a workplace. For me, it's mainly that I go by bike to my ordinary workplace. Mostly I cycle to work. That half-hour gets me started mentally. And when I

get to work, I always have a cup of coffee and shower as well, to get going. At home, it doesn't work to just jump out of bed to sit in front of the computer or by the phone or start reading. I need something to get me started. And it might be the case that I have breakfast, I do something to, kind of, get started, washing up, hanging up washing or whatever, right, maybe read the paper a bit.

(Administrator of environmental issues, male)

In answer to the question of how they end their teleworking day, some respondents described procedures such as going over work that had been completed, what work is to be done the next working day and tidying up the desk area. However, there were also indications that the end of a teleworking day was governed by other family members coming home:

My son comes home around four and my husband works till later. Most often, when he comes home I realise: 'It is that late!' Because he finishes at half five and he comes home maybe at six or half six. And then I sort of: 'Ops!'

(Remedial Educationalist 2, female)

According to Hall and Richter (1988: 220), the daily commute to and from work has 'an important psychological function in that it gives people a chance to get "into" work in the morning and to "unwind" in the afternoon'. This seems reasonable since commuting to the workplace involves distance, a sort of 'boundary land' in space, time and activity, and may therefore facilitate mental switching. Looking at the differences between having a regular workplace and teleworking at home, it seems that teleworkers do not have this distance and boundary land in space, time or activity. The rites of passage seem to function as a replacement for commuting and its psychological aspect; they also seem to facilitate the mental shift from one domain to the other (Ashforth et al. 2000; Mirchandani 1999).

Flexibility, permeability and boundaries with whom or what

It appears that the above concept of boundaries implicitly entails a further component, namely that boundaries are created and directed towards someone or something. For instance, reflecting on the rituals discussed above, it is possible to say that they are a way of building (mental) boundaries for oneself (towards the self), as well as a way of ensuring that one actually physically and/or mentally enters the workplace. Boundaries can also be directed towards environmental elements, family members, neighbours, colleagues, clients and customers. The idea that boundaries are created and directed towards something or someone follows the implication that boundaries can differ in terms of their flexibility and permeability (Clark 2000). Flexibility suggests that 'a border may contract or expand, depending on the demands of one domain or the other', while permeability 'is the degree to which elements from other domains may enter' (Clark 2000: 757, 756). For instance, the case of working during a lunch break in urgent situations or simply working overtime is a form of flexibility in time. Likewise, using the living room for waged work represents flexibility in space. Finally, the ways described above of dovetailing household activities, for example doing the laundry during work breaks, can be seen as flexibility in activity. The 'subjects' of boundaries (against whom they are erected) appear to influence the flexibility and permeability. For instance, a boundary may be impermeable to colleagues in the sense that they are not allowed to call during lunchtime on a teleworking day, whereas it is permeable to clients.

> It often happens that – because I say to people that they can call me on Friday and that it doesn't matter at what time, because I'll be available. And it feels really good to be able to say that. So it's not uncommon that the phone rings in the middle of my lunch break ...
> I: And you don't tell them not to do that?
> It really depends on who it is. If it's a workmate I can tell them, like, but if it's someone from a school, then I take the call.
>
> (Remedial Educationalist 1, female)

However, the relationship can also be reversed, as the following quotation illustrates:

> There are several motives for teleworking – the possibility of working at home. One reason is that there is, there was a need of peace and quiet because of the way the job was. Especially here at the Advisory Customer Service, you don't have – it's an open-plan office and visits from customers ... so there is a need of peace and quiet if I for example have to read up on something or I have to write something. If I have to read or write, I want peace and quiet. I connect my voice mail box, saying that I will be back the next day or later in the afternoon. I don't say that I'm working at home – I don't want anyone to be able to contact me. But my colleagues know that they can phone, of course.
>
> (Administrator of environmental issues, male)

Furthermore, the interviews in this study revealed cases where boundaries that had previously been set were now moved to a new point. Perhaps the clearest example is a case in which a previously selected day for working at home (Friday) was changed to another work day (Wednesday), after the individual had experienced problems with family members who had special expectations for Fridays.

> There are expectations from others if I'm at home on a Friday: 'When you're at home anyway.' And Fridays are a bit special, you know. My husband can come home earlier on Fridays; the children expect more from me on Fridays than on Mondays. Because then it is a Friday.
>
> (Remedial Educationalist 2, female)

In this case, Friday seemed to entail special expectations since it is the start of the weekend and some people finish work or school earlier and, consequently, having it as the day on which to work at home gave rise to greater problems. As a solution to this problem, a different day was adopted for teleworking and the boundaries were moved. This example reflects one way of coping with the new stresses and strains that occur when individuals work at home.

In sum, these issues illustrate how different groups and relationships may have an influence on the dynamics of creating boundaries in home-based telework. That is, whether and how boundaries are created depends on several aspects, such as type of activity, the character of the relationship (for example emotions, dependency, power) towards whom it is created, and the situation given.

Concluding remarks

This chapter has examined a social situation in which traditional boundaries between work and home are contested, namely home-based telework. The study interviewed teleworkers who have a contract with their employer to work at home up to two weeks per month. In relation to their employers, the fact that they were allowed to perform their work in their homes made the home-based teleworkers feel that they were trusted. This trust motivates them to put in extra efforts to get the work done, including using private equipment. It also makes it seem important to them to re-establish boundaries between waged work and other activities at home. The boundaries were set up to ensure the continuation of the trust relationship. On the other hand concerning friends, neighbours and even family, the participants tended to experience distrust and suspicion that they are not really working when they are at home. A consequence of this perceived distrust from the social environment seems to be a need for legitimacy. By way of response, the participants created boundaries. Boundaries between work and home are re-established in order to legitimise working at home in relation to family, friends and neighbours.

In general, people seem to establish and maintain mental boundaries in order to create social order. They also seem to have the need to compare themselves with others (Thomsson 2002) through categories such as women and men, full-time and part-time employees, or work and leisure. On the whole, this need may be seen as the requirement to orientate themselves in a landscape of categories. The act of comparing consists of an act of building categories which in turn is an act of establishing boundaries around certain things that seem to have some features in common. Thus, creating categories and boundaries makes it easier for individuals to create social order in a 'messy world'.

In the more specific case of home-based telework it was found that although the way that participants constructed their workplaces differed due to individual preferences and social and environmental circumstances, boundaries played a crucial role for them all. One respondent (headmaster, male) tried to stick rigidly to the schedules of his regular workplace, following the timetable exactly for when to begin, when to have coffee breaks and when to stop working. He explained that he preferred keeping work and home separate. More commonly, however, the teleworkers would alternate work and domestic activities in a way that was most effective for their working conditions, that is, taking breaks when it suited their work process or when a break was needed mentally. From a critical perspective, the working arrangement of home-based teleworking can be interpreted as a bilaterally selected 'invasion' of the home and private sphere during certain hours, whereas the work domain might represent a 'greedy institution' with a 'long arm' (Coser 1974; Meissner 1971). Nevertheless, many of the postulated advantages of home-based teleworking, for example less commuting or flexibility in everyday domestic arrangements, were also mentioned by participants. Consequently, the greed is subtle in nature and related to the degree of mental engagement and commitment needed for waged work or home and household work (cf. Hochschild 2001).

The process of creating boundaries in this boundaryless agreement seems to be an act of creating order for the individual and others. This ordering includes adjusting to the needs, expectations and assumptions of the individual, their employer and their environment. Boundaries are re-established in search of order in a potentially chaotic situation – a need for a boundary between work and the rest of life.

The research identified three types of boundaries – space, time and activity. Space boundaries are established by reserving a room or part of a room for work, while time boundaries are created by schedules for when to work. Both time and space boundaries are permeable to some extent and are not very problematic to maintain. Activity boundaries between work tasks and other tasks tend to be more difficult and are also more emotionally loaded, especially with guilt, than the other two types of boundaries. Suspicions from the teleworkers' social surroundings are, further, more intense in relation to this type of boundary. These differences between types of boundaries may be due to the fact that there are less clear and established norms concerning activity boundaries for work than time and space boundaries. In the literature, mental boundaries are also discussed, however it is more reasonable to analyse these processes as mental *aspects* of time, space and activity boundaries. Crossing those boundaries tends to be associated with a mental switch, although the level of concentration needed for work and home tasks respectively exerts an influence on the process. In conclusion, the current study has contributed to further knowledge on certain aspects of the dynamics of work and non-work interactions, the crucial roles of boundaries and the struggles in home-based telework.

Acknowledgements

This study is part of a larger research project called 'Boundaryless work – or the new boundaries of work' supported by the Department of Psychology, Stockholm University and the Swedish Council for Working Life and Social Science. We are also grateful for the support of the municipality of Karlstad, Sweden.

REFERENCES

Ahrentzen, S. (1989) 'A Place of Peace, Prospect and … a P.C.: The Home as Office', *Journal of Architectural and Planning Research*, 6, 271–88.

Ahrentzen, S. (1990) 'Managing Conflict by Managing Boundaries: How Professional Homeworkers Cope with Multiple Roles at Home', *Environment and Behavior*, 22, 723–52.

Allen, S. and Wolkowitz, C. (1987) 'Homeworking: Myths and Realities', London: Macmillan.

Armstrong, N. (1999) 'Flexible Work in the Virtual Workplace: Discourses and Implications of Teleworking' in A. Felstead and N. Jewson (eds) *Global Trends in Flexible Labour*, London: Macmillian.

Aronsson, G. and Karlsson, J.Ch. (2001) *Tillitens ansikten*, Lund: Studentlitteratur.

Ashforth, B.E., Kreiner, G.E. and Fugate, M. (2000) 'All in a Day's Work: Boundaries and Micro Role Transitions', *Academy of Management Review*, 25:3, 472–91.

Büssing, A. and Broome, P. (1999) 'Vertrauen unter Telearbeit', *Zeitschrift für Arbeits- und Organisationspsychologie*, 43:3, 122–33.

Buunk, B.P., de Jonge, J., Ybema, J.F. and de Wolff, C.J. (1998) 'Psychosocial Aspects of Occupational Stress' in P.J.D. Drenth, H. Thierry and C.J. de Wolff (eds) *Handbook of Work and Organizational Psychology*, Vol. 2, Work Psychology, East Sussex: Psychology Press.

▶

▶

Clark, S.C. (2000) 'Work/Family Border Theory: A New Theory of Work/Family Balance', *Human Relations*, 53, 747–70.

Coser, L.A. (1974) *Greedy Institutions: Patterns of Undivided Commitment*, New York: Free Press.

Distansarbetsutredningen (1998) 'Distansarbete, betänkande', *Statens Offentliga Utredningar*, 1998:115, Stockholm: Fritzes offentliga publikationer.

Eriksson, B. (1998) *Arbetet i människors liv*, Forskningsrapport 98:10, Karlstad: Karlstad University Press.

Felstead, A., Jewson, N. and Walters, S. (2003) 'Managerial Control of Employees Working at Home', *British Journal of Industrial Relations*, 41:2, 241–64.

Felstead, N. and Jewson, N. (2000) *In Work, at Home*, London: Routledge.

Forester, T. (1989) 'The Myth of the Electronic Cottage', *Computers and Society*, 19:2, 4–19.

Foucault, M. (1977) *Discipline and Punish*, Harmondsworth: Penguin.

Frone, M. (2003) 'Work-Family Balance' in J.C. Quick and L.E. Tetrick (eds) *Handbook of Occupational Health Psychology*, Washington DC: American Psychological Association.

Giddens, A. (1984) *The Constitution of Society*, Cornwall: T.J. Press.

Glaser, B.G. (1978) *Theoretical Sensitivity*, Mill Valley: Sociology Press.

Glaser, B. and Strauss, A. (1967) *The Discovery of Grounded Theory: Strategies for Qualitative Research*, Chicago: Aldine.

Grzywacz, J.G. and Marks, N.F. (2000) 'Reconceptualizing the Work-Family Interface: An Ecological Perspective on the Correlates of Positive and Negative Spillover between Work and Family', *Journal of Occupational Health Psychology*, 5, 111–26.

Hall, D.T. and Richter, J. (1988) 'Balancing Work Life and Home Life: What Can Organizations Do to Help?', *Academy of Management Executive*, 11, 213–23.

Hartig, T., Kylin, C. and Johansson, G. (2007) 'The Telework Tradeoff: Stress Mitigation vs. Constrained Restoration', *Applied Psychology: An International Review*, 56:2, 231–53.

Harvey, M. (1999) 'Economies of Time: A Framework for Analysing the Restructuring of Employment Relations' in A. Felstead and N. Jewson (eds) *Global Trends in Flexible Labour*, London: Macmillan.

Hochschild, A.R. (2001) *The Time Bind*, New York: Holt.

Holm, E., Lindgren, U. and Malmberg, G. (2004) *Arbete och tillväxt i hela landet – betydelsen av arbetskraftsmobiliseringen*, A2004: 022, Östersund: ITPS.

Hultén, K. (2000) *Datorn på köksbordet. En studie av kvinnor som distansarbetar i hemmet*, Diss., Lund: Sociologiska Institutionen.

▶

Huws, U., Korte, W.B. and Robinson, S. (1990) *Telework: Towards the Elusive Office*, Chichester: Wiley.

Jahoda, M. (1979) 'The Impact of Unemployment in the Thirties and Seventies', *British Psychological Society Bulletin*, 32, 309–14.

Johansson, G., Isaksson, K. and Sjöberg, A. (1996) 'Drivkrafter för arbete – attityder och värderingar i arbetskraften' in Arbetsmarknadspolitiska kommittén (ed.), *Statens Offentliga Utredningar*, 1996:34, Stockholm: Fritze.

Kahneman, D. (1973) *Attention and Effort*, New Jersey: Prentice-Hall.

Larsson-Sjöberg, K. (2003) 'Mamma, pappa, styvpappa – barn' in M. Bäck-Wiklund and T. Johansson (eds) *Nätverksfamiljen*, Stockholm: Norstedts.

Meissner, M. (1971) 'The Long Arm of the Job: A Study of Work and Leisure', *Industrial Relations*, 10, 239–60.

Mirchandani, K. (1998) 'Protecting the Boundary: Teleworker Insights on the Expansive Concept of "Work"', *Gender and Society*, 12:2, 168–87.

Mirchandani, K. (1999) 'Legitimizing Work: Telework and the Gendered Reification of the Work-Nonwork Dichotomy', *Canadian Review of Sociology and Anthropology*, 36, 87–107.

A Nippert-Eng (1996) *Home and Work*, Chicago: University of Chicago press.

O'Driscoll, M.P., Ilgen, D.R. and Hildreth, K. (1992) 'Time Devoted to Job and Off-Job Activities, Interrole Conflict, and Affective Experiences', *Journal of Applied Psychology*, 77, 272–79.

Österåker, M. (2003) *Arbetsplatsens betydelse – från självklarhet till medvetenhet.*, Diss., Helsingfors: Yliopistopaino.

Policy dokument, Distansarbete (Home-based telework) (1997), Karlstads Kommun, Cirkulär 9/97.

Rifkin, J. (1995) *The End of Work*, New York: Putnam.

Starrin, B., Larsson, G., Dahlgren, L. and Styrborn, S. (1991) *Från upptäckt till presentation*, Lund: Studentlitteratur.

Stenbeck, M. (1983) 'Lönearbetets organisation' in J.Ch. Karlsson (ed.) *Om lönearbete. En bok i arbetssociologi*, Stockholm: Norstedt.

Steward, B. (2000) 'Changing Times: The Meaning, Measurement and Use of Time in Teleworking', *Time and Society*, 9:1, 57–74.

Stokols, D. (1976) 'The Experience of Crowding in Primary and Secondary Environments', *Environment and Behavior*, 8, 49–86.

Sztompka, P (1999) *Trust. A Sociological Theory*, Cambridge: Cambridge University Press.

Thompson, E.P. (1967) 'Time, Work-Discipline and Industrial Capitalism', *Past and Present*, 38, 56–97.

Thomsson, H. (2002) *Reflexiva intervjuer*, Lund: Studentlitteratur.

van Gennep, A. (1965) *The Rites of Passage*, London: Routledge.

Zerubavel, E. (1981) *Hidden Rhythms: Schedules and Calendars in Social Life*, Chicago: University of Chicago Press.

Zerubavel, E. (1991) *The Fine Line: Making Distinctions in Everyday Life*, Chicago: University of Chicago Press.

Frustrated Ambitions: **11**
The Reality of Balancing
Work and Life for Call
Centre Employees

Jeff Hyman and Abigail Marks

Introduction

Fundamental shifts in employment in the service sector and in telephonic call
centre services in particular have been well-documented (Bolton and Houlihan
2005; Glucksman 2004; Taylor and Bain 1997, 2001, 2005). The rapid growth
of this 'front-line' service sector work has been accompanied by contrasting
claims for its implications for employees. While Castells claims that there will
be 'greater freedom for better-informed workers' (2000: 257), the same employees are also said to be subordinated to the 'cult of the customer' in which service
delivery acts as the fulcrum for market advantage (Taylor 1998). Castells's thesis
suggests that conditions of employment can be designed to promote 'freedom'
in terms of job satisfaction, health and well-being, career and training opportunities, and the establishing of appropriate borders between the demands
of work and domestic life. Several studies have indicated links between work
autonomy and job satisfaction (see for example Holman 2004) and that product market strategies and consequent labour utilisation policies, including flexible working practices, combine to replace earlier 'sweat-shop' configurations
of call centre work (for example Deery et al. 2004; Kersley et al. 2006; Wood et
al. 2006). Nevertheless, recent findings also indicate that even where so-called
high commitment practices have been adopted in call centres, these operate
within prescribed managerial parameters (Halliden and Monks 2005; Kinnie
et al. 2000).

Our aim in this chapter is to extend research horizons beyond the workplace to review both employment practices, practices that can differ significantly from formal stated policies (see for example Hoque and Noon 2004),

and the implications of these practices for employees and their non-working lives. In so doing, the rhetoric of flexible work will be contrasted with employee views which display tensions inherent in maintaining any sort of equilibrium between the domains of work and non-work. Through the voices of employees we present a broader picture of how work can dominate and distort people's non-working lives and ambitions and in so doing confront prescriptive formulations for achieving balance between work and life as espoused by employers and governments. Based on interviews conducted with employees in four call centres, this chapter demonstrates the reality and frustrations experienced by workers in their attempts to construct meaningful, fulfilled work that complements and enriches their domestic lives.

Life and work in the modern economy

The contemporary workplace is held to be typified by widespread use of flexible information technologies in service and sales work providing the foundation for an expanding cohort of 'knowledge workers' (Frenkel et al. 1999). Nevertheless, current developments in the nature of paid work are by no means straightforward. Some authors have suggested that the contemporary economy is characterised by a polarisation of employment between secure, interesting, knowledge-based occupations and mundane, unskilled and insecure jobs (Goos and Manning 2003). Other commentators claim, based on the ideas of *inter alia*, Drucker (1993) that 'Western economies are becoming knowledge economies' (May et al. 2002). Yet other authors have been more circumspect, suggesting that while a polarisation may be occurring, the majority of new jobs are shifting inexorably towards being knowledge-based or, at the very least, higher value-added (Frenkel et al. 1999; Moynagh and Worsley 2005). This latter position is certainly an image that politicians are eager to project, concomitant with a general emphasis on 'education, education, education', and more specific policy ambitions to further expand tertiary education to provide for university level participation by at least half the 18–30 age cohort by 2010 (Wolf 2002). In Scotland, where the research was conducted, economic aspirations towards a 'smart, successful Scotland' (Scottish Executive 2004) are founded on a ready supply of labour that is highly educated and highly skilled. It is an open question, however, whether jobs are becoming more knowledge-intensive or employers are simply raising entry-level qualifications for occupations that previously did not require a degree (Warhurst and Thompson 2006; see also Fleming et al. 2004). In our study, certainly, over a quarter of survey respondents had either graduate or post-graduate qualifications.

For proponents of the new knowledge-based economy, the foundation for the alleged shift is an information technology revolution (Castells 2000) that helps to transform growing numbers of companies into 'knowledge' or 'learning' organisations and their employees into 'knowledge workers'. The advance of so-called knowledge work is linked with purported organisational shifts into high involvement work regimes in order to secure effective performance and commitment from these workers (see for example Huselid 1995). Discounting the hyperbole, a common trend across the EU has been the rise in high technology, information-driven organisations, typified by a central characteristic: a principal factor of production is provided by human capital (DfES 2001).

Some authors (for example Frenkel et al. 1999) claim that even low-level knowledge workers enjoy enhanced employment opportunities and an improvement in working life and indeed work-life balance, many others would question this perspective. To counterbalance the lack of substantive change in work, a contemporary hook to attract and retain employees may be provided by workplace temporal flexibility, offering employees the promise of more freedom to work hours which suit their domestic circumstances and caring responsibilities. Such provision can also be linked with efforts to raise employee commitment (Wood 1999). As we show below, call centres frequently offer temporal flexibility in terms of shiftworking and part-time opportunities. Many employers proclaim that this combined commitment and work-life balance revolution is already 'mission accomplished' (CBI 2005).

Though temporal flexibility is common, its application need not necessarily benefit the operatives to whom it is directed. In an occupation with shiftwork and/or informal extensions of the working day (as is the case with our call centre organisations) a requirement for complex coping strategies to ensure effective work-life balance emerges (Baldry et al. 2007). Such coping strategies not only relate to work continuity and provision of child care, but also to other elements of securing a reasonably fulfilled life, such as personal and professional development opportunities. While some writers (for example Belt 2002) have identified that the career aspirations of call centre workers often reflect a traditional company career, these aspirations are rarely accommodated by the institutional or organizational infrastructure. Call centres' predominantly flat structures restrict hierarchical promotion, and companies pay little more than lip service to personal development (Baldry et al. 2007). With work-life balance looking increasingly precarious with the shift towards 24 hour working, ability to develop skills in non-work time becomes increasingly problematic. Any ambitions for a new career or career development become constrained by poor work-life balance.

It is between these disputed areas that the present study aims to illuminate further in the specific context of call centres. The chapter then addresses broader issues that these frustrations entail for employee well-being.

Call centres in Scotland: a profile of four organisations

Scotland has been portrayed, at least internally, as an exemplar of an aspiring knowledge economy and there is little doubt that the economy is changing: service work in all its manifestations has been continually expanding while manufacturing, as in the rest of the UK, appears to be in decline. Call centres are a case in point. In the UK, wherever customer servicing can be conducted remotely, call centres have emerged as the dominant model (Baldry et al. 2007; Taylor and Bain 2005). Whether call centres form part of the knowledge revolution in terms of their demands on employees is debatable, but what is certain is that large numbers of jobs in these centres have been established, many offering the promise of a worthwhile career or even golden future for those with the necessary attributes.

In Scotland, the sector grew from 16,000 employees in 1997 to 46,000 by 2000 (Taylor and Bain 1997, 2001) and expansion continued less dramatically thereafter to 56,000 by 2003 (Taylor and Bain 2005). Expansion in the call centre workforce has taken place alongside a broadening of its activities. While financial services, media/telecommunications, travel, IT and utilities employ the largest numbers, growth in outsourcing has also been dramatic, and new public sector services, such as medical and health help-lines, now suggest that rather than constituting a single 'call centre industry' the sector has evolved 'to cover the full spectrum of marketing, selling and serving' (Glucksman 2004: 796). With this growth and diversification it has been suggested that the call centre labour process displays similar variability and early identification of a single sector with similarly uniform tight supervisory and electronic control systems (Fernie and Metcalf 1997) is now conceding ground to more sophisticated analyses. These analyses reveal that with varying requirements made of employees by organisations operating in different product markets (see for example Bolton and Houlihan 2005; Callaghan and Thompson 2002; Collin-Jacques 2004; Taylor et al. 2002), there is at least some telephonic service work apparently characterised by employee discretion and the use of product or service knowledge.

Our analysis draws on data collected through workplace and home/ community based interviews with 91 employees from four call centres. In addition, a comprehensive employee survey was conducted with 855 responses. For this chapter, only passing reference to the survey will be made (for more details see Baldry et al. 2007). The four call centres studied operated in financial services, travel, telecommunications/entertainment and outsourcing. All four companies commenced operations between 1995 and 1998, during the period of the UK call centre sector's swiftest expansion. These centres were intended to generate significant cost savings and enhanced revenue as a result of the centralisation of hitherto geographically dispersed front office servicing or sales operations and through the creation of entirely new operations.

Moneyflow employed 170 workers at its Glasgow call centre and specialised in provision of mortgages, insurance and unsecured loans. 'Volume' and 'value' workflows could be distinguished, reflecting bifurcated services that provided non-secured and secured loans respectively, corresponding to the 'unregulated' and 'regulated' sides of the business. Thejobshop was an outsourced call centre also located in Glasgow whose on-site employment levels fluctuated between 320 and 400 agents as operations conducted on behalf of clients expanded and contracted. The core, preferred clients provided the greatest revenue and promoted Thejobshop's quality reputation, while smaller business clients took advantage of low start-up costs realised through the utilisation of spare capacity and the exploitation of a flexible internal labour market. Contractual agreements between Thejobshop and clients, closely allied to the type of service or product offered, influenced the nature of work organisation. Entcomm, a large US multinational employing 530 people, provided its UK customers with a range of services related to its cable-delivered telecommunications and entertainment products, including enquiries, billing, payments, booking or changing packages, repairs and maintenance. Holstravel was a large, long-established travel and holiday organisation employing 340 workers at its call centre in central Scotland. In addition to product diversity, the companies exhibited differences in managerial emphases on quality and quantity and in working time arrangements, which together confirmed that, despite common defining characteristics, call centres and their workflows are not uniform.

'Time is a Thief': working hours and shift patterns

Historically, shiftworking has been associated with the medical and caring professions, emergency services and manufacturing and the majority of research derives from these sectors (Ritson and Charlton 2006). Indeed, manufacturing has typically been the largest employer of shiftworkers and from this sector there have been many reports of adverse health and social outcomes (for example Colquhoun and Rutenfranz 1980; Smith and Barton 1994). Organisational rationales for shiftworking in manufacturing tend to centre on the reduction of operating costs by more fully utilising machinery (Rosa and Colligan 1997). However, in call centres, an additional reason is emerging: with global marketing strategies, technology improvements and customer demands, many organisations have moved towards 24 hour working to offer customers improved service. This increase in service hours has swollen the numbers of shiftworkers.

In the UK, the total number of employees working atypical shift patterns in 2000 exceeded 16 per cent of the population and more employees in the services now work shifts than in manufacturing (IDS 2000).

While there is a substantial and expansive body of work on the negative impact of formal shift patterns – particularly on home life – in the medical professions and in manufacturing (for example Bohle and Tilley 1998; Smith and Barton 1994), there is very little that examines the effects of atypical working hours for front-line service workers. This neglect is despite 24-hour shift patterns becoming the reality for many employed in the call centre sector (Baldry et al. 2007).

Not surprisingly, our case studies displayed a variety of shift arrangements well beyond conventional clerical service working hours (see Table 11.1). The extent to which working hours bleed into time that is traditionally for family and friends is indicated by the 63 per cent of agents who reported working 'always' or 'frequently' on Saturdays and the 42 per cent who work on Sundays, with as many as 76 per cent working evenings and 39 per cent working nights. There are variations between the call centres related to the nature of the sector, to the product and the specific service provided. In the holiday/travel firm Holstravel and in the entertainment/telecommunications organisation Entcomm shift diffusion was even more pronounced. For example, at Holstravel 79 per cent of agents 'frequently' or 'always' worked Saturdays and 74 per cent worked Sundays, while at Entcomm 77 per cent did likewise on Saturdays.

Employee shift patterns were calibrated to correspond to volumes of incoming calls. At Holstravel separate teams would commence work between 11.00 h and 13.00 h at 15- or 30-minute intervals and, later, part-time shifts would begin at 16.00 h, enabling maximum agent availability during peak periods of customer

Table 11.1   Call centre operating hours

Call Centre	Moneyflow	Thejobshop	Entcomm	Holstravel
Operating hours:				
Monday–Friday	07.00–22.00	07.00–24.00	07.00–23.45	24 hours
Saturday	09.00–17.00	07.00–24.00	09.00–23.45	24 hours
Sunday	None	07.00–24.00	09.00–23.45	24 hours
Week total	73 hours	119 hours	120 hours	168 hours
% of respondents who frequently/ always work:				
Weekday evenings	76	57	78	76
Weekday nights	23	25	27	70
Saturday	49	35	77	79
Sunday	4	24	39	74

demand, particularly in the evenings. Though practice varied in the formal terms and provisions of working hours for their employees, a common characteristic in our case studies was the expansion of working time and a management expectation that operatives should be flexible in order to staff required shifts. These demands inevitably damaged any security in terms of domestic or social arrangements.

For example, at Moneyflow, staff core hours were expanded from 08.00 h to 21.00 h to 07.00 h to 23.00 h for new staff. Saturdays were included as regular shifts. Existing staff worked 140 hours over a four-week period, with standard eight-hour shifts, though these shifts could be adjusted either way by a maximum of two hours to 'meet business needs'. New staff had revised contracts with maximum ten-hour shifts, and management had discretion to vary start and finish times by up to two hours with 48 hours' notice. For all staff, there was a requirement to work additional hours, again in accordance with 'business needs'. Indeed, such practices were not untypical. The length, numbers and types of shifts were usually determined by the employer, and, as a consequence, shiftworkers experience social problems – needing to arrange their lives around the shifts and not the other way round. This issue is important, and we expand upon it later.

Shifts at Thejobshop varied according to requirements of individual accounts, so that hours fluctuated according to the account. Transfer of employees between accounts was both expected and practiced. At Entcomm contracts stated that staff were required to work a flexible 24-hour shift pattern over a seven day period and that shifts could be changed by management with 'reasonable notice'. Shift patterns at this company could be complex. Employees were hired at Holstravel on the basis of a 37.5-hour week over a five day period that 'may contain a provision for Sunday working'. In addition, in some areas of the call centre, a continuous four days on–four days off 12-hour shift system was implemented. For a minority of employees, particularly young single adults, the opportunity to have a number of days off in succession was seen to benefit their non-work lives. Yet, as we show below, for many more employees, this benefit was not achieved.

'Hanging in the Balance': impact of work on life

Work-life balance is about people having a measure of control over when, where and how they work. It is achieved when an individual's right to a fulfilled life inside and outside paid work is accepted and respected as the norm, to the mutual benefit of the individual, business and society.

(Work Foundation 2007: webpage)

Much of the rhetoric from the work-life balance debate concerns the rights and ability of employees to prioritise different aspects of life and personal responsibility in order to achieve balance (Bunting 2004). The debate suggests that flexible work arrangements offer choices for balancing work and non-work commitments (Eikhof et al. 2007). Yet such positive evaluations overlook the structural constraints many workers face. As already noted, shift patterns are for the most part determined by organisations and not individual employees. For employees with caring commitments in particular, the 24/7 flexibility requirements of large parts of the service sector often eat into family life (Legge 2005).

In our study, shift arrangements were only viewed positively by employees if they perceived that they had some control over the shift patterns they worked or the hours were seen to be compatible with other life demands. Some women workers viewed shift arrangements positively as such arrangements complied with child-care arrangements. For the most part however, non-conventional shift patterns led to a great deal of interference in employees' home lives. It is not just the specified contractual hours that are relevant here, it is both the actual number of hours worked and, particularly, their predictability and timing that are important in terms of compatibility with domestic life. In general, the time-flexible regimes and associated shift patterns were perceived by employees to be more of a hindrance than a help in organising their domestic affairs.

> We are not happy with our shifts. Our shifts have changed three times in the past three or four weeks and our shifts are getting worse and worse. We've only got about five or six Saturdays off in the space of about four or five months, which is not a lot. The shifts are getting worse and a lot of people aren't happy with that as well.
>
> (Entcomm-I-21)

Lack of control over shift patterns was frequently exacerbated by the introduction of new IT arrangements which gave individual employees minimal choice or discretion over shift arrangements. Organisation of shifts was often dictated by detailed, but questionably accurate, predictions of call volumes generated by computerised management information systems. Indeed, the use of these software packages caused additional problems with shift patterns. Employees were unable to put in requests for consecutive days off, which meant that time to spend with family became even more constrained. As one operator explained: 'We used to always know maybe the same days for the four days on. We never used to have sort of staggered days' (Holstravel-I-13).

The most frustrating aspect for employees was the inability to balance the demands of variable and non-standard hours with non-work life. This constraint applied not just to employees with families but also to employees with partners who also worked shifts.

I feel it knocks me out in my personal life. The 12.30 shift pattern is really, you don't start 'til 3.45 in the afternoon then finish at 12.30 at night ... They [husband and daughter] are in their bed when I get home ... so for a whole week I don't see anyone.

(Entcomm-I-03)

In addition, managerial expectations of unpaid overtime were commonly reported in the call centres, although these were not identified by respondents as being as disruptive as shiftwork. Nevertheless, together with unpredictable shift patterns and weekend working, these expectations compounded the pressures felt by employees.

'Where Do I Go Now?': careers, promotion and training

There has been renewed interest in careers, originating from the widespread debate about career implications of those organisational and social changes that threaten traditional assumptions about work. Many scholarly attempts to assign meaning to contemporary employment have adopted terms such as 'new' or 'boundaryless' careers (Arthur and Rousseau 1996). Yet from our evidence contemporary working patterns are more 'bounded' or constrained by the shift patterns and structures that are imposed on people's working lives.

Most call centre operatives faced the often daunting prospect of having to conduct their basic call-handling duties indefinitely, while some hoped job opportunities might arise elsewhere within the company, for example in the dwindling numbers of high street retail branches or in IT:

I know within my team ... I feel if they were give opportunities they would probably take them. It's just the type of job it is. It's a kind of, it sounds terrible to say, but you just sometimes feel that it's a dead end job.

(Entcomm-HI-02)

Career theory argues that the best career opportunities for women arise through intra-organisational mobility (for example Valcour and Tolbert 2003). Yet the palpable lack of opportunities either internally or externally was a recurring theme in our interviews, leading the previously quoted operative to comment plaintively: 'I just wish I could do something different. I wish I could get off the phones.'

The lack of career development for those employees who completed any available team leader development training also was found to act as a demotivator. Despite employees being allowed to work part-time, non-standard hours tended to constrain vocational choices and opportunities. Training courses tended to be offered on a full-time basis only and promoted posts were also full-time and frequently not open to job share agreements:

> There was an opportunity that came up just last week for (team leader) training ... basically the position was full-time and there was no way you could have it part-time. So I actually typed an email off to one of the call centre managers and I express my concern again that there was opportunities coming up, but again they were full-time and there was no way of getting on to them. So basically, he was very good, he went to see the training department, well he said he was being very good, and he said to me to apply for the job, but I wouldn't get it.
>
> (Entcomm-HI-02)

Many of our respondents talked about career ambitions and career changes ranging from acting to physiotherapy. However, external labour market opportunities were also constrained. It was frequently mentioned that shift patterns were unsuited to the needs for regular attendance at evening or part-time courses and home study was equally problematic as out of working hours many call centre workers found themselves exhausted:

> At one time I did think about social work and there is quite a lot of studying that you need to do, there is all sorts of different courses that you would need to do before you would be accepted into that sort of work. So I had thought about that but the shifts at work would make it impossible to do any sort of academic studies.
>
> (Entcomm-HI-03)

Consistent with earlier studies (for example Eagle et al. 1998) of women trying to balance work, families and evening classes, for those employees who did take the plunge and opt for part-time study, the impact on their lives was only too apparent. These employees were not only failing to balance social and family lives with work commitments, they were also constrained in their ability to change careers:

> I feel tired all the time at work ... if you guys hadn't come over tonight I'd probably would still be at work trying to finish everything ... I'm putting more time into work than I should be ... Just with my studying and work being quite stressful at the moment my normal sort of life's been put on a back burner.
>
> (Moneyflow-HI-15)

It is instructive to look in more detail at the experience and growing disillusionment of the above operative, a 27-year-old female science graduate who was continuing her studies on a part-time basis. Having grown up in a small village and from a working class background, she was one of the few from her school cohort who had progressed to university. After graduating and without an established job she started work 'on the phones' and quite soon after was asked to train a batch of new operatives. Very soon, this new responsibility became an integral part of her job: 'it's like in my performance agreement ... they have just sneakily given me a new agreement which says I train new staff as well as doing all my normal parts of the role. So it's pretty much' (Moneyflow-HI-15). While enjoying the additional training responsibility, she felt both overworked and unfulfilled: 'I still don't really like putting in too many extra hours at work because you are not really appreciated a lot for it.' Moreover, she could not manage normal leisure activities as her non-work life was being constrained by her need to study. She remarked that it was months since she had picked up a book. As with other respondents she also worried that she had not made the most of herself: 'I kind of want people to think that I am better than I am kind of thing. At school I did really well and everything but it was still scumbag from [a poor suburb of Glasgow] ... Hopefully, by the time I'm 30 I'll be in something better than this' (Moneyflow-HI-15).

This employee was by no means the only graduate working in the four call centres. From our survey of 855 respondents, over a quarter (N = 283) possessed either graduate or postgraduate qualifications and many part-timers were undergraduates. Many full-time workers with degrees had similar tales to tell, of poor working conditions, little hope for development or advancement and stunted 'careers' typified by frequent horizontal job shifts.

Increases in the numbers of graduates in the labour market have resulted in a glut of prospective candidates for graduate positions and subsequently in an intensification of competition for such posts (Doherty et al. 1997). As Scott-Clark and Byrne (1995) indicated, the expansion of higher education has resulted in a 'graduatisation' of many jobs previously filled by non-graduates. The Higher Education Statistics Agency reveals that 38 per cent of those who entered work in 2003 were in 'non-graduate' employment six months after finishing their course (HESA 2003). Combining this evidence with the fact that career progression opportunities are no longer vertical and hierarchical but increasingly horizontal in nature (Herriot 1992; Nystrom and McArthur 1989), it can be concluded that not only will more graduates enter relatively unskilled front-line service work but will also have little opportunity other than to remain in such an employment position. This reality however, has been found to contradict the expectations of the graduate population (Doherty et al. 1997). More importantly, the reality directly contradicts the Scottish Executive's statement that

Scotland needs more graduate labour (Biggart et al. 2005). Our study clearly demonstrates the extent of non-casual graduate employment in call centre occupations and the restrictions such employment entails for internal career progression or for transfer to more challenging work.

'Voices in My Head': stress and health

There are mixed findings as to the extent to which call centre workers succumb to the health issues that are seen to be 'the norm' for shiftworkers in manufacturing and nursing (for example Rosa and Colligan 1997). Ritson and Charlton (2006) found no evidence for either increased errors in the workplace for call centre agents working anti-social shifts or excessively high stress levels. Yet our studies show that call centre workers do feel exhausted and stressed as a result of their job (Hyman et al. 2003). Nearly half of the 855 survey respondents experienced feelings of stress 'quite often' or 'all the time'. In addition, over a third of employees reported thinking about the job quite often or all the time when away from the workplace. Of respondents with care responsibilities, a higher 52 per cent reported being stressed. This feeling of exhaustion further diminishes their capacity to enjoy, benefit from or engage with their non-work lives.

Stress may arise, however, from a number of sources. Firstly, and as described in the previous section, we identified the lack of career opportunities and the perception that the current employment situation is 'as good as it is going to get'. Secondly, again as previously noted, there is inter-role conflict with caring responsibilities. Thirdly, as Taylor et al. (2003: 449) have convincingly argued, much of the stress caused is work-induced and results from a combination of 'targets, call volumes, repetitiveness, and lack of breaks'. Finally, there is the emotional performance that is required from the majority of call centre workers, which for many also seeps into their home life with caring and family responsibilities described by Hochschild with Machung (1989) as *The Second Shift*. As we have addressed the former two factors above, discussion will focus on the latter two causes.

Research confirms the negative impact of call centre practices on employees (Taylor et al. 2003). Chalykoff and Kochan (1989) found that high levels of monitoring lead to depression and poor overall well-being. We too found evidence of emotional impairment attributable to working in call centres:

> I think it's a stressful job ... I think call after call – I mean, I used to go home at night and didn't want to speak for a couple of hours, you know ... If the phone went at home, I didn't want to answer ... because you had been speaking all day.
>
> (Moneyflow-I-07)

Furthermore, Holman (2002) noted that the most negative impact on employee well-being was the perception of lack of control over *how* a task is undertaken. Feeling out of control of timings at work can lead to increased anxiety and depression (ibid.). Zapf et al. (2001) found that the necessity for emotional work in call centres is one of the greatest stressors. Employees are often required to display emotions in order to influence customers (for example empathy and friendliness) that contradict their own emotions. This emotional dissonance was found to be the most significant stressor for call centre workers (Holman 2002). Our own findings demonstrate the emotional pressure put on employees: 'Sometimes if you have had a really bad day with constant calls ... it is very tiring. I've been exhausted and grumpy when I've went home' (Entcomm-I-09). Workers were subject to feelings of exhaustion and not being able to 'switch off' after work and, more seriously, feelings of stress and, occasionally, even adverse health consequences.

> I think a lot of people tend to think, oh you are only sitting answer a phone, you know. I don't think people that don't work in a call centre realise how stressful it is ... we are there to represent the company and to give customer service but people don't realise that if you are given dog's abuse all the time it can become very stressful.
>
> (Entcomm-HI-02)

It is clear that call centre work not only affects work-life balance and career aspirations, it has wider implications for employee well-being.

Concluding discussion

Employment in call centres remains buoyant and is unlikely to diminish. Only recently, a number of centres were relocated to the UK following less than successful initiatives in overseas outsourced operations. With their integrated use of telephony, highly sophisticated software and service orientation, call centres are central to the operation of the 'new economy'.

There was little to suggest from our case studies and interviews with operatives that the new forms of working prevalent in call centres were being matched by new styles or approaches to management. In many respects, there appeared to be a direct transmission from 'old' economy styles of employee management to this new sector. This evolutionary continuity was associated with, and reinforced by, gradual but observable shifts from value-based (requiring specific and tacit skills and knowledge) to volume-based work in a number of the centres, where call response targets, sales targets and other measurable and qualitative performance indicators tightened under increasingly pressurised competitive commercial conditions. There were, therefore, clear signs of Taylorised work intensification, squeezing out any porosity from the working day (and night). There was, moreover, equally clear evidence for extensification of work, with few if any signs of the much-hyped high involvement systems of working offering heightened voice, task choice or time discretion to employees.

Despite the promise, work-life policies and practices were notable by their absence. If anything, employee control over working time, a vital asset for employees to integrate work with their domestic lives, was becoming ever more constrained through impersonal shift-matching IT systems and extended centre access times resulting in substantial quantities of paid and unpaid overtime. As we have argued elsewhere, a pervasive feature of call centre work is that the onus is placed on employees to adjust their lives and those of their families in accordance with organisational needs (Hyman et al. 2005). These compound pressures served to provide a generally pressurised work environment, especially resonant for employees attempting to negotiate individual work-life boundaries. Stressful working conditions seeped into the domestic and social lives of call centre employees and hampered their activities.

There was clearly little expressed job satisfaction and opportunities for internal advancement or shifts to careers consistent with qualifications were limited in number and scope. For call centre workers, and especially for the substantial minority who were well-qualified and for those whose job and geographical mobility was restricted, the limitations represented by routinised, intensified and unpredictable work presents a major hurdle in attaining a more fulfilled life. As well as the basic 'information transfer' tasks identified in the substance of much 'knowledge' work (Warhurst and Thompson 1998), the pressures applied to these workers may have exerted more debilitating and unsettling effects. In their study of call centres, Deery et al. found that emotional exhaustion derived from, firstly, lack of job satisfaction, itself related to 'promotional opportunities, skill use and pressure on wrap-up time' and, secondly, too high work loads (2004: 218–9). These key impositions were clearly evident in the increasingly competitive environment in which our call centres operated.

For these employees, 24/7 working and constantly changing shift patterns coupled to an exhausting and tightly controlled work regime help to restrict engagement in life-enhancing leisure, social and academic activities through exhaustion, time starvation, stress and absence of personal control between the boundaries of work and domesticity. While many workers derive satisfaction from their domestic and social lives, there is little evidence of enrichment or opportunity provided from the bulk of these jobs. Therefore, the prescriptions and forecasts of a genuine recasting of work and social relations through participation in the knowledge economy are seriously deficient. Despite the promise of 'new' work improving employees' working lives and expanding opportunities for all, we found the reality to be very different. Although some employees reaped the benefits of temporal flexibility, for many, anti-social shift patterns and 24 hour working not only impacted on relationships with family and friends but also constrained career and promotion opportunities, increased individuals' stress and damaged broader well-being. While the 'new' economy has been welcomed by some authors, whether as a way forward for renewal of post-industrialised economies or as a means of offering a more enlightened and beneficial approach to managing employees increasingly equipped with tertiary qualifications, analysis of the actual work and working conditions offers rather less scope for optimism. Rather than enriching lives or offering life-enhancing opportunities to educated women, the prognosis for the psychical and physical well-being of people working in the new economy, or at least in substantial sections of it, does not appear to be good.

Acknowledgements

The chapter is based on data collected for a project funded under the ESRC's Future of Work Initiative – 'Employment and Working Life Beyond the Year 2000: Two Emerging Employment Sectors'. The full team for this project was Peter Bain, Chris Baldry, Dirk Bunzel, Gregor Gall, Kay Gilbert, Jeff Hyman, Abigail Marks, Gareth Mulvey, Dora Scholarios, Philip Taylor and Aileen Watson. The late Harvie Ramsay was instrumental in setting up the project.

REFERENCES

Arthur, M.B. and Rousseau, D.M. (1996) 'The Boundaryless Career: A New Employment Principle for a New Organizational Era' in D.M. Rousseau and M.B. Arthur (eds) *The Boundaryless Career*, Oxford: Oxford University Press.

Baldry, C., Bain P., Hyman, J., Taylor, P., Scholarios, D., Marks, A., Watson, A., Gilbert, K., Gall, G. and Bunzel, D. (2007) *The Meaning of Work in the New Economy*, Basingstoke: Palgrave Macmillan.

Belt, V. (2002) 'A Female Ghetto? Women's Careers in Call Centres', *Human Resource Management Journal*, 12:4, 51–66.

Biggart, A., Dobbie, F., Furlong, A., Given, L. and Jones, L. (2005) *24 in 2004 – Scotland's Young People: Findings from the Scottish School Leavers Survey*, Edinburgh: Scottish Executive Education Department.

Bohle, P. and Tilley, A.J. (1998) 'Early Experience of Shiftwork: Influences on Attitudes', *Journal of Occupational and Organizational Psychology*, 71, 61–79.

Bolton, S. and Houlihan, M. (2005) 'The (Mis)representation of Customer Service', *Work, Employment and Society*, 19:4, 685–703.

Bunting, M. (2004) *Willing Slaves*, London: HarperCollins.

▶

▶

Callaghan, G. and Thompson, P. (2002) '"We Recruit Attitude": The Selection and Shaping of Routine Call Centre Labour', *Journal of Management Studies*, 39:2, 233–54.

Castells, M. (2000) *The Rise of the Network Society*, Oxford: Blackwell.

CBI-Pertemps (2005) *Employment Trends Survey*, London: Confederation of British Industry.

Chalykoff, J. and Kochan, T. (1989) 'Computer-aided Monitoring: Its Influence on Employee Job Satisfaction and Turnover', *Personnel Psychology*, 42, 807–34.

Collin-Jacques, C. (2004) 'Professionals at Work: A Study of Autonomy and Skill Utilization in Nurse Call Centres in England and Canada' in S. Deery and N. Kinnie (eds) *Call Centres and Human Resource Management*, Basingstoke: Palgrave Macmillan.

Colquhoun, W.P. and Rutenfranz, J. (1980) *Studies of Shiftwork*, London: Taylor and Francis.

Deery, S., Iverson, R. and Walsh, J. (2004) 'The Effect of Customer Service Encounters on Job Satisfaction and Emotional Exhaustion' in S. Deery and N. Kinnie (eds) *Call Centres and Human Resource Management*, Basingstoke: Palgrave Macmillan.

DfES (2001) *Skills Dialogues: Listening to Employers*, Nottingham: Department for Education and Skills.

Doherty, N., Viney, C. and Adamson, S. (1997) 'Rhetoric or Reality: Shifts in Graduate Career Management?', *Career Development International*, 2:4, 173–9.

Drucker, P. (1993) *Post-Capitalist Society*, New York: Harper.

Eagle, B., Maes, J. and Miles, E. (1998) 'The Importance of Employee Demographic Profiles for Understanding Experiences of Work-Family Conflict', *Journal of Social Psychology*, 138:6, 690–709.

Eikhof, D.R., Warhurst, C. and Haunschild, A. (2007) 'What Work? What Life? What Balance? Critical Reflections on the Work-Life Balance Debate', *Employee Relations*, 29:4, 325–33.

Fernie, S. and Metcalf, D. (1997) *(Not) Hanging on the Telephone: Payment Systems in the New Sweatshops*, Centre for Economic Performance, London School of Economics.

Fleming, P., Harley, B. and Sewell, G. (2004) 'A Little Knowledge is a Dangerous Thing: Getting below the Surface of the Growth of "Knowledge Work" in Australia', *Work, Employment and Society*, 18:4, 725–47.

Frenkel, S., Korczynski, M., Shire, K. and Tam, M. (1999) *On the Front Line*, Ithaca: Cornell University Press.

▶

▶

Glucksman, M. (2004) 'Call Connections: Varieties of Call Centre and the Divisions of Labour', *Work, Employment and Society*, 18:4, 795–811.

Goos, M. and Manning, A. (2003) 'McJobs and Macjobs: The Growing Polarization of Jobs in the UK' in R. Dickens, P. Gregg and J. Wadsworth (eds) *The Labour Market under New Labour*, Basingstoke: Palgrave Macmillan.

Halliden, B. and Monks, K. (2005) 'Employee-centred Management in a Call Centre', *Personnel Review*, 34:3, 370 83.

Herriot, P. (1992) *The Career Management Challenge*, London: Sage.

Higher Education Statistics Agency (HESA) (2003) *Destinations of Leavers from Higher Education 2002/3*, London.

Hochschild, A.R. with Machung, A. (1989) *The Second Shift*, New York: Avon.

Holman, D. (2002) 'Employee Stress in Call Centres', *Human Resource Management Journal*, 12, 35–50.

Holman, D. (2004) 'Employee Well-being in Call Centres' in S. Deery and N. Kinnie (eds), *Call Centres and Human Resource Management*, Basingstoke: Palgrave Macmillan.

Hoque, K. and Noon, M. (2004) 'Equal Opportunities Policy and Practice in Britain: Evaluating the "Empty Shell" Hypothesis', *Work, Employment and Society* 18:3, 481–506.

Huselid, M. (1995) 'The Impact of Human Resource Management Practices on Turnover, Productivity and Corporate Financial Performance', *Academy of Management Journal*, 38, 635–72.

Hyman, J., Baldry, C., Scholarios, D. and Bunzel, D. (2003) 'Work-Life Imbalance in Call Centres and Software Development', *British Journal of Industrial Relations*, 41:2, 215–39.

Hyman, J., Scholarios, D. and Baldry, C. (2005) 'Getting on or Getting by? Employee Flexibility and Coping Strategies for Home and Work', *Work, Employment and Society*, 19:4, 705–25.

Income Data Services (IDS) (2000) *Pay, Conditions and Labour Market Changes*, IDS Studies Report No. 816.

Kersley, B., Alpin, C., Forth, J., Bryson, A., Bewley, H., Dix, G. and Oxenbridge, S. (2006) *Inside the Workplace*, London: Routledge.

Kinnie, N., Hutchinson, S. and Purcell, J. (2000) 'Fun and Surveillance: The Paradox of High Commitment Management in Call Centres', *International Journal of Human Resource Management*, 11:5, 967–85.

Legge, K. (2005) *Human Resource Management*, Basingstoke: Palgrave Macmillan.

▶

▶

May, T.-M., Korczynski, M. and Frenkel, S. (2002) 'Organizational and Occupational Commitment: Knowledge Workers in Large Corporations', *Journal of Management Studies*, 39:6, 775–801.

Moynagh, M. and Worsley, R. (2005) *Working in the 21st Century*, Swindon: ESRC.

Nystrom, P.C. and McArthur, A.W. (1989) 'Propositions Linking Organizations and Career', in A.M. Hall and B. Lawrence (eds), *Handbook of Career Theory*, Cambridge: Cambridge University Press.

Ritson, N. and Charlton, M. (2006) 'Health and Shiftworking in an Administrative Environment', *Journal of Managerial Psychology*, 21:6, 131–44.

Rosa, R.R. and Colligan, M.J. (1997) 'Plain Language about Shiftwork', www.cdc.gov/niosh/Pdfs/97-145.pdf.

Scott-Clark, C. and Byrne, C.A. (1995) 'Degree of Dismay', *Sunday Times*, 29 January, 1.

Scottish Executive (2004) *A Smart, Successful Scotland*, Edinburgh: Scottish Executive.

Smith, L. and Barton, E. (1994) 'Shiftwork and Personal Control: Towards a Conceptual Framework', *European Work and Organizational Psychologist*, 4:2, 101–20.

Taylor, P. and Bain, P. (1997) *Call Centres in Scotland: A Report for Scottish Enterprise*, Glasgow: Scottish Enterprise.

Taylor, P. and Bain, P. (2001) *Call Centres in Scotland in 2000*, Glasgow: Rowan Tree Press.

Taylor, P. and Bain, P. (2005) 'India Calling to the Far Away Towns: The Call Centre Labour Process and Globalisation', *Work, Employment and Society*, 19:2, 261–82.

Taylor, P., Baldry, C., Bain, P. and Ellis, V. (2003) '"A Unique Working Environment": Health, Sickness and Absence Management in UK Call Centres', *Work, Employment & Society*, 17:3, 435–58.

Taylor, P., Mulvey, G., Hyman, J. and Bain, P. (2002) 'Work Organization, Control and the Experience of Work in Call Centres', *Work, Employment and Society*, 16:1, 133–50.

Taylor, S. (1998) 'Emotional Labour and the New Workplace' in P. Thompson and C. Warhurst (eds) *Workplaces of the Future*, Basingstoke: Palgrave Macmillan.

Valcour, P.M. and Tolbert, P.S. (2003) 'Gender, Family, and Career in the Era of Boundarylessness: Determinants and Effects of Intra- and Interorganizational Mobility', *International Journal of Human Resource Management*, 14:5, 768–87.

▶

▶

Warhurst, C. and Thompson, P. (1998) 'Hands, Hearts and Minds: Changing Work and Workers at the End of the Century' in P. Thompson and C. Warhurst (eds) *Workplaces of the Future*, Basingstoke: Palgrave Macmillan.

Warhurst, C. and Thompson, P. (2006) 'Mapping Knowledge in Work: Proxies or Practices?', *Work, Employment and Society*, 20:4, 787–800.

Wolf, A. (2002) *Does Education Matter?*, London: Penguin.

Wood, S. (1999) 'Family-friendly Management. Testing the Various Perspectives', *National Institute for Economic Research*, 168, 2/99, 99–116.

Wood, S., Holman, D. and Stride, C. (2006) 'Human Resource Management and Performance in UK Call Centres', *British Journal of Industrial Relations*, 44:1, 99–124.

Work Foundation (2007) 'Employers and Work-Life Balance', http://employersandwork-lifebalance.org.uk/work/faqs_a1.htm.

Zapf, D., Seifert, C., Schmutte, B., Mertini, H. and Holz, M. (2001) 'Emotion Work and Job Stressors and Their Effects on Burnout', *Psychology and Health*, 16, 527–45.

12 Recreational Use or Performance Enhancing? Doping Regulation and Professional Sport

Tilda Khoshaba

Introduction

Academic interest in the relationship between sport and work was sparked by Bero Rigauer's (1980) *Sport and Work,* in which he argued that the pressure exerted upon athletes for faster, higher and stronger performances had caused their dehumanisation, inevitably transforming them into the tool of a tightly ordered social system and corrupting the purpose and function of sport. As a result, Rigauer declared that sport is work and that, as with other work, sport has become specialised, bureaucratised, inhumane and repressive. As such, he argues that for both the athlete and the worker, 'bureaucracy acts to formalise relationships between the administrator and those being administered, and as such it tends to reinforce the principles and effects of rationalisation and specialisation' (p. 39). Consequently, and as with other workers, Rigauer has continuously argued that the athlete has become a commodity: 'one speaks of ... a million-dollar ballplayer', to which Rigauer comments that 'behind these quantifications, the living human, with his special qualities, disappears' (p. 17).

The regulation of an athlete's 'work' has increased with the professionalism and commercialisation of sport, which, according to Striegel et al. (2002) coincided with the increasing usage of performance-related substances. Although formal testing of athletes has occurred since the late 1950s, it was not until the introduction of the World Anti-Doping Agency (WADA) and the acceptance of the World Anti-Doping Code in 2003 that drug testing started to encroach upon the private lives of athletes. WADA puts forward two arguments for testing: firstly, that doping is a form of cheating and, secondly, that doping damages the health of athletes. However, the way in which testing procedures have evolved has undoubtedly resulted in the loss of control for athletes over their working and non-working lives, while at the same time increasing the power of WADA over athletes and their representatives. It is the encroachment into athletes' private lives that is examined in this chapter. Two aspects of this encroachment are analysed in particular: firstly, how doping regulations permit a transgression of the boundary between work and non-work with physical invasions of privacy and, secondly, how athletes' non-working, private lives are prescribed with the inclusion of not only performance enhancing but also recreational drugs. Much of the material presented is from secondary sources; however primary data is included that is drawn from the author's recently completed doctoral research (Khoshaba 2007). These anonymised interviews encompassed several athletes participating in the various footballing codes as well as several sports administrators and representatives from player associations. Access to such individuals would not have been possible had it not been for the direct involvement of the researcher in the sport. This involvement also enabled the generation of the interview material presented in this chapter, much of which is not usually discussed in the public domain. Unless otherwise stated, all unsourced quotes presented in the chapter are drawn from these interviews over 2006–7.

The capacity to encroach upon athletes' private lives and blur the boundary between work and non-work place and activities is derived from WADA's institutional power not only in the professional sporting community but also within the legal structures of the countries that have agreed to comply by its code. From an Australian perspective, the Australian government created the Australian Sports Anti-Doping Authority (ASADA) in 2006, which is deemed to be an integrated anti-doping organisation having its functions outlined in the Australian Sports Anti-Doping Authority Act (2006) and the Australian Sports Anti-Doping Authority Regulations (2006). In order for the Government to gain the cooperation of all sporting codes, the now former Australian Minister for Arts and Sport, Senator the Hon Rod Kemp (2005) argued that

> As a condition of funding or other support, the Government will require sporting organisations to submit to the operations of ASADA, including its anti-doping investigations and presentation of cases at hearing. Sports will be able to present the case at a hearing and use its own hearing tribunal if ASADA is satisfied that the sport has a robust and transparent process for its own hearing of doping matters.

According to the Athletes Association of Australia (AAA), which comprises the representational bodies of cricket, Australian Football, netball, swimming, soccer, rugby union and rugby league, the independence of Australian sports has been removed and placed in the hands of government bureaucrats. This reality became clear with the five o'clock morning drug raid on the family home of Penrith Panther rugby league forward Frank Pritchard in 2006. The raid was condemned by AAA, which argued that such invasive measures and the manner in which tests are being conducted not only cast a presumption of guilt over all athletes but is challenging the notion of what can be regarded as working hours and the workplace for professional athletes.

By analysing doping in sport and its regulation, this chapter demonstrates that WADA and its subsidiary organisations have removed the independence and privacy of athletes by regulating both their working and non-working lives. As such the work-life boundary has become blurred for professional athletes and this blurring hinders these athletes' private life outside of their profession. It is this loss of Rigauer's 'living humans' that is both the focus of this chapter as well as the concern of athletes and those who seek to represent their interests both on and off the field.

Doping, sport and the introduction of doping regulation

The term doping is derived from the Dutch word 'dop', which is the name of an alcoholic beverage made from grape skins used by Zulu warriors in order to enhance their prowess in battle (Buti and Fridman 2001). The term became prevalent at the turn of the twentieth century when it was used in relation to discussions of the illegal drugging of racehorses. However, the practice of enhancing performance through foreign substances or other artificial means is as old as competitive sport itself. Ancient Greek athletes are known to have used special diets, including sheep's testicles in order to boost the bodies' testosterone levels, and stimulating potions to fortify themselves so that any injuries sustained would be both minimal as well as fast healing. During the Roman era, it has been documented that horses were fed substances that were believed to make them run faster in chariot races, while gladiators ingested substances such as strychnine[1] that supposedly increased endurance so that their fights were more spectacular: that is violent and bloodied. Such substances also provided them with an enhanced opportunity for survival it was claimed (see Donohoe and Johnson 1986; Voy 1991).

The use of performance enhancing substances continued to be a feature of sport, whether at the amateur, semi-professional or professional level. However, the last half of the nineteenth century saw the beginnings of modern medicine and, not coincidentally, a significant growth in the use of drugs to improve athletic performance. It was during the first part of the twentieth century that drug use in sport began to be regarded as commonplace. Swimmers, long distance runners, sprinters and cyclists used substances such as strychnine, cocaine, nitroglycerine and caffeine in an attempt to gain a competitive edge over their opponents. By the mid-twentieth century sport had become 'big business', providing a significant source of entertainment, sponsorship and employment. Such growth contributed to the escalation of drug-related incidents, a number of which resulted in the death of professional athletes. By the late 1920s restrictions regarding drug use in sports were necessary for maintaining the integrity, image and the spirit of sport, as well as preventing deaths (Killanin and Rodda 1976).

In 1928 the international governing body of sport responsible for establishing standard rules for sports and ensuring adherence to these rules, the International Amateur Athletic Federation, became the first international sport federation to ban the use of substances believed to be able to enhance athletic performance. However, the restrictions were ineffective as there were no tests that could detect substance use. Meanwhile the problem was made worse by synthetic hormones, which were growing in usage for doping purposes during the 1950s. This usage derived from pharmaceutical companies developing anabolic androgen steroids (AAS) intended originally as a treatment for weight loss in cancer patients. However, such steroids were equally effective in improving body mass, particularly that of athletes, and were first used by athletes requiring physical strength, such as weight-lifters. The problem of doping intensified in the 1960s and 1970s and it became increasingly apparent that a regulatory approach was required. Brewer (2002) argues that it took the death of 23-year-old Danish cyclist Knud Enemark Jensen during competition at the Olympic Games in Rome 1960 for international organisations to recognise that unless a regulatory framework was established and employed, doping would continue to escape undetected and result in the further deaths of athletes.

The first international anti-doping development occurred in the same year, when the Council of Europe (a group of 21 West European nations) tabled a resolution against the use of doping substances in sport. In 1965 France and Belgium enacted doping laws aimed at curbing both the use of performance enhancing substances as well as the supply of drugs, by way of punishing those athletes who tested positive. The punishment was in the form of sanctioning that excluded athlete participation in particular events as well as suspension from competition for a period of time (Bird and Wagner 1997). Such a regulatory framework was based on a negative list enumerating all banned substances and to be enforced by random blood or urine testing of athletes both in and out of competition. However, enforceability was problematic as testing for substances was infrequent and not sufficiently sensitive to clearly identify positive samples.

As the credibility of the International Olympic Committee (IOC) began to be questioned, it sought to re-assert its credibility by passing a resolution in

1967 that established the Medical Commission, tasked solely with controlling the doping of professional athletes. Simultaneously the IOC integrated doping into its Olympic Rules and published a list of prohibited doping classes, including stimulants, narcotics, anti-depressants and tranquillisers. However, the naming of substances and stating their usage as illegal failed to quell substance use, as sporting nations found new methods, techniques and drugs to enable the enhancement of performance. Franke and Berendonk (1997) detail the programme initiated by the German Democratic Republic (GDR) in the 1970s which was titled 'efficient talent screening'. Cowan and Kicman (1997) claim that this programme was supplemented by a 'pre-competition bridging programme' that saw GDR athletes switch from AAS to testosterone weeks before competition and that was, at that time, not detectable in the testing regime. Underwood (1979) claims that the GDR was not alone and states that over a long period of time American team sports, namely football, encouraged the use of performance enhancing substances as a means of increasing stamina and providing a more 'entertaining contest'.

In 1998 a scandal erupted at the Tour de France when an official of the Festina Cycling Team was arrested by French customs officers for possession of illegal prescription drugs including narcotics, EPO, hGH, testosterone and amphetamines. Based on the investigations following Willy Voet's arrest, two weeks later the French police raided the hotel rooms of numerous cycling teams and discovered copious amounts of doping products in the possession of another team, TVM. It has since been argued that the doctors employed by both the Festina and TVM teams were central figures associated with the distribution of drugs and with monitoring the doping programme of their respective teams (Waddington 2000). As athletes participating in the event were made aware of developments within the investigation, they staged a collective 'sit-down-strike' on the seventeenth stage of the Tour, protesting the heavy-handed tactics of the French police and particularly the invasion of athlete privacy. The scandal attracted international attention and, according to Waddington, highlighted the need for the creation of an independent international body that could both develop and enforce a uniform standard for the definition of, and testing for, doping that would preside across the majority, if not all, international sports.

After the events of 1998, numerous governments threatened to increase their involvement in doping regulations, resulting in the IOC and the international federations (fearing a loss of their influence and power over international sport), agreeing to concessions which resulted in a World Conference on Doping in Sport, held in Lausanne, Switzerland in 1999. The subsequent Lausanne Declaration argues that doping practices are a contravention of sport and medical ethics as well as constitute violations of the rules established by the Olympic Movement. However, the major outcome was the creation of

WADA, with its chairman Richard Pound arguing that 'until we get to the point where everybody understands that it is wrong to use doping, it is very important that everybody knows that there are very reliable tests in existence. The tests are getting better and there are testing protocols that are better' (quoted in Hanstad and Loland 2005: 1).

Drug testing and the encroachment into athletes' lives

Denham (2000: 56) argues that the hysteria that surrounds doping in sport continues to be flamed by the media, particularly in the US, using 'emotional language and pictures, as well as the testimony from reformed (rehabilitated) former professional athletes as scientific fact, that drug use in professional sport is a matter worthy of public policy' and so in need of increased regulation. A similar approach is evident in Australia. Thorpe (2003) notes that the historical emergence of the discourse of crisis within the Australian sports sector, particularly in relation to doping, can be regarded as a government strategy.

WADA and the relevant national drug control agencies (which act as policing bodies) spend enormous amounts of money and time on the testing of elite athletes, an activity that they claim is justified based on six key principles of sport: morals, ethics, equity, health, social and image. However, such arguments have been refuted by sport ethicists, including Malloy and Zakus (2002), who claim that WADA is a controlling body that is using the welfare argument to justify an increasing regulatory approach on doping as well as expanding drug testing to include substances that athletes may decide to use during non-competitive hours for non-work recreational purposes. Now included as prohibited are recreational drugs such as marijuana, cannabis and amphetamines. Consequently, regulation has expanded to encompass the lifestyles and life decisions of athletes outside the pool, field or track. Some athletes question this direction when other regulatory issues seem more pressing. As one rugby union player explained: 'I find it really weird that WADA was created to clean out cheats: what should have been created was an anti-corruption agency to clean out sports administration – but then again why would they do that?' Other athletes, according to Katz (2001), almost unanimously publicly endorse the approach taken by governing bodies. This endorsement includes the belief that interventions are for the benefit of the individual athlete. Moreover, athletes use the perceived crisis to monitor and question the behaviour of their peers, while dissenting voices feel constrained by the fear of public sanction and ostracism.

The Athlete Associations of Australia (AAA) was established as a peak athletes' representative body that could have greater access to resources to challenge the doping regulatory bodies that sought to impinge on their members' personal freedoms and working conditions. As Frank Pritchard explained about his visit from the regulatory authorities:

> There was a knock at the door around 5.00 a.m. ... I was having a bit of a sleep in because training was at 9.00 a.m. so I thought what the heck ... I got out of bed onto to see my mum standing there with these two guys. The first thing I thought of was who died? To cut a long story short they said they were from ASADA and wanted to talk to me so I took them to my room. They told me to give them a sample. It's the first time this has happened to me and anyone else in [rugby] league and it's an invasion of my privacy but from what I hear it won't be the last.

The AAA were concerned about the protocols and processes employed by ASADA in relation to the testing of Australia's athletes both in and out of competition, and the regulatory authorities right to invade the privacy of athletes in the way that the Frank Pritchard incident highlighted. The AAA was (and remains) convinced that the testing body is both ignorant of professional sport and its operations. As such ASADA's credibility among athletes is low. After the Frank Pritchard incident, AAA sought to engage in an open dialogue with both ASADA and the Australian Government in an attempt to raise and deal with their concerns.

These concerns firstly included ASADA's policies relating to home testing. Although it is understandable that the anti-doping community seek the achievement of 'pure performance', it however needs to be noted that ASADA has failed to provide details of their policy in relation to home testing (whether occurring within 'normal' hours or outside of these times). In addition, the actions of ASADA are not in line with their international counterparts, which have recently legislated testing times. An example of this difference is the introduction of legislation in France that specifically regulates the times at which athletes may be subjected to drug testing in their homes. Moreover ASADA's position is both a breach of the WADA Code and UN Conventions. Attempts by the AAA in 2006 to seek clarification on home testing in Australia received a limited response. It is interesting to note that ASADA are yet to supply any Australian sporting code with either the policy or a simple fact sheet detailing its testing protocols. Their inability to do so causes suspicions about the testing procedures and creates a hostile environment between the testing body, the athletes and their representatives. By not divulging the requested information to sporting codes, it appears that ASADA either has no codified policy or, if it has, it wishes to control not only the testing process but the level of knowledge that can be attained about that process within Australian sport. As Tony Dempsey, CEO of the Rugby Unions Players Association states: 'if sporting codes and the players unions' get hold of the so-called code we will have the opportunity to further examine and highlight the questionable behaviour and tactics employed by them, and they can't have that now can they.'

The AAA is also concerned about there being no advance notice of testing. The WADA COde stipulates that acceptable calling times for 'no advance notice testing' are between the hours of 7.00 a.m. and 9.30 p.m. However, if an athlete has been difficult to contact during these hours, ASADA officers have the authority to enter the home premises of the athlete before 7.00 a.m. or after 9.30 p.m. This approach again breaches international conventions about agreed privacy rights of individuals set out and protected through Article 12 of the UN's Universal Declaration of Human Rights and Article 17 of the International Covenant on Civil and Political Rights. The notion of 'no advance notice testing' allows doping officials to enter the residences of athletes with no prior warning. With the WADA Code and hence ASADA, such an approach could not be taken because doing so would breach individual freedoms. The UN Conventions are intended to ensure that no one should be subject to arbitrary interference in relation to individual and family privacy, and, additionally, that there should be no attacks upon a person's honour and reputation. The 'no advance notice testing' thus breaches the international covenants to which WADA claimed that it adhered. Yet again, however, the lack of clarification and guidance from ASADA has enabled AAA to question its validity and credibility as a doping body.

This continued criticism has been met with distain from both the Australian Government and the doping agency, reinforcing Katz's point about restricted dissent through the use of public criticism and ostracism. As Mathew Rodwell, CEO of the Rugby League Professionals Association, argues:

> I don't get why it would be unreasonable to suggest that a protocol for the implementation of no advance notice testing be developed and signed off with a sport before it is carried out. I seriously can't see why this would be such a problem.

Relatedly, AAA has also raised with ASADA their concerns about not providing for the right of an athlete to have an independent witness present at the time of the drug test. Dempsey claims that

> We had a meeting with ASADA August 2006 on this issue. ASADA have yet to provide us with a reasonable explanation in relation to how this issue is overcome when conducting home tests ... the only thing they have said is no doping windows will be created as it signals to athletes when they can be tested ... we are now half-way through 2007 and I don't see an explanation appearing anytime soon.

ASADA is in a position to alleviate the concerns of athletes, sports governing bodies and player representative groups should they develop a framework based on cooperation rather than just seeking a regulatory approach. In doing so ASADA could assist sports governing bodies to educate athletes about the processes involved and the consequences of doping, which would prove beneficial in the overall fight against doping as it would place all concerned parties in a more informed position. Such an approach was discussed in the 2007 Tour de France – 'the most scandal ridden since 1998' according to Friebe (2007: 12) in which a number of athletes tested positive for performance enhancing substances and whole teams were withdrawn from the race. Such athletes are foolhardy at best within the current regulatory regime and interestingly now seem to be incurring the wrath of teammates as peer disdain is enlisted for the first time as a 'new weapon' in 'the war on doping' (ibid.). However, the fact remains that a lack of athlete and sporting body education programmes relating specifically to doping negatively impacts on the overall sporting image as well as the ability of athletes to function effectively in professional sport. However, from an Australian perspective, the CEO of ASADA, Richard Ings, has continually stated that the doping agency will not change its approach as their main objective is to create 'pure performance' and in doing so the adoption of procedures and processes are for the achievement of this goal, and not for the creation of a comfortable environment for sports administrators and athletes (see also www.asada.gov.au/news/bulletins).

WADA and ASADA have established a position of power and control over sports and professional athletes in Australia that not only seeks to regulate athletes' performance at work but also their personal lives, both prescribing and invading those lives. The programmes and activities of ASADA do not simply operate through the conducting of drug testing to detect and eliminate the use of performance enhancing substances; rather, they attempt to govern doping practices through the administration of a disciplinary regime (Foucault 1977) that creates, maintains and enforces a culture of control, surveillance and punishment. This regime is unhappily recognised by athletes, as one A-League soccer player complained:

> What they want to do is test what we eat and what we drink, next they will probably tell us what we can wear and who we can and cannot sleep with ... when will they get it that we athletes are just blokes who work for a living, have families and do what everyone else does ... then again they probably didn't make it to the big time so they want to screw those who did.

The situation that is being created in professional sport is forcing players to not only strongly reflect upon their activities during working hours but also during their own personal time. As one rugby league player noted:

When I go out I make sure that I have the full product description of what I eat and what I drink ... and if I can't see the make up of a product on its packaging I am asking. I am so paranoid that even when I go to a restaurant I ask the waiter for a breakdown of the ingredients used ... how nuts is that?

The final concern relates to the continuously growing list of prohibited substances, which according to Beamish and Ritchie (2005) includes substances for which performance enhancing capabilities are yet to be scientifically measured. According to the AAA, ASADA has neglected to forward any empirical and triangulated data to support the need to conduct testing on a number of substances. Much evidence on some substances that have been identified as performance enhancing is contradictory. The most controversial element of WADA and its Code has been the expanding list of prohibited substances, which now incorporates recreational as well as performance enhancing drugs, and there is, as yet, no satisfactory answer from ASADA as to why the prohibited list now includes recreational substances. Just as importantly in terms of encroachment into athletes' private lives, there is no evidence to suggest that testing on the private premises of athletes can identify certain fast metabolising substances any better than testing in the 'workplace'.

Considering that WADA's determination of the substances on the prohibited list and methods of testing are final and are not capable of challenge by an athlete or other interested parties, it is critical that WADA's determination be based upon objectively assessed standards that can be justified to those who are subject to the operation of the Code whether by contract or legislative fiat. In addition, WADA should, in the interests of transparency and accountability, publish the reasons why particular substances and methods have been included on the prohibited list. As Beamish and Ritchie (2005) argue, such an approach would assist in dealing with the debate about the inclusion of such substances as cannabis and cocaine, particularly against the background of considerable medical and scientific evidence that some recreational drugs are not performance enhancing to athletes competing in a wide range of individual and team sports.

The debate over the inclusion of recreational drugs has intensified in Australia since Wendell Sailor[2] was banned for two years, effectively ending his rugby union career, after he tested positive for Benzoylecgonine, a metabolite of cocaine, after a test conducted by ASADA in 2006. According to Wilson and Derse (2001), although cocaine is listed as a prohibited substance in the WADA Code due to its so-called ability to enhance performance as a stimulant as well as constituting a health risk to athletes, the evidence that WADA relies on is defective in its framework and therefore flawed in its findings. If one extends the concerns raised by Wilson and Derse to other substances that appear on the list, it can be argued that the process undertaken for substance inclusion is also defective and therefore needs to be independently reviewed by organisations not influenced by the internal politics or vested interests of WADA and the IOC. Such an undertaking would allow athletes to generate an appreciation for WADA, its objectives and the nature of its testing processes. As the regime for the eradication of doping currently operates, athletes have concerns about the lack of privacy that they are afforded. Montgomery (1999) argues that the 365 days of the year approach to drug testing under the auspices of new and sophisticated drug testing methods has created a culture of surveillance in which an athlete's movements are restricted and monitored at all times. Athletes argue that the conditions of their employment have taken over their family and personal lives. As one rugby league player noted: 'because of the testing and the types of drugs they are testing for when does my working day finish ... does it even finish? I am so not sure ... [it's] pretty bloody confusing. I don't even know what I can eat or drink anymore because apparently everything is performance enhancing.' Another player argued: 'my existence is now in the hands of ASADA and I just want to get control of my own life back. If that's too much to ask. Maybe professional sport is not for me ... because I don't think a bloke on a construction site is told to piss as much as I do.'

In addition, it has been revealed that WADA has given itself the authority to preserve the urine and blood samples of athletes for up to 20 years so that with the availability of new drug testing methods, the samples will undergo further examination in the future, allowing WADA to strip an athlete of any medals they have won over their sporting career. This possibility accentuates the view that WADA is about control and punishment rather than creating an environment of drug free sport. 'I can't believe that they are going to hold onto my samples for that long,' said one rugby union player, 'every year they add substances to the prohibited list ... so by 2027 if bananas are placed on the list because they increase energy levels will I have to give back my medals? ... What if I am dead will they exhume me to get them or will they change my stone to say "Here lies a cheat?" ... seriously those guys in charge have no clue, because if they did they wouldn't treat us like shit.' Such sentiments being expressed by players are no longer isolated and are in fact becoming common both domestically and internationally. As a Great Britain player noted during the 2006 rugby league Tri-Nations series, 'I used to think that Australia was a nice place to visit both from a tourist and a sporting view, but after going through the new doping test regime for the last six weeks I am hoping that the next tour takes place when I am retired ... In England we are tested, but what the guys have to go through here makes me think that a rugby league player has no time off, and that is so wrong.'

Conclusion

While athletes and their representatives remain advocates of drug free sport, it is critical that they are fully aware of their rights and entitlements and that their privacy is protected in the desire to establish 'pure performance' in Australian and international sport. In this respect it is crucial that WADA and ultimately ASADA are transparent, accountable and are committed to discussing and drafting effective and reasonable policies with the input and consultation of athletes and their representatives that allow athletes to lead private lives. At present, the boundaries that athletes once enjoyed in relation to work and non-work time and place have been removed by the creation of WADA and the enforcement of its code by ASADA. To be tested 'anywhere and anytime' without prior notification creates an environment of uncertainty and discomfort for athletes, and as one noted: 'my wife works full-time and I have an 18 month old daughter. I could be changing her, feeding her or playing with her when the guys from ASADA walk in. So do they provide babysitting services while I empty my bladder ... but then what if my kid doesn't like them?' Considering the history of doping and the way in which sporting federations sought its minimisation, it can be concluded that these federations' past ineffectiveness as well as the under-regulation of doping has laid the foundation for what athletes are dealing with in the modern era of sport: that of over-regulation.

This chapter has argued that the introduction of WADA and its doping code has created a great deal of anxiety and confusion among athletes, their representatives and their respective governing bodies. Since its inception, WADA and its subsidiary agencies have failed to alleviate the concerns that have been particularised by organisations such as the AAA in that their intervention is negatively affecting the ability of professional athletes to sustain a private life. Athletes' personal lives are being severely encroached, so much so that the spatial and temporal boundaries between work and private lives are not just being transgressed but dissolved. These personal lives are being both physically invaded and prescribed, and some activities proscribed. Although this chapter has not questioned the overall objectives of WADA, what it has questioned, are both the policing tactics that it has employed and the way in which such tactics have removed the boundary of work and non-working hours in the lives of professional athletes. As one rugby league player pointed out: 'It's one thing to stamp out doping, but come on, what they are doing now, it's beyond ridiculous. At our club we have been told to keep a whereabouts diary so if ASADA come looking they know where we are – so I write dear diary today I am going shopping at Westfield's ... what's next, an ankle bracelet?'

Notes

1. Strychnine is a colourless, crystalline compound that is both a stimulant and a convulsant, or agent that causes uncontrolled fits or spasms, and its action can be nearly instantaneous.
2. Sailor was a dual international in the codes of rugby league and rugby union throughout the 1990s to 2006.

REFERENCES

Beamish, R. and Ritchie, I. (2005) 'From Fixed Capacities to Performance-Enhancement: The Paradigm Shift in the Science of Training and the Use of Performance-Enhancing Substances', *Sport in History*, 25:3, 412–33.

Bird, E. and Wagner, G. (1997) 'Sport as a Common Property Resource: A Solution to the Dilemmas of Doping', *Journal of Conflict Resolution*, 41, 749–66.

Brewer, B. (2002) 'Commercialization in Professional Cycling: 1950 to 2001: Institutional Transformations and the Rationalization of Doping', *Sociology of Sport Journal*, 19, 276–301.

Buti, A. and Fridman, S. (2001) *Drugs, Sport and the Law*, Queensland: Scribblers Publishing.

Cowan, D.A. and Kicman, A.T. (1997) 'Doping in Sport: Misuse, Analytical Tests and Legal Aspects', *Clinical Chemistry*, 43, 1110–13.

Denham, B.E. (2000) 'Performance-Enhancing Drug Use in Amateur and Professional Sports: Separating the Realities from the Ramblings', *Culture, Sport, Society*, 3, 56–69.

Donohoe, T. and Johnson, N. (1986) *Foul Play? Drug Use in Sport*, Oxford: Blackwell.

Foucault, M. (1977) 'Nietzsche, Genealogy, and History' in D.F. Bouchard (ed.) *Michel Foucault: Language, Counter-Memory, Practice: Selected Essays and Interviews by Michel Foucault*, Oxford: Basil Blackwell.

Franke, W.W. and Berendonk, B. (1997) 'Hormonal Doping and Androgenization of Athletes: A Secret Program of the German Democratic Republic Government', *Clinical Chemistry*, 43, 1262–79.

Fridman, S. and Buti, T. (1999) 'Drug Testing in Sport: Legal Challenges and Issues', *The University of Queensland Law Journal*, 20:2, 153–86.

Friebe, D. (2007) 'Contador Maintains His Grip on the Tour', *Sunday Telegraph*, sports supplement, 29 July, 12.

Hanstad, V.D. and Loland, S. (2005) *What is Efficient Doping Control?*, Oslo: Norwegian School of Social Sciences.

▶

▶

Katz, S. (2001) 'Michel Foucault' in A. Elliott and B.S. Turner (eds) *Profiles of Contemporary Social Theory*, London: Sage.

Kemp, The Hon. Rod. (2005) 'New Body to Take Up the Fight against Drugs in Sport', media release, Ministry for Arts and Sport, 23 June.

Khoshaba, T. (2007) 'Blood, Sweat and Tears: A Study of the Rugby League Professionals Association', unpublished doctoral thesis, Faculty of Economics, University of Sydney.

Killanin, Lord En and Rodda, J. (1976) *The Olympic Games: 80 Years of People, Events and Records*, New York: Collier Books.

Malloy, D.C. and Zakus, D.H. (2002) 'Ethics of Drug Testing in Sport – An Invasion of Privacy Justified?', *Sport, Education and Society*, 17:2, 203–18.

Montgomery, P. (1999) 'IOC Credibility Questioned as Drug Meeting Starts', *New York Times*, 3 February, D1.

Rigauer, B. (1980) *Sport and Work*, New York: Columbia University Press.

Striegel, H. Vollkommer, G. and Dickhuth, H.H. (2002) 'Combating Drug Use in Competitive Sports: An Analysis from the Athletes' Perspective', *Journal of Sports Medicine and Physical Fitness*, 442 , 354–9.

Thorpe, S. (2003) 'Crisis Discourse in Physical Education and the Laugh of Michel Foucault', *Sport, Education and Society*, 8:2, 131–51.

Underwood, J. (1979) *The Death of an American Game: The Crisis in Football*, Boston: Little, Brown and Company.

Waddington, I. (2000) *Sport, Health and Drugs: A Critical Sociological Perspective*, London: E & FN Sponn.

Wilson, W. and Derse, E. (eds) (2001) *Doping in Elite Sport: The Politics of Drugs in the Olympic Movement*, Champaign: Human Kinetics.

Voy, R.O. (1988) 'Clinical Aspects of the Doping Classes' in A. Dirix, H.G. Knuttgen and K. Tittle (eds) *The Olympic Book of Sports Medicine*, Oxford: Blackwell.

Voy, R.O. (1991) *Drugs, Sports, Politics*, Champaign: Leisure Press.

Name Index

Subject Index